Magical, Mysterious
LAKE OF THE WOODS

National Library of Canada Cataloguing in Publication

Robertson, Heather, 1942-
Magical, Mysterious Lake of the Woods / by Heather Robertson and Melinda McCracken.

Includes bibliographical references.
ISBN 1-896150-26-8

1. Lake of the Woods--History. I. McCracken, Melinda, 1940-2002 II. Title.

FC3095.L34R63 2003   971.3'11   C2003-905414-4

Heartland Associates Inc.
PO Box 103 RPO Corydon
Winnipeg, MB R3M 3S3
hrtland@mts.net
www.hrtlandbooks.com
5 4 3 2 1

Credits

Editor
Barbara Huck

Editorial assistance
Peter St. John, Debbie Riley

Design and maps
Dawn Huck

Prepress
Avenue 4 Communications,
Winnipeg, Canada

Printing
Printcrafters, Winnipeg,
Canada

Cover illustration
Sunset, Lake of the Woods,
by Walter J. Phillips

Back cover photographs
by Gary Gobeil

On behalf of Melinda McCracken, Heartland Associates Inc. wishes to express its gratitude to Manitoba Culture, Heritage and Tourism for assistance from its Heritage Grants Program.

Magical, Mysterious
LAKE OF THE WOODS

by Heather Robertson and
Melinda McCracken

Heartland Associates, Inc.
Winnipeg, Canada

Printed in Manitoba, Canada

ACKNOWLEDGEMENTS

WE ARE ENORMOUSLY GRATEFUL to all the many people who took us on guided tours, allowed us to photograph their homes, camps, boathouses and themselves, gave us new contacts and shared with us their scholarship, stories, photographs and family archives. This history could not have been written without the earlier diligent research and publications of the area's historical societies, or without the wonderful resources of the museums and cultural centres: Chapple Museum in Barwick, ON; Grand Council Treaty # 3 Cultural and Research Centre in Kenora, ON; Kay-Nah-Chi-Wah-Nung Historical Centre in Long Sault Rapids, ON; Lake of the Woods Museum in Kenora; Lake of the Woods County Museum in Baudette, MN, and Warroad Heritage Center in Warroad, MN. Kenora's Taiga Institute, journalist Bryan Phelan and the staff, past and present, of Ontario's Ministry of Mines and Minerals and Ministry of Natural Resources have generously assisted with research, maps, plans and scientific studies. Tourism Kenora provided information and encouragement, while the Hudson's Bay Company Archive in the Manitoba Archives in Winnipeg, MB, the Manitoba Museum in Winnipeg and the Royal Ontario Museum in Toronto were all important resources.

Water lilies cluster on a pond at Sioux Narrows.

DENNIS FAST

DENNIS FAST

Autumn sets the forest afire near Hoyland, Minnesota.

TO MELINDA (1940–2002)

MELINDA, LIKE ALL OF US, loved the Lake. She could always be found in the morning sunshine out on the deck, sitting in a lawnchair. Her red-painted toenails would be pressed against the railing; her straw hat bent down as she narrated into her notebook. Even before my mother got together with Heather to tell the stories that linger at Lake of the Woods, she was weaving tales of her own at our cottage in Clearwater Bay. The best yarns were spun over the requisite late afternoon gin and tonic. Melinda would begin with the time she and her then-boyfriend Jim motored their scooter across Europe, and would move on to her heady hippie days working at the *Montreal Gazette*. There was the time she took her lobster for a walk around the block before it suffered a tasty death. And didn't the people stare when she was the first to bare her beautiful legs in an oh-so-daring mini skirt?!

When my grandparents, Edith and William McCracken, bought our cottage in 1959, Melinda, like most young people, was ready to take full advantage. As a young woman, she and her life-long pal, Myf, drove from Toronto to the Lake in Melinda's new convertible. They arrived glowing with sunburns and excitement, having picked up hitchhikers only to ask them to hop out at the bottom of the hills so the car could make it to the top, and then run up and hop back in again.

As time marched on, the Lake was always our family retreat from the pressing demands of the rest of the world. Edith, also affectionately known as Nana, would always lead my Mom and me in card games after the dinner dishes were washed up. We started with "Go Fish" and from there moved on to Crazy Eights, Gin Rummy, and my personal favourite, Canasta. Melinda was a good sport, but never 100 per cent enthusiastic, probably because Nana usually "wholloped" us (as she would say). When Trivial Pursuit came out in the Eighties, Melinda put some of her journalistic knowledge to good use and redeemed herself as the unfailing champion.

As a teenager and an only child at a quiet cottage, I asked my mother to send me to what I heard was a fun camp where the food was actually good – YM-YWCA Camp Stephens. I wanted to learn to canoe the way she could. Melinda watched me go off to camp for four years as a camper and seven years as a staff member. I can remember one nervous sleepless night before my first ever two-week canoe trip when she stayed up with me all night singing Rolling Stones songs because I was so excited. When I co-led the women's six-week canoe trip, I will always remember her proud face watching us as we told the crowd at the return ceremony about our adventures in the enchanting Canadian Shield.

Melinda was honoured and excited to take part in this book with her other life-long pal, Heather Robertson. She spent the last year of her life doing what she loved – telling stories about a part of the world that was dear to her heart with her good friend. She adored boating down to Big Traverse Bay to look for Massacre Island, and poring over La Vérendrye's journals. Her voice is now joined with the many who loved the Lake and touched our hearts with their stories. If I listen early in the morning sunshine, I can still hear her: "Tell them."

By Molly McCracken

TABLE OF CONTENTS

INTRODUCTION

L AKE OF THE WOODS has had many names. The
Cree, who lived to the north, called it Ministick
Sakahegan, Lake of Islands, but the French, who
arrived in the seventeenth century, misunderstood it as
Mistick Sakahegan or Lac du Bois, Lake of the Woods.
Jacques de Noyon, a *coureur de bois* who reached the lake
in 1688, called it Lac des Assiniboiles for the Assiniboine
guides who brought him there. The Ojibwe, or Anishinabe,
reaching the lake down the Rainy River from the east,
named it Sakahegan Pekwaonga, Lake of the Sand Hills
after the dunes and sandbars at the river's mouth. Two bays,
Shoal Lake and Whitefish Bay were long thought to be separate lakes, and the name Clearwater Lake was once given
to the lake's entire northern half. The Ojibwe called the
neck of rock separating Lake of the Woods from the
Winnipeg River, Wazhushk Onigum Keewatin, "northern
portage to the muskrat country", an ancient campsite that
became the village of Keewatin; Rat Portage is English for
Wazhushk Onigum. The lake's many names express its
multiple personalities. In a story called "The Magic Lake",
Minnesota writer Earl Chapin explains the lake's peculiar-
ities with a myth:

> Lake of the Woods was created by a lesser god of
> the Crees in a fit of whimsy. Being a magic lake,
> its waters are of many colours, sometimes tawny,
> sometimes the colour of black tea, and some-
> times as thick and green as pea soup. It is said
> that the wendigo became so enamoured of his
> handiwork that he transformed himself into
> an image of rock so he might forever remain to
> marvel at what even a lesser god might do
> when the spirit is strong within him.
>
> 'I'll make a garden of this lake,' said the
> wendigo, and he did. He brought maples and
> planted them among the northern pines. Amid
> the shrubs and grasses that sleep through winters
> of many moons, he mixed alien plants to remind
> him of lands of earlier spring. And on the most
> barren of all his islands he planted cactus where
> of winter nights trees are riven by the intense cold.
>
> 'I'll hide a treasure in this lake,' said the
> wendigo, and he did. He salted the shores of the
> islands with gold and silver, with beryls, mica,
> feldspar, zinc-blende, galena, antimony, iron,
> cobalt, mispickle and fool's gold. He was a clever
> spirit, and a perverse one. It is said that on sum-
> mer nights when thundercaps climb like bastions
> above the mirror lake, one can still hear his sar-
> donic laughter reverberating among the hills. 'I'll
> make a maze of this lake,' he said, 'to confound
> those who might seek to drive my people from
> it, and I will place puzzles here that will perplex
> men forever more.' And he did.
>
> 'Here,' said the wendigo, looking upon his
> handiwork, 'I have created a paradox of beauty
> and desolation, of riches and poverty, of bounty
> and starvation. I have made this lake to provide me
> with amusement for today and for my tomorrows.'

Since time remembered, the Aboriginal people of
Lake of the Woods have placed offerings of food and clothing,
dishes, tobacco and religious items on rock ledges for the

Morning mist on Rushing River.

spirits who dwell within. In many of the lake's eastern bays, sheer rock faces have been painted with handprints and small, stylized figures that appear to represent people, weapons, animals, canoes, mythical beasts or abstract forms. In 1957, Canadian artist Selwyn Dewdney began to measure, sketch and photograph these pictographs and compare them to similar rock paintings as far east as Agawa Bay on Lake Superior. The paint, he concluded, was red ochre or iron oxide mixed with bear's grease, sturgeon oil, bird's egg,

beeswax, blood or spit. He could not determine the paint's age, but he described these "mysterious red markings of a vanished culture" as "stone age art older than the bricks of Babylon."

Yet one of the red ochre drawings on Lake of the Woods shows a European pallisade with a flag; another, a boat with a sail, might represent the 1870 passage of British troops to crush the Red River Resistance. Some pictographs have been drawn over, others defaced. Who made them, and are they spiritual symbols, hunting charms, graffiti, astronomical charts, or messages? Some archaeologists believe they depict Midewiwin medicine lodge rituals, but the artists may have painted hieroglyphs on rocks much as they did on birchbark. John Tanner, an Irish American captive who lived as an Ojibwe from 1790 to 1823, described in his memoir how these notes were read:

"As I was one morning passing one of our usual encamping places, I saw on shore a little stick standing in the bank, and attached to the top of it a piece of birchbark. On examination, I found the mark of a rattlesnake with a knife, the handle touching the snake, and the point sticking into a bear, the head of the latter being down. Near the rattlesnake was the mark of a beaver, one of its dugs touching the snake. This was left for my information." The animals were totems, and Tanner quickly deduced that his adoptive Ojibwe brother, a member of the rattlesnake clan, had killed a man whose totem was a bear, and "that he was dead, and not wounded merely, was indicated by the drooping down of the head." Tanner recognized the beaver as Net-no-kaw, the mother who had bought him as an eleven-year-old child and raised him as her own son. To Tanner, birchbark drawings were "perfectly explicit and satisfactory", white paint around a totem's mouth signified hunger, and "if the figure of a man appears without any designatory mark, it is immediately understood that he is a Sioux or at least a stranger."

Lake of the Woods was a summer campground for the Ojibwe. Tanner says, "we started to come to an island called Me-nau-zhe-taw-naun in the Lake of the Woods where we had concluded to plant corn. On our way we stopped at a place to make sugar, then we went to visit the traders. I hunted for about a month, then went back into the country I had left, all the Indians remaining behind to clear the ground where they intended planting corn." From Lake of the Woods, he says, "the Indians have a road to go to Red River which the white men never follow; this is by way of the Muskeeg or swamp carrying place." Paddling up the Swamp River, they dragged their canoes over a quaking bog to a small stream choked with cow parsley. Here they trapped beaver, and, in spring and fall, feasted on ducks and geese. The weather, however, was fickle. Tanner describes being caught by an early winter storm on his way home from an excursion against the Sioux, as the Ojibwe called the Dakota people from the south:

There were six of us to return together to Lake of the Woods. Heavy snow and severe cold came upon us at the Muskeeg carrying place; the trees cracked with the cold, but the water in the swamp was not yet frozen hard enough to bear. Our canoes, however, could not be pushed through. The utmost exertion of our strength would not avail to move them. We were hungry and much fatigued, and sat deliberating what was best to be done when we discovered our women coming from the Lake of the Woods and dragging their light canoes through water, ice and snow above their knees. Our wives laughed at us, telling us it was more like old women than like warriors returning to their village, to sit shivering in a canoe which could move neither way through fear of a litle water and ice. They had brought us a supply of corn, sturgeon and other food. With them we returned to our last encampment, then went down the Red River with the intention of spending the winter there.

LAKE OF THE WOODS was at the centre of a complex network of rivers and trails that stretched as far west as the Souris River, where the people hunted buffalo, down the Red River to Lake Winnipeg and the rivers leading to Hudson Bay and east to the Great Lakes and the St. Lawrence River. The Lake of the Woods watershed therefore bustled with commerce, with much of the business done by women. In his *Travels and Adventures in Canada and the Indian Territories between the years 1760 and 1776*, fur trader Alexander Henry, a New Englander based in Montreal, describes his first trip west of Rainy Lake in July 1775:

> On the thirtieth, we reached Lake of the Woods, or Lake des Isles, at the entrance of which was an Indian village of a hundred souls where we obtained a further supply of fish. Fish appeared to be the summer food. From this village, we received ceremonious presents. The mode with the Indians is first to collect all the provisions they can spare, and place them in a heap; after which they send for the trader and address him in a formal speech. They tell him that the Indians are happy in seeing him return to their country; that they have been long in expectation of his arrival; that their wives have deprived themselves of their provisions in order to afford him a supply; that they are in great want, being destitute of every thing, and particularly of ammunition and clothing; and that what they most long for is a taste of his rum, which they uniformly denominate *milk*.

> The present, in return, consisted of one keg of gunpowder, of sixty pounds weight; a bag of shot and another of powder, of eighty pounds each; a few smaller articles and a keg of rum. In a short time, the men began to drink, while the women brought me a further and very valuable present, of twenty bags of rice. This I returned with goods and rum, and at the same time offered more for an additional quantity of rice. A trade was opened, the women bartering rice while the men were drinking. Before morning, I had purchased a hundred bags of nearly a bushel measure each.

A PROSPEROUS CAMP and a good party; Henry had also cast an appreciative eye on the Rainy River: "Its banks are level to a great distance, and composed of a fine soil, which was covered in luxuriant grass. I was greatly struck by the beauty of the scene, as well as with its fitness for agricultural settlements."

Fourteen years later, in 1789, another Montreal trader, Alexander Mackenzie, praised the Rainy River as one of the finest rivers in the northwest. "To the north, its banks are clothed with fine open groves of oak, with the maple, the pine and the cedar. The southern bank displays the maple, the white birch and the cedar, with the spruce, the alder and various underwood. Its waters abound in fish, particularly the sturgeon, which the natives both spear and take with drag-nets. But notwithstanding the promise of this soil, the Indians do not attend to its cultivation, though they are not ignorant of the common process, and are fond of the Indian corn when they can get it from us."

Mackenzie noted the abundance of wild rice, but a scarcity of Natives; between Lake Superior and Red River the Aboriginal population did not appear to exceed 300 warriors and their families. "Among the few whom I saw," Mackenzie wrote, "it appeared to me that the widows were

A. SHERRIFF SCOTT OR EDWIN C. GUILLET / NATIONAL ARCHIVES OF CANADA / C–024654

An illustration, conceived more than 150 years later, of Alexander Henry at Lake of the Woods in 1775.

more numerous than the men." The Ojibwe, Cree and Assiniboine were engaged in a long war with the Dakota, a prairie nation from the south that they called *nadowessioux*, meaning "snakes". Mackenzie also recalled that in 1782 "small-pox spread its destructive and desolating power, as the fire consumes the dry grass of the field," throughout the midwestern continent: "The fatal infection spread around with a baneful rapidity which no flight could escape, and with a fatal effect that nothing could resist. It destroyed with its pestilential breath whole families and tribes. To aggravate the picture may be added the putrid carcases which the wolves, with a furious voracity, dragged forth from the huts, or which were mangled within them by the dogs whose hunger was satisfied with the disfigured remains of their masters."

LAKE OF THE WOODS, Mackenzie wrote, "was formerly famous for the richness of its banks and waters, which abounded with whatever was necessary to a savage life. The French had several settlements in and about it; but it might be almost concluded that some fatal circumstance had destroyed the game, as war and the small-pox had diminished the inhabitants, it having been very unproductive in animals since the British subjects have been engaged in travelling through it."

The most fatal circumstance, as Mackenzie knew, was the fur trade itself. The violence, greed and drunken debauches of the North West Company, in which Mackenzie was a partner, were notorious. In the decades that followed, open warfare with the Hudson's Bay Company erupted, particularly after the HBC established an agricultural colony of Scots at Red River (now Winnipeg) in 1812.

As the fur traders were joined by surveyors and geographers, the antiquity of the place began to be recognized. One was U.S. Army officer, Major Joseph Delafield, the American agent for the International Joint Commission marking the boundary between Lake Superior and Lake of the Woods. In August of 1823, Delafield was travelling down the Rainy River in search of his surveyor, John Ferguson. Instead, he met the chief astronomer, Canadian David Thompson, his son Samuel and their companion, Dr. John Bigsby, paddling upriver. The voyageurs' highway was getting crowded and many of the newcomers left their impressions of the lake.

"Towards sunset meet a brigade of four canoes," Delafield wrote in his diary. "They approach in fine style, abreast of each other, the crews all singing and paddling in their best manner. They proved to be part of a larger brigade from the Athabaska Country, bringing down packs, and discharged clerks with their families, and broken-down and super-annuated voyageurs, and freemen, all to seek their fortunes in some new mode of life. It was a wholesome lesson for my men to witness the industry, activity and

labor of these crews on the portages. It was the best conducted strife (for it was a race) that I can imagine. The portage was made upon the trot at every instance. Of three canoes that went thro' whilst I was present, I did not hear a word spoken."

At the head of Manitou Rapids, Delafield made a discovery: "On the N. shore is an ancient clearing of half a mile extent upon the river front, that appears to have been a spot visited by the Indians in the Spring to fish, from time immemorial. The poles of many wigwams are here with some of their mats, canoe wood, etc. concealed in the bushes, as if they would soon return. Not a soul is now here. There is a very regularly shaped mound of earth at this place that may be artificial, but nobody knows the fact." Below the rapids, Delafield searched the south shore "for the white earth which, mixed with sturgeon's oil, the natives and Canadians use as paint; the former for their persons, the latter for their canoes."

DR. BIGSBY, an English physician and geologist, missed the Manitou Mounds; he was too busy swatting mosquitoes. "We slept, or tried to do so, in these meadows. The mosquitoes were in billions. As soon as the tread of man gave notice of his approach, I saw them rising to the feast in clouds out of the coarse grass around. We burnt the grass after watering it and lived in the smoke. Although the heat was very great, we wore gloves, veils, and caps over the ears. My pantaloons were tied close down to the boots, or the creatures would have crept up the legs." David Thompson noted in his own journal: "Plenty of musketos but not very bad." Thompson, fifty-three, had been travelling the northwest from Hudson Bay to the Pacific Ocean for more than thirty years; his wife, Charlotte, was Métis, and he spoke Cree fluently. Bigsby describes "Mr. Astronomer Thompson" as "a firm churchman" who held Sunday services for his canoemen.

Thompson, instructed to find the most northwestern point of Lake of the Woods, headed up the west shore. "Towards the Rat Portage," Bigsby observed, "the country rises, and the scene becomes precisely that of the Thousand Islands on the St. Lawrence, so exquisitely beautiful when seen on a calm evening when the shadows are long. The Rat Portage, its outlet, we reach by a narrow cul-de-sac, 600 yards long, ending in a grassy swamp, the portage lying between two eminences, naked but for burnt pines, a few cypress trees and poplars. This cul-de-sac is 120 yards broad at the portage, and is made offensive and foul by dead insects, the croaking of frogs and the plague of mosquitoes." Climbing a hill, however, Bigsby beheld, on the other side, the Winnipeg River, "a magnificent sheet of water flowing down a prolonged woody valley. Wild islands of granite stud the west side of this basin, whose shores are high and naked, and backed by three ranges of lofty hills, either bare or covered with bright young verdure."

The Ojibwe were greatly admired by both the French and later British for their outstanding abilities as canoeists.

THE SURVEYORS HAD BARELY LEFT when a reconnaissance expedition of the U.S. Army, led by Major Stephen H. Long, came up the Winnipeg River and camped at Rat Portage. The expedition's young geologist and historian, William Keating, described one the river's waterfalls in the contemporary language of Romantic literature:

> After having passed over numerous rocks, which form diversified cascades, the water is suddenly received into a basin enclosed by high rocks, where it is forced to sojourn awhile by the small size of the aperture through which it issues; here the waters present the character of a troubled ocean, whose waves rise high and beat against the adjoining shores, and against the few rocky islands in the midst of this basin; it is to this character that the spot owes the name which it receives from the natives, 'the fall of moving waters'. We reached them in time to watch the beautiful effect of the setting sun, whose beams reflected by the stream imparted to it the appearance of a sea on fire. This was soon replaced by the moon, which cast a more placid light, and heightened the charm of the scenery by the melancholy mantle which it spread over it. A scarcity of vegetation contributes to the picturesque effect. We have here a spare growth of aspen, birch, spruce and other evergreens, whose size, generally small, adds to the wild and barren appearance of the rocks. Our tents were pitched so that we had a view of the splendid effect arising from the play of the moonbeams upon the surface of this ocean-like basin, and our eyes were constantly bent upon it until the noise of the cataract lulled us to sleep.

Keating commented on "the great abundance of fish on the river; they were frequently seen leaping out of the water. Over these falls eagles and hawks soared high in the air, watching for the easy prey they derive from the numbers of fish that are wounded or killed by being hurried against the rocks by the irresistible force of the current." He observed wooden crosses on the shore marking where voyageurs had drowned, and learned why:

> When in the afternoon the wind blew high, and the heavens were darkened with clouds, the scene became almost terrific; the waves arose, and it required the fullest confidence in the skill and experience of our guide to hush all apprehension as we observed him make for a projecting point where a small eddy, barely 30 feet in length, presented the only landing place for the canoes. Our paddlers strained every nerve; at last, having, by strong and quickly repeated strokes of the paddle, reached the eddy, one of the men immediately jumped into the stream to stop the frail bark and prevent it from being dashed against the shore; two men were scarcely able to keep the canoe in place as its bow touched the rocks while the stern was still in the rapid. She was quickly unloaded, and raised from the waters, and while the men were transporting the baggage across, we stopped on the rock to watch the progress of the other canoes, which were conducted with equal skill to the landing place.

Not every traveller found the scenery picturesque. On June 6, 1846, Toronto artist Paul Kane noted:

> It was a remarkable fact that the trees on each side of the [Rainy] river, and part of Lake of the Woods, for full 150 miles of our route, were literally stripped of foliage by myriads of green caterpillars, which had left nothing but the bare

WALTER J. PHILLIPS / NATIONAL ARCHIVES OF CANADA / C-110910

For nearly two centuries, artists and photographers have found the beauty of Rushing River, on the lake's north-east corner, to be almost irresistible. In 1931, Walter J. Phillips created this dramatic woodcut of the cascade.

branches; and I was informed that the scourge extended to more than twice the distance, the whole country wearing the dreary aspect of winter at the commencement of summer. As it was impossible to take our breakfast on land, unless we made up our minds to eat them, dropping incessantly as they did from the trees among our food, and the ground everywhere covered with them en masse, we were compelled to take it in our canoes."

A quiet cove on Lake of the Woods.

KANE, ON A SKETCHING trip to the west coast, was one of the lake's first tourists; he was soon followed by big game hunters, government agents, botanists, engineers, land speculators and, in 1870, the British troops bound for Red River. Their advance scout, Captain William F. Butler, worried that Métis insurgents might ambush the troops on the lake, built a York boat at Rat Portage and set out in search of the expedition on July 31st:

> That portion of the Lake of the Woods and through which we now steered was a perfect maze and network of island and narrow channel; a light breeze from the north favoured us, and we passed gently along the rocky islet shores through unruffled water. In all directions there opened out innumerable channels, some narrow and winding, others straight and open, but all lying between shores clothed in a rich and luxuriant vegetation; shores that curved and twisted into mimic bays and tiny promontories, that rose in rocky masses abruptly from the water, that sloped down to meet the lake in gently swelling undulations, that seemed, in fine, to present in the compass of a single glance every varying feature of island scenery. Looking through these rich labyrinths of tree and moss-covered rock, it was difficult to imagine that winter could ever stamp its frozen image upon such a soft summer scene. The air was balmy with the scented things which grow profusely upon the islands; the water was warm, almost tepid, and yet despite of this the winter frost would cover the lake with five feet of ice, and the thick brushwood of the islands would lie hidden during many months beneath great depths of snow.
>
> Among the Indians the lake holds high place as the favourite haunt of the Manitou. The strange water-worn rocks, the islands of soft pipe-stone from which are cut the bowls for many a calumet, the curious masses of ore resting on the polished surface of rock, the islands struck yearly by lightning, the islands which abound in lizards although these reptiles are scarce elsewhere – all these make the Lake of the Woods a region abounding in Indian legend.
>
> On the second morning, we began to get out into the open waters. A thunderstorm had swept the lake during the night, but the morning was calm and the heavy sweeps were not able to make much way. Suddenly, the wind veered round to the northwest. We set sail for a strait known as the Grassy Portage, which the high stage of water in the lake enabled us to run through without touching ground. Beyond this strait there stretched away a vast expanse of water over which the white-capped waves were running in high billows from the west. On we swept over the high-rolling billows with a double reef in the lug sail. Before us, far away, rose a rocky promontory, the extreme point of which we had to weather to make the mouth of Rainy River. Keeping the boat as close to the wind as she would go, we reeled on over the tumbling seas. Our lee-way was very great, and for some time it seemed doubtful if we would clear the point; as we neared it we saw that there was a tremendous sea running against the rock, the white sprays shooting far up into the air. The wind had now freshened to a gale and the boat laboured much, constantly shipping sprays. At last we were abreast of the rocks, close hauled, and yet only a hundred yards from the breakers. Suddenly, the wind veered a little, or the heavy swell which was running caught us, for we began

to drift quickly down into the mass of breakers. The men were all huddled together in the bottom of the boat and for a moment or two nothing could be done. 'Out with the sweeps!' I roared. All was confusion; the long sweeps got foul of each other, and for a second everything went wrong. At last three sweeps were got to work, but they could do nothing against such a sea. We were close to the rocks, so close that one began to make preparations for doing something – one didn't well know what – when we should strike. Two more oars were out. How they did pull! And it told; in spite of wave and wind we were around the point, but it was only by a shade. An hour later we were running through a vast expanse of marsh and reeds into the mouth of the Rainy River.

Colonel Garnet Wolseley and his troops rowed out on the lake from the marsh a few days later. Wolseley wrote:
A large sand-bar has formed in the Lake of the Woods immediately across the mouth of the river, upon which great seas, rolling in from the ocean-like lake beyond, broke with a loud roar, sending up clouds of spray in an angry fashion. Looking out westward as we passed between the bar and the shore, where the water was calm as a harbour, the lake was covered with 'white-horses'. No open boat could have crossed the bar; so we turned northward, keeping near shore, but between it and a line of sandy dunes. These sand-banks extended some six or eight miles, running tolerably parallel with the shore, and from a thousand to two thousand yards from it. The water was very shallow at places, and as we got towards the end of the protecting sand-banks, the force of the waves increased, so that all chance

of beating to windward under sail was out of the question. We were forced to put into a rocky island partly covered with trees, where we were detained two days by a heavy westerly gale – a severe trial to our patience. When we did get off, some of us were without guides in crossing the lake, and as the maps were altogether wrong, many wandered about at the northern extremity of the lake searching in vain for the mouth of the Winnipeg River.

WOLSELEY HAD AMPLE TIME to admire "the fine, perpendicular cliffs tinted with many shades of red," and the island gardens "where the Indians, from time immemorial, have been in the habit of growing potatoes and maize." The lake's water, he noted, "is, except at a very few places, of a dark-green colour, and almost opaque from a profuseness of confervoid growth [algae]. These confervae are minute, needle-shaped organisms, of a bright green hue, and about half an inch in length. They are in such quantities at places that the water resembles green pea-soup. When pressed between the teeth they have a pungent flavour like mustard. Our mosquito nets were here very useful for straining the water, but it was not fit for drinking until boiled."

The lost commander's emotions can only be imagined; in a magazine article, he summed up this experience in one sentence: "To lose one's way upon an expanse of water like the Lake of the Woods, and to wander about in a boat, as the writer did, through its maze of uninhabited islands, where no sound was to be heard but the dip of the oars at regular intervals, or the distant and weird-like whistle of the loon, is to experience the exquisite sensation of solitude in all its full intensity." Wolseley was not as solitary as he felt; a passing Ojibwe guided his boat to Rat Portage.

The lake spirits were having a little sport with the British, but the storms, stirred up by Mi-shi-pi-zhiw, the Great Water Lynx, might have drowned them. Offerings on rock ledges may commemorate lives lost. Old fishermen tell of boats catching fire and sinking, swamping in storms or smashing on the treacherous reefs; the lake bottom is littered with wrecks. Many reefs are named for the men who drowned or the boats that sank there; boaters are now cautioned to carry charts and not travel after sunset. In winter, lake travellers who stray on to soft ice may disappear; all that was found of one man who walked to the post office was a packet of letters frozen in the ice beside a black hole.

The lake's mood changes with the seasons, the weather and the daily cycle of the sun. Artist Walter J. Phillips visited Lake of the Woods at all times of the year. Phillips painted the white pine, with its "wheel-shaped branches of dark-green needles," the birch, "whose opalescent bole reflects the colours of surrounding things," and the poplar, "with twisted branching, delightfully capricious, and dancing leaves – a medley of dark green discs, spinning golden guineas, oval mirrors the colour of the sky. I shall never forget the extraordinary sensation of standing in a copse of young poplars whose leaves, seared by an early frost, had turned an even yellow. The trees were high enough to form a partial canopy that obscured the burning blue sky, and I was shrouded, enwrapped, enmeshed and circumvested in gold."

Phillips also appreciated the subtle colours of early spring: "A few meandering channels cleft the ice – strips of blue in pallid harmony of grays, snow lay in white accents on the sheltered shores of the islands and beneath the trees, which were brown in hue. In the foreground were yellow tufts of dead grasses amidst the snow. The only greens of any brilliance were in the mosses on the rocks."

Though he rarely tired of trying, Phillips found it impossible to reproduce in watercolour the reflections of the sky on the water, "never still, never the same and moving rhythmically. Sometimes clouds appear upon it as a multitude of small ovals, enveloping others of different colour or tone. They appear and vanish in a flash, and dance with an

abandon that inspires all beholders. There is the sheen of the sun on the ripples – countless images of the sun that dazzle and glitter with a blinding brilliance." But he found the lake's greatest beauty in the sky itself:

> The evening sky over the end of the bay is laced with wisps of golden cloud. The moon is low on the horizon. We are between the sun and the moon, and this is the golden hour. The suffusion of light creates soft harmonies and in a measure mitigates the chromatic crimes our neighbours have committed on their boathouses. The shadows are cool and enhance the brilliance of the light. The wispy clouds deepened to crimson as we sat.

A FINE SUNSET, Phillips acknowledged, yet, "here at Lake of the Woods majestic cumulous clouds often rise in the eastern skies in the evening. Tinted by the sun, they reflect its last rays – gold, orange, red, and the last ghostly gray in the night. The limpid shadows that reveal its contours, the thoughts that its magnificence inspires, why, with this object of splendour in the heavens, who would look at a sunset?"

After sunset, summer nights become alive with the rhythmic thrumming of nighthawks' wings, and the hoots, scurrying, snufflings, shrieks and howls of nocturnal hunters and their prey. On calm nights, loons' yodels carry for miles; during storms, thunder crashes overhead, and forks of lightning seem to rend the rocks, silhouetting whitecaps and tossing trees. Away from the water, the woods are inky, but near the lake, even on a cloudy, moonless night, the stars cast a pale radiance. When the sky is clear, the shining dome of the universe is reflected in the water. Northern lights shimmer in wispy green curtains, or writhe in huge, multicoloured coils; in the summer of 2003, Mars smouldered like a hot coal in the southeast. Sometimes, as the eastern sky flushes, the moon yet rides high in the west, slowly fading into the blue as songbirds celebrate the sunrise.

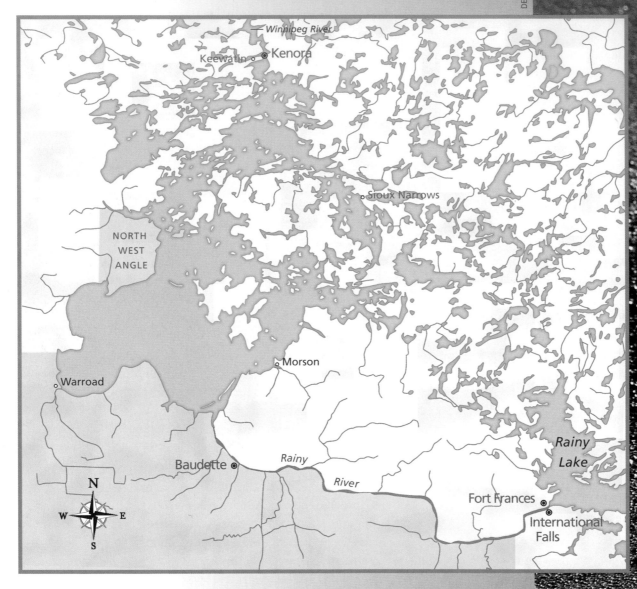

Winnipeg River

Keewatin ○ ◉ Kenora

○ Sioux Narrows

NORTH
WEST
ANGLE

○ Morson

○ Warroad

Baudette ◉

Rainy

River

Rainy
Lake

Fort Frances ◉

International
Falls

N
W ✦ E
S

Remnants of Earth's creation are evident in
many places around Lake of the Woods.

THE **CREATION STORY**

THE
CREATION
STORY

IN THE BEGINNING, about 4.5 billion years ago, cosmic gases and dust particles swirled together, releasing tremendous heat, to form the molten blob we call Earth. Over the next billion years, Earth began to cool and its hot, heavy liquid core became covered by a semi-solid mantle of lighter material topped by a thin crust. As the crust cooled and hardened, hot gases and lavas, under tremendous pressure beneath, burst through cracks and fissures to create mountainous volcanoes. This volcanic activity lasted about another billion years, a time geologists call the Archean eon of the Precambrian period.

DENNIS FAST

Earth's first rocks were formed during this time, among them the basalts and granites of Lake of the Woods.

"This was a violent place in Precambrian times," says Dick Beard, geologist with the Ontario ministry of Northern Development and Mines from 1974 to 1998. "It was very, very active volcanically. There were volcanoes every thirty to fifty miles." The volcanoes spewed out two kinds of lava, or magma: "The first kind is the dark basaltic rock, formed from a very thin lava that pours out of volcanoes in flat beds. It's not very spectacular, the lava just flows down the sides of the volcano. The second kind of lava is called rhyolite. It's very thick, so when it tries to poke up through the volcano's vent, it gets stuck and builds up pressure. So you get an explosive volcano that throws great chunks of rhyolite into the air. When that kind of lava solidifies, it's lighter, coarser, more like a granite."

Granites, shading from grey to beige to white, sometimes tinged red or pink with iron oxide, solidified beneath or inside the volcanoes. Hard and coarse-grained, they pushed up into the volcanic surface rock to form intrusive masses geologists call plutons or batholiths. The force of the intrusions bent and buckled the surrounding rock, releasing subterranean gases and liquids as described by nineteenth-century geologist Dr. George Bryce: "The contorted strata of the rocks ... had many crevices, faults, fissures, broken seams, cracks and openings in their structure. The intrusive rocks would liberate in their upheaval great bodies of lava, steam and boiling water from the vast depths below. These would have metals in a state of solution. The cooling down of the materials thus carried in makes the veins." When Dr. Bryce gave his talk to the Manitoba Historical and Scientific Society in 1881, veins of gold had recently been discovered at Lake of the Woods.

Shrouded in dark, roiling rain clouds, Earth was swept by violent storms during the volcanic period; lightning crackled and thunder boomed over the red glow of the

KITCHE MANITOU

I N *OJIBWE HERITAGE*, Basil Johnston gives a spiritual version of the Creation story. He tells how Kitche Manitou, the Great Spirit, fulfilled his vision: "Out of nothing he made rock, water, fire and wind. Into each one he breathed the breath of life. On each he bestowed with his breath a different essence and nature. Each substance had its own power which became its soul-spirit. From these four substances Kitche Manitou created the physical world of sun, stars, moon and earth.

"To the sun, Kitche Manitou gave the powers of light and heat. To the earth he gave growth and healing; to waters, purity and renewal; to the wind music and the breath of life itself. On earth, Kitche Manitou formed mountains, valleys, plains, islands, lakes, bays and rivers. Everything was in its place; everything was beautiful.

"Then Kitche Manitou made the plant beings. These were four kinds: flowers, grasses, trees and vegetables. To each he gave a spirit of life, growth, healing and beauty. Each he placed where it would be most beneficial, and lend to earth the greatest beauty, harmony and order.

Eddy Cobiness painted in several styles, each independent of the others. Perhaps the one that most reflects his Ojibwe heritage is this technique, which is reminiscent of both ancient rock paintings and modern x-ray technology.

"After plants, Kitche Manitou created animal beings, confering on each special powers and natures. There were two-legged, four-legged, winged and swimmers.

"Last of all, he made man. Though last in the order of creation, least in the order of dependence and weakest in bodily powers, man had the greatest gift – the power to dream.

"Kitche Manitou then made the Great Laws of Nature for the wellbeing and harmony of all things and all creatures. The Great Laws governed the place and movement of the sun, moon, earth and stars; governed the powers of wind, water, fire and rock; governed the rhythm and continuity of life, birth, growth and decay. All things lived and worked by these laws."

"MALE & FEMALE CARIBOU" BY EDDY COBINESS / COURTESY OF HELEN COBINESS AND THE WAH-SA GALLERY

Cobiness

eruptions. Earth's crust was under water, the volcanic cones poking up above the storm-lashed waves, and the waves and incessant rain washed volcanic ash and debris, called tuffs, down the sides of the cones. Submerged, these fine grains solidified into basins of layered, sedimentary rock surrounding the volcanoes.

As the virgin rock cooled and hardened, it was baked and squeezed by Earth's internal convulsions, processes geologists call metamorphosis and orogeny – mountain building. Intense heat and pressure transformed the rocks' chemical and mineral characters: a basalt might become a soft soapstone, or a crumbly sedimentary rock a hard chert or glass-like mica. All are present at Lake of the Woods. Road and railway cuts reveal how, as Earth's crust heaved and sighed, granite was tossed up, turned sideways, twisted, kneaded, layered and invaded by molten material, transformed into a new rock known as gneiss.

Until 2.5 billion years ago, the lake's morphing rocks were also on the move. During a period of tectonic activity – the shifting of Earth's layered crust – that lasted for about 300 million years, the volcanic and sedimentary rocks of the Lake of the Woods region, under pressure from granite masses to the north and south, buckled, sheared and folded to form an elongated series of ridges and basins called a "greenstone belt" running in an east-west direction. This wave-like formation can be seen in aerial photographs and geologists' maps, which show the lake's islands, the tips of underwater greenstone ridges, strung out in a series of arcs.

George Mercer Dawson, in mid-career. Despite considerable physical disability, Dawson was an insightful scientist and an intrepid traveller.

THE NORTHERN EDGE, or fault line, of the greenstone belt was discovered by sharp-eyed geologist George M. Dawson during his meticulous survey of Lake of the Woods in 1872. Dawson was travelling by canoe, and when he came to cross Rat Portage at the foot of Portage Bay, he noticed that the rock at the southern end of the path, "worn smooth by the feet of the voyageurs of old time", was greenish-black, but at the height of land it became light, pinkish-grey granitoid gneiss. "The junction is so close that one may actually lay the hand on it," Dawson reported, "and the separating line is remarkably straight and even." Dawson followed the fault for about 100 metres to the west, then located it again above the waterfall at the lake's eastern outlet.

The rocks of Lake of the Woods are among the oldest on Earth, but the lake itself is a relatively new-born remnant of glacial Lake Agassiz, shaped by thousands of years of glaciation and erosion. Apart from the discovery of fossilized algae in Archean rock, geologists can only speculate about the area's history from the time the rocks solidified, about 1.7 billion years ago, to the last period of glaciation, the Wisconsinan, which began about 100,000 years ago. No fossilized crustaceans or dinosaur bones have been found here. Evidence elsewhere suggests, however, that Earth's climate fluctuated dramatically, and central North America was alternately covered by tropical seas, jungles and savannahs, and was later buried beneath thousands of metres of ice. It is likely that the ancient granites and greenstones of Lake of the Woods, and of all northern Ontario, were at one time covered with limestone, shale and sandstone formed from sediment

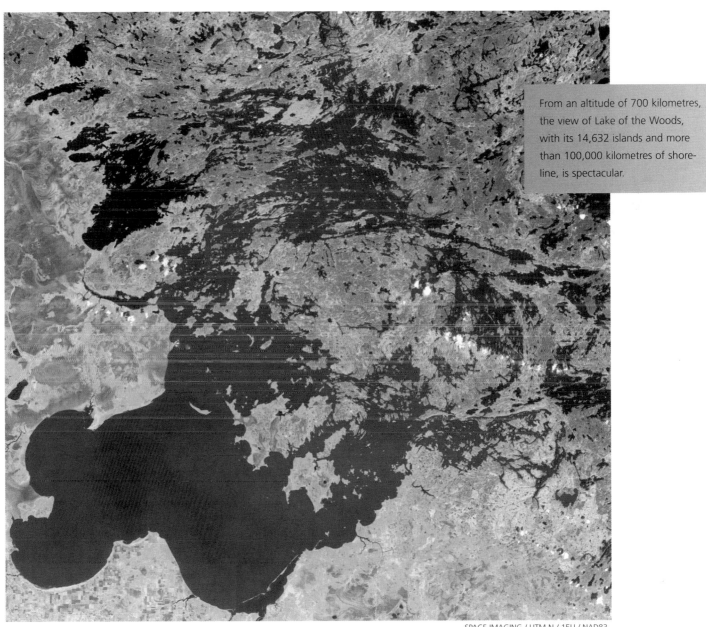

From an altitude of 700 kilometres, the view of Lake of the Woods, with its 14,632 islands and more than 100,000 kilometres of shoreline, is spectacular.

SPACE IMAGING / UTM N / 15U / NAD83

left by the vast inland seas; as Earth's crust sagged and heaved, these sediments and soft rocks eroded away into the rivers, lakes and oceans.

THE ROUNDED HILLS and bare granite outcrops characteristic of the northern part of Lake of the Woods appear to be the remains of mountain ranges worn low and smooth by eons of abrasion and erosion. Certainly they bear the scars of the great Laurentide ice sheet that covered eighty per cent of Canada until it began to melt away about 13,000 years ago. As it advanced and retreated, ceaselessly moving, the glacier dislodged rock fragments that became frozen in the ice. Like a heavy, rough-soled boot, the glacier scoured, sanded and polished the landscape, scraping it down to its bare bones, leaving long grooves, called striations, gouged in the rock. Rocks cracked apart by the frost and the weight of the ice were ground into gravel, sand and clay, or rounded into boulders that were often stranded, like giant eggs, in unexpected places: limestone boulders were dragged hundreds of kilometres from the west and deposited on the lake's southwest shores. The glacier also left curious "potholes" at several places on the shore, deep holes in bedrock so perfectly circular that they look man-made. Dick Beard explains them as a phenomenon caused by glacial meltwater: "Water cleared off the glaciers very fast, like rapids. If a boulder got stuck in a little crack in the rock under the glacier, the fast water swirled that rock around, making a pothole. The water kicked out that rock, then another rock came in and swirled around. These potholes are up to five feet deep."

The ice sheet, divided pincer-like into the Labrador lobe on the east and Keewatin lobe on the west, pushed and dragged with it vast quantities of rock, sand, soil and clay; when it melted, this debris became the bottom and shoreline of glacial Lake Agassiz. For much of its existence, Lake Agassiz was landlocked: contained within the Arctic watershed, it could drain only to the north where the retreating ice sheet blocked all exits to Hudson Bay. As well, Earth's crust, depressed several hundred metres under the glacier's weight, began to rebound, a process called isostatic uplift that continues today.

Geomorphologist Dr. Brian Phillips has studied its impact on the formation of Lake of the Woods: "The once horizontal shorelines of Lake Agassiz were deformed, the

vertical displacement increasing to the northeast. In spite of the land's downward slope to Hudson Bay, Lake of the Woods lies on a surface that has risen and developed a relative tilt to the south." Phillips measured the height above sea level of an old Lake Agassiz shoreline running roughly from the Rainy River to Kenora; it rose from 350 metres at the Rainy River to 375 metres near Kenora, a tilt of about one metre in four kilometres (or just over three feet every two-and-a-half miles). The tilt forced Lake Agassiz's trapped water to flow to the south, carrying with it the glacier's load of till, sand, clay and flotsam that eventually formed a thick layer of sediment. When Lake Agassiz finally drained north, leaving Lake of the Woods, in Phillips' words, "a little puddle", the accumulation of sediment made the southern half of the lake shallow and murky, with a low, sandy shoreline that shifted with the winds, a striking contrast to the craggy

CARL GUSTAF LINDE / LAKE OF THE WOODS MUSEUM, KENORA

With its sandbars, meandering channels and wetlands, the southwest shore of Lake of the Woods, an obvious legacy of Lake Agassiz, is a world apart from the rest of the lake.

islands, deep water and a powerful current that sucked the lake into the Winnipeg River to the north.

Centuries of wind and waves sculpted the soft sediment of the lake's southern shore into bays and lagoons, beaches and sand spits, as well as the Sable Islands that shelter the mouth of the Rainy River. The broad stretch of shallow open water, no more than ten metres (or about thirty feet) deep, is lashed by summer storms and strong, steady winds; waves as high as three metres pound the shore, and high winds create a "wind tide." Phillips explains: "When the wind blows over a water surface it extends a horizontal stress on the water, driving it in the direction of the wind. This wind effect can result in the piling up of water at the leeward end of an enclosed water body, and a lowering of the water level at the windward end."

In a sandy environment almost any variation in wave action or water level alters the form of the beach. Moderate winds and waves push sand from the lake bottom towards the shore, building the beach, while choppy storm waves comb down the beach by dragging sand offshore. Waves breaking at an angle move the sand along the shore. "Beaches have been described as rivers of sand," says Phillips. "A beach provides the best natural protection against erosion of the shoreline, absorbing wave energy by compliantly changing the form and slope of the beach face for every size of and direction of wave attack."

Erosion has been transforming the south and western shorelines of Lake of the Woods since the lake came into being. In 1872, a summer of high water, geologist G.M. Dawson commented: "A more forbidding and desolate region can scarcely be imagined. In some places, low, swampy savannah fronts directly on the lake, and this I have seen fringed, after a gale, by a belt many feet in width of brown, vegetable pulp, equally impossible to walk on, and impassable for the canoe. The lake is perpetually extending its border southward and westward among the swamps, sandhills and lagoons by which it is surrounded. Tamarack swamps are in some places so rapidly encroached on that the trees may be seen along the shore bending forward at every angle and falling into the lake." The lake's basin may be tilting as little as thirteen centimetres (or about five inches) a century, but the tilt is irreversible.

EROSION IS PART of the lake's natural cycle. However, at the end of the nineteenth century, a new shoreline was created when dams were built across the lake's northern outlets. The water level rose more than a metre. In low-lying areas, the dammed lake flooded forests, wild rice beds, hay meadows, fish spawning grounds, campsites, farms and homes, and the water never receded. Old beaches, once able to restore themselves during periods of low water, were permanently submerged; sand spits broke into islands, islands became reefs. A "prehistoric mound" on Sable Island, mapped in an 1886 geological survey, disappeared. Phillips believes that the mound might have been there for 2,000 years, but Sable Island itself, shaped by waves and currents, is migrating south; in 2002, half a kilometre of the island disappeared under water. The south shore of Lake of the Woods, destabilized, choked with silt and debris, is drowning.

Lowering the lake's summer level by .6 metres (slightly less than two feet) would reduce damage from waves and wind tides, but would lower water jeopardize the efficiency of the hydro electric dams at the lake's outlets and on the Winnipeg River? In 1872, before hydro, G.M. Dawson, dismissing the southwestern lakeshore as "utterly useless", proposed a bolder solution: "Should land for agricultural purposes ever become of value in this region," he advised, "a great area of the bottom of the lake might be laid dry, at comparatively small expense, by removing the rocky barrier at Rat Portage, the water being thus lowered about eighteen feet."

Though he was never completely satisfied with his efforts, others have marvelled at Walter J. Phillips' ability to capture the lake's ancient and ever-changing beauty.

THE KENORA BISON – THE LAST OF ITS KIND?

MARCH 25, 1980: Spring is in the air. In a damp peat bog near upper Laurenson's Creek east of Kenora, local contractor Nick Serduletz is dredging up peat to sell as topsoil. The frosty plume of his breath floats upwards and dissolves in the misty air. The growl of his backhoe is the only sound in the bog's gloom.

Serduletz's shovel bites into the peat at the 4.5-metre depth where he's been working. When the shovel surfaces, something in it catches his eye. That rusty brown lump, what is it? Scrap iron? Rock? Root? Two shapes stick out of it like horns on either side. Serduletz shuts off the backhoe and climbs down to take a closer look. The object appears to be the skull of an animal, but this horned monster doesn't resemble any animal Serduletz has ever seen. "I told my friends," Serduletz joked later, "I dug up the Devil himself."

Serduletz reported his find to district archaeologists Grace Rajnovich and C.S. "Paddy" Reid. They hadn't seen anything like it either. Sifting through the peat where the skull had been found, they recovered a partial skeleton – sixty-one bones and fourteen teeth – stained brown but well preserved. The depth of the peat on top indicated that the beast had died there

a long time ago, but when? And what was it? They sent the skull, teeth and bones to mammologists George Lammers and Jack Dubois at the Manitoba Museum in Winnipeg.

The excited scientists tentatively identified the skull as *Bison crassicornis*, a species of bison that became extinct more than 10,000 years ago, but radiocarbon dating of a rib established that the bison died 4,270 years BP (Before Present, with 1950 used as the baseline date), plus or minus sixty-five years. After paleobiologist Jerry McDonald of the United States National Museum of Natural History examined the skeleton, the scientists agreed that it was a *Bison antiquus occidentalis,* a bison native to North America that lived between 11,000 and 4,000 BP. The Kenora bison was the youngest of this species ever found. The only bison skeleton unearthed in Ontario's boreal forest, it had died 280 kilometres north and sixty-five kilometres east of the previously known limits of bison range.

The bison, a mature, adult male, had suffered; both jaws had been broken, apparently by a severe blow, earlier in its life, and while the fractures had healed, its teeth showed evidence of moderate but chronically inadequate nutrition at the time of its death. How did it die? Nothing indicated that it had been killed by predators. No spear points or arrowheads were found on the site, and the bones showed no signs of having been gnawed or torn apart by carnivores.

The skull of Kenora's *Bison antiquus occidentalis* not only raises a host of questions, but provides some answers. Whether he was the last, lonely one of his kind, or one of a small, dwindling herd, it seems clear that the area along the Winnipeg River (where other, older skeletons have been found) and around Lake of the Woods was a haven for a species on the edge of extinction.

THE MANITOBA MUSEUM / # V1687 / # 595

Analysis of the abundant, well-preserved seeds and pollen in sediment within the bison's skull and the peat bog created a portrait of the bog as it had been when the bison died. Botanist John McAndrews of the Royal Ontario Museum found proof of larch trees, swamp birch and blackberry shrubs, with a preponderance of water and marsh plants. McAndrews concluded that "the bison died in a water-lily covered pond one or two metres deep that was bordered with a marsh dominated by shrubs; wetland conifers, likely spruce and larch, grew nearby. The pond subsequently filled in and the site became bog forest." McAndrews' analysis of pollen evidence from nearby Hayes Lake indicated that between 9,200 and 3,600 years BP, bison would have been able to browze in an open woodland rich in herbs, oak savanna and alders, but as the climate cooled, stands of

The 'Fall of the Moving Waters' was one of many cataracts on the upper Winnipeg River. Eight or nine thousand years ago, it's possible that bison grazed within the sound of the falls; later, the falls bewitched and bedevilled early paddlers. Ultimately, they all were dammed to create hydroelectric power.

pine and spruce overran the meadows and deciduous forests. The Kenora bison may have drowned, foundered in the mud, succumbed to disease or old age, but its grave in a wetland suggests that Lake of the Woods was a doomed last refuge; even before 5,000 years ago, *Bison antiquus occidentalis* had been extirpated from the open plains. The last survivors lived on for a time on the fringes of the eastern prairies and, apparently, at the Lake of the Woods. Was the Kenora bison the very last of its kind?

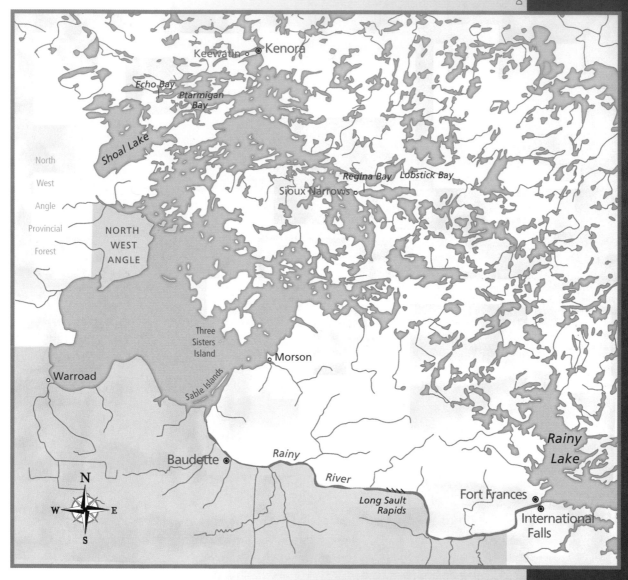

Keewatin ○ ● Kenora

Echo Bay

Ptarmigan Bay

Shoal Lake

North West Angle Provincial Forest

NORTH WEST ANGLE

Regina Bay   Lobstick Bay

Sioux Narrows ○

Three Sisters Island

○ Morson

Warroad ○

Sable Islands

Rainy

Baudette ◎

River

Rainy Lake

Long Sault Rapids

Fort Frances ◎

○

International Falls

N
W   E
S

Ring-billed gulls, right, stand watch over the lake; they are among
hundreds of species of flora and fauna that have made Lake of
the Woods their home since the end of the last glaciation.
Over time, changes in climate, variations in water levels and
population pressures have all left a mark on the lake's
plant and animal communities.

FOREST MEETS MEADOW

A florescent autumn maple, left, lights the ancient bones of the Earth along the Rainy River.

Working in a variety of media, Walter J. Phillips never tired of attempting to capture the primaeval landscapes of Lake of the Woods; this watercolour dates from 1927.

inhospitable to any other form of life. It is so prolific that populations can reach more than several billion per acre. Springtails are good composters and recyclers of decaying vegetation, and they provide food for many species of ants, beetles and small animals. Most springtails are inconspicuous, but hordes of hopping snow fleas often cover snow banks in late winter and early spring.

ANTS AND BEETLES, predatory, omnivorous, adaptable and aggressive, would have followed; ants are one of the most numerous creatures on earth, beetles and weevils

are the largest order of families in the entire animal kingdom. Both can fly, and, unlike other winged insects, they are equipped with sturdy legs that enable them to dig, climb, grasp and scurry across the ground at remarkable speeds. They are protected by a hard carapace, in beetles often an iridescent green, blue or gold, that frustrates predators and allows them to burrow under debris or into the earth for shelter. Many beetles spend most of their lives underground as eggs, larvae and pupae. Beetles are found in and on the ground, on plants and trees and crawling, burrowing, diving, scavenging and whirling on and in the water.

Many insects, along with algae, aquatic plants and fish, came north by water from the Mississippi River watershed, which briefly drained Lake Agassiz into the Gulf of Mexico. Among the most numerous, and unusual, of these insects were the ancient, primitive mayflies, or "fish flies", and the caddisflies. Both larvae thrive in clean, moving water, and, as adults clumsily plopping on to the surface of a lake, or as underwater nymphs, they are gobbled up by fish, especially lake trout, a fish found only in cold, deep water. Mayflies, with their soft, translucent bodies, Tinkerbell wings and two delicate filaments extending from the rear abdomen, emerge from the water with one single purpose: to molt, mate and die. Since their airborne lives are so brief, they are known as "emphemeroptera", and when swarms of mayflies molt, copulate and die at once, their rotting bodies form reeking, wave-washed windrows on the shores.

Caddisflies, drab, moth-like insects, emerge from what looks to be a tiny, living bundle of sticks that staggers along the lake bottom. Each caddisfly larva, as soon it hatches from an egg, begins to construct a protective case from silk, sand grains, bits of leaves, twigs, shell and anything else it can find in the neighbourhood. As the larva grows, the case enlarges to fit and eventually becomes a snug home where the larva pupates into an adult. Trout will eat the larvae, sticks, sand and all.

FROGS AND TOADS TOO CAME NORTH, able, by slowing their winter metabolism to near-death rates, to survive long months burrowed in the mud. Embryo clams, snails, crayfish and other crustaceans, hitching rides on the scales of migrating fish, moved in to populate the shallows of the warming lake. Here, they provided easy pickings for the stately, vigilant great blue heron; nearby, the indefatigable sandpiper kept shorelines impeccably free of insect life. Bugs, seeds and berries attracted grey jays, chickadees, juncos, cedar waxwings and song sparrows. Dabbling ducks nested in the sedges, feeding on invertebrate embryos and pondweeds; loons, deep-diving fish eaters, nested on shallow, mossy depressions in the rocks by the shore, their eerie calls answering each other across the water. Ravens, given their hardiness, talent for scavenging and mythic reputation as messengers, may have been the first birds to venture this far north and to stay over the winter.

There is, as yet, no evidence that mastodons, mammoths or other giant species inhabited Lake of the Woods, but a spruce forest would have attracted woodland caribou, moose, wolves and grouse. During the prairie era, herds of bison seem to have grazed where dense forests now stand and after the bison came elk, bears and white-tailed deer. Warm, shallow water stimulated the growth of marsh plants that provided habitat for sturgeon, pike, muskellunge, perch and walleye (or pickerel). Wild rice, a grass that grows in fairly shallow, slow-moving water, may have migrated to the lake at this time. Pine forests would have been populated by squirrels, stands of poplar by beaver.

The diversity of the Lake of the Woods landscape – forest, rock, muskeg, meadow, sand – makes it a biological phenomenon. Boreal forest, with its mix of pine, birch, spruce, poplar and balsam fir, grows on the thin, rocky soil to the north and east of the lake. Here the undergrowth is a tangle of alder and mountain maple, yew, hazel, honeysuckle, mountain ash, prickly rose and wild raspberry; the ground is covered with bunchberry, wild sarsparilla, wild lilies, bed straw, violets and wood anemones; in May, marsh marigolds, bright as daffodils, bloom in low, wet areas.

But, to the southeast, huge hardwood trees grow in the Rainy River Valley, trees normally found on the Great Lakes and St. Lawrence River: black and red ash, red maple, yellow birch, basswood and elm, all mixed with white cedar, tamarack and the ubiquitous poplar. This is a fertile forest full of chokecherries, cranberries, strawberries and acorn-bearing bur oaks. In autumn, the leaves of the trees and shrubs turn incendiary shades of red, orange and gold; even the tamarack blanches pale yellow and sheds its needles. In the marsh, or fen, at the river's mouth, the autumn sedges, grasses and reeds form an undulating quilt of soft browns and honey golds. Apart from some rocky outcrops, this marsh continues around the lake's south shore to the west, where the lake oozes away into a Great Bog.

Plants grow at Lake of the Woods that are found nowhere else in Ontario, and nowhere else in Canada's boreal forest. In preliminary field studies in the area between 1994 and 1998, biologists W.D. Bakowsky and M.J. Oldham of Ontario's Ministry of Natural Resources identified five prairie and savannah sites they classified as

Standing more than a metre tall, right, with a wingspan of almost two metres, the great blue heron is North America's largest heron and among its tallest birds.

Where bison and caribou once grazed, white-tailed deer now are found in large numbers.

GUY FONTAINE

THE MANITOBA MUSEUM

ON LAKE OF THE WOODS

-Linde-

A WOODLAND CARIBOU SEEKS GREENER PASTURES.

Clockwise from top left: A great grey owl zeroes in on its prey, a rare piping plover guards its eggs on a pebble-strewn beach and a blue jay fluffs its feathers to keep out the winter cold.

"extremely rare". One, a mesic, moist prairie adjacent to Manitou Rapids and the Long Sault Rapids on the Rainy River, they described as of "immense significance, as it represents the only known occurrences of this vegetation in northwestern Ontario." Moreover, this vegetation is "globally rare, having been almost entirely lost due to agricultural and residential land use." Here, in addition to common prairie species – smooth aster, northern bedstraw, hairy meadow-rue, snakeroot and golden alexanders – they found oval-leaved milkweed, a plant previously thought to have been extirpated from Ontario. As a bonus, they identified a globally rare dragonfly, the green-faced clubtail, last seen, in southern Ontario, in 1925.

INVESTIGATING FIFTEEN OPEN, south-facing slopes next to water, Bakowsky and Oldham discovered sixty species of provincially rare plants, including eight never recorded before in northwestern Ontario: early buttercup, prairie smoke, Venus's looking-glass, rough pennyroyal, creeping lovegrass, Pennsylvania pellitory, hooked buttercup and spring forget-me-not. Twenty-eight species of prairie grasses and wildflowers were catalogued: big and little bluestem, needlegrass and prairie onion on the dry sites, sunflowers and goldenrod in the bur oak savannahs. Native hairy golden aster and purple prairie-clover, previously thought to have been imported, were found in Echo Bay, near Shoal Lake on the west, but the richest communities of prairie and southern exotics occupied island locations in Ptarmigan Bay, Regina Bay and Lobstick Bay on the lake's northern shores, regions commonly assumed to be inhospitable forest.

On Lake of the Woods, plants from the west and the south mingle with northern natives to form a unique environment; a tiny cactus, the fragile prickly pear, clings to shallow soil and rocky crevices on the lake's western shores. Prairie vegetation has lured meadowlarks, blackbirds, magpies and other western birds to nest at Lake of the Woods, among

them a rare, endangered species, the piping plover. A stocky little grey-and-white shorebird with a distinctive black collar, the piping plover scavenges tasty tidbits washed up by the waves. It nests in the open, laying its eggs in a shallow depression in the gravelly beach. While plovers have excellent camouflage, and use broken-wing feint tactics to distract

DENNIS FAST

predators, their exposed nests, easily washed away by high waves, are vulnerable to raids from gulls, crows and other predators. A census in 1996 counted 698 pairs of piping plovers breeding on the Canadian prairies, predominantly in Saskatchewan, and one pair in Ontario: this pair was nesting on an island in Lake of the Woods. Normally, there are four to six plovers on the Ontario side of the lake, with another forty to fifty in Minnesota. Plovers once nested on the Sable Islands, but recently abandoned this site.

American white pelicans reach the eastern edge of their breeding grounds at Lake of the Woods, nesting in colonies on bare rock outcrops called the Three Sisters Islands. Like

Braving a cool spring, American white pelicans return to breed. Only thirty years ago, these majestic birds were listed as "threatened"; today they are back in large numbers.

IMAGES THIS PAGE: GUY FONTAINE

Astoundingly graceful in flight, given their size, pelicans have been compared to C-130 Transports.

plovers, pelicans lay their eggs in the open, but pelicans have the advantage of size and numbers; as many as 16,000 breeding pairs crowd together on the rocks in the spring. Big and bulky, with black-edged wings spanning three metres or more, nesting pelicans hover over their fledglings, spreading their wings like beach umbrellas to protect their broods from other birds and the blazing sun. Waddling on land, or bobbing on the water like oversize bathtub toys, pelicans, with their strange pouches, look a little foolish; in flight, flocks of pelicans soar and wheel in military formation with spectacular grace. Only hawks and the maligned turkey vultures ride the winds as well as the pelicans; the bald eagle, the lake's most prestigious and imposing bird, will hover, as silent as its shadow on the ground, but eagles usually fly purposefully with regular strokes of their powerful wings.

PELICANS KEEP CONSTANT COMPANY with their skinny, long-necked sooty cousins, double-crested cormorants. Opposite as they appear to be, pelicans and cormorants fish together on an assembly line. Gathering in flocks that can number into the thousands, cormorants, strong divers, scare schools of small fish to the surface, gobbling their fill in pursuit, while the pelicans, unable to dive, cruise in parallel lines, scooping up the frantic fish as they churn to the surface. Beaks full, the pelicans in front of the lines fall back to the rear, giving the pelicans behind their turn until all stomachs are bursting or the fish have escaped.

Eastern birds also nest at Lake of the Woods. In a 1978 study of the North West Angle Provincial Forest and southeastern Manitoba, ornithologist Robert Ferguson found, in addition to the tree swallows, wrens, nuthatches, sparrows and chickadees he expected in a spruce forest, dozens of birds more characteristic of a deciduous, eastern Ontario

forest: eastern phoebe, eastern wood pee wee, rose-breasted grosbeak, common grackle, pine warbler, American woodcock and scarlet tanager, and the last three were nesting at the western limits of their breeding grounds.

From early March, when eagles and crows return, until late August, when the warblers fly south, the birds' songs, squabbles and conversations create the lake's impromptu music; once loons strike up an evening chorus, they may continue intermittently until warblers and song sparrows tune up at dawn. Even in winter, birds remain. On December 18, 1999, the twentieth annual Kenora Christmas bird count recorded 3,619 birds representing thirty-four species, among them: 768 ravens, 604 chickadees, 576 evening grosbeaks, 513 common redpolls, 330 pine grosbeaks, 255 grey and blue jays, 127 waxwings, seventy-three woodpeckers and a cardinal. And since the lake rarely entirely freezes where the current is strong, there was a wintering population of ducks and loons.

Warblers, flycatchers and other carnivorous forest birds come to the Lake of the Woods watershed to feed on its banquet of bugs: the terrain is so ideally suited to certain species they swarm by the billions. Female black flies choose to lay their eggs in cool, shallow running water; mosquitos prefer warm, quiet ponds rich with algae. Lake of the Woods offers both. Black flies and mosquitos live primarily on nectar, but females require a stiff drink of blood to mature their eggs. Unlike the mosquito, which sucks, the black fly bites a hole in its victim's skin.

Flies, including the vicious deer fly, are known to munch on birds and turtles, but their most accessible, vulnerable

prey are the forest's animals. Shy woodland caribou have been driven from the Lake of the Woods area to the spruce forests farther north, while white-tailed deer, which have steadily pushed their range north and west, die in great numbers during cold winters. Muskrats drown when high water floods their lodges. But beaver, hares, wolves, foxes, moose and black bears have long made Lake of the Woods their home. Black bears sleep through the winter, but when the black bear doesn't sleep, it eats. Small for a bear, but strong and smart, a black bear patrols its expansive territory shovelling down whatever comes to hand: berries, with leaves and twigs, nuts, insects, spruce needles, roots, fish, rodents, rabbits, carrion and garbage. Garbage, exotic fast food for a bear, has created a respectful bond with the black bear's greatest territorial rival: people.

Down-covered ducklings are able to walk and swim just hours after birth. Black bears, such as this portly youngster, are omnivorous and adaptable and often seem almost human.

DENNIS FAST

GUY FONTAINE

43

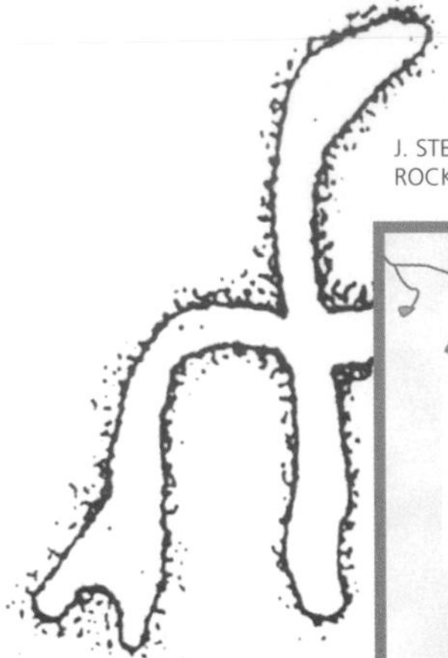

J. STEINBRING, E. DANZIGER & R. CALLAGHAN /
ROCK ART RESEARCH 1987 / VOL. 4, NO. 1

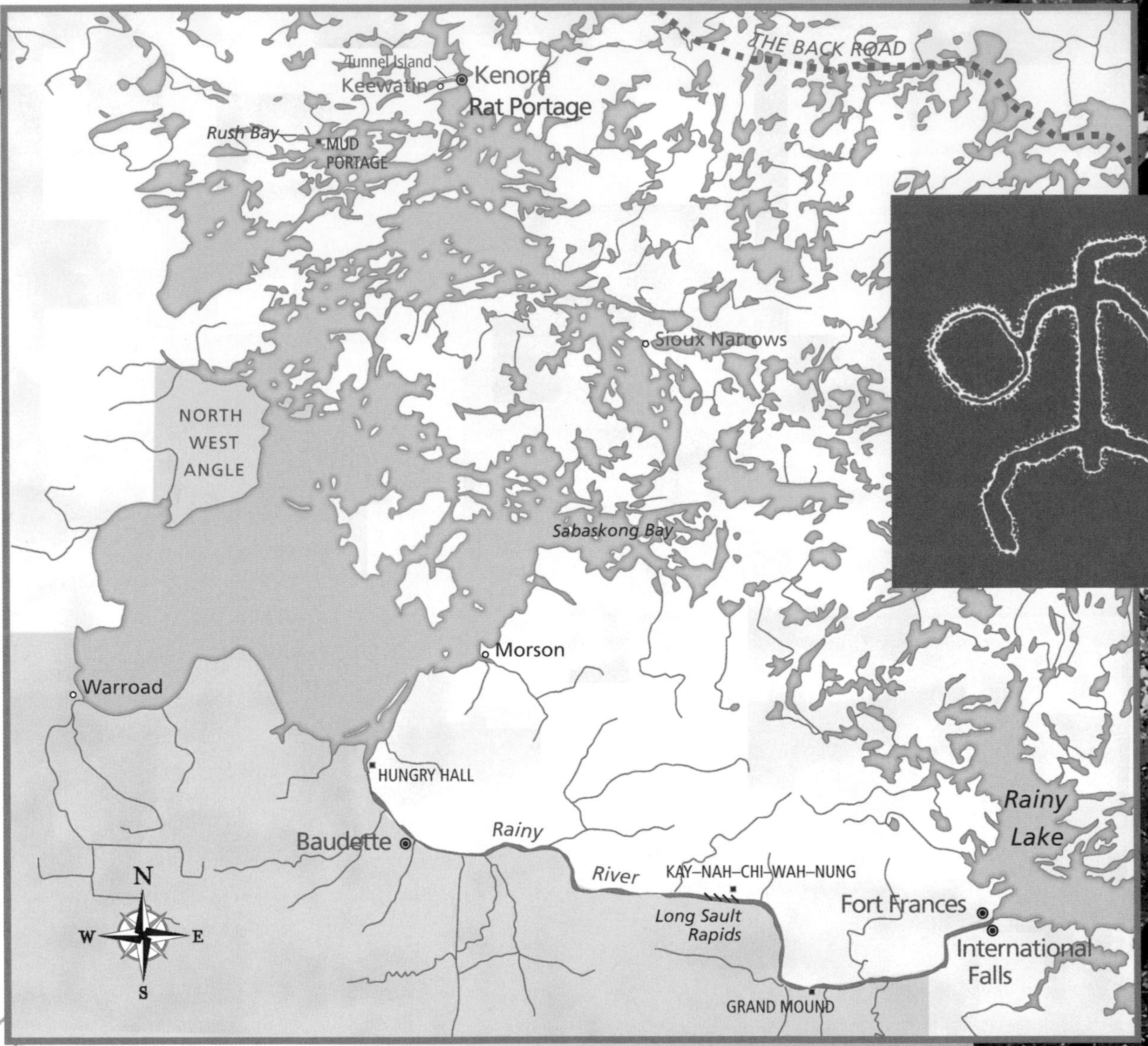

DENNIS FAST

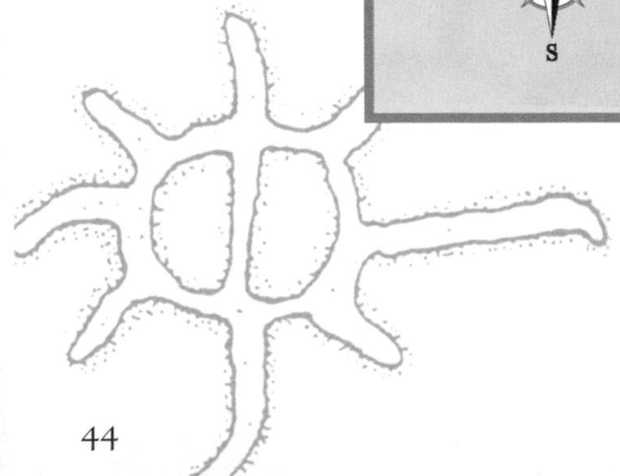

THE BACK ROAD

Tunnel Island
Keewatin
Kenora
Rat Portage

Rush Bay
MUD
PORTAGE

Sioux Narrows

NORTH
WEST
ANGLE

Sabaskong Bay

Morson

Warroad

HUNGRY HALL

Rainy
Baudette

Rainy
Lake

River   KAY–NAH–CHI–WAH–NUNG

Fort Frances

Long Sault
Rapids

International
Falls

N
W   E
S

GRAND MOUND

Petroglyphs, right, identified as representative of
the Clearwater Bay Style, were found at the Mud
Portage Site. These, as well as a multitude of
points and tools uncovered at the site, are
evidence of the long human occupation
around Lake of the Woods.

THE **FIRST PEOPLES**

Hanging Rock Island, one of a series of woodcuts created by Walter J. Phillips in 1934, illustrates the lake's timeless landscape of rock, trees and water.

and traders moving all over the landscape. Well, if those people are moving all over God's half-acre, why not these people? The first people were coming here from the southwest, south and southeast, out of North Dakota, Minnesota, Wisconsin.

HARD EVIDENCE OF PLANO MIGRATION into Lake of the Woods was found in the 1970s in a ploughed field on a farm northeast of the mouth of the Rainy River. The Sandmoen site, named for the property's owners who uncovered the artifacts, is the only Plano site discovered in the western Rainy River/Lake of the Woods area. Archaeologist C.S. "Paddy" Reid identified two long, oval projectile points gouged obliquely in characteristic Plano fashion, a stone knife and the tip of an unidentified weapon or tool. Reid linked the style of the projectile points to Plano weapons found in the Agate Basin in Colorado, yet both weapons and tools were manufactured from local materials, chert and quartz. The lake's numerous outcrops of flaking, flint-like stone would have attracted these people to the area, and Reid believes the Sandmoen site, on a ridge near the lakeshore, represents a well-established, long-term campground.

Among the earliest of these waves of immigrants was a group of people who brought with them an unusual, bright orange rock now called Hixton silicized sandstone. This stone has provided precise information about their origins: "It comes from the southwestern corner of Wisconsin," says Bill Ross. "There's a huge quarry there. The stone is a very distinctive colour, and it's the only material I am aware of that looks like that. It was used extensively throughout southern Wisconsin, primarily in Paleo times, but later too. Up here, it's used only in Paleo times, until about 7,000 years ago. I think over time, and distance, they were losing their connections with their origins."

DDENNIS FAST

Lake of the Woods provided everything early peoples needed. Included in the region's bounty were furs for winter warmth, and such treats for the eye as a rednecked grebe and its chicks, the latter borne safely above the water.

GUY FONTAINE

Harvesting wild rice, above, was relatively easy from a canoe, while drying and winnowing it (inset) rendered it into a light, portable food that kept for years.

valley, where, over centuries, prosperous feudal-style chiefdoms, characterized by monumental earthworks and mortuary mounds, were based on the cultivation of corn, squash and pumpkins. Manitoba archaeologist Leo Pettipas believes that these newcomers to the north may have been driven out of their homeland by overpopulation or warfare, or they may have rebelled against the slave labour required to build these pharaoh-like structures. Perhaps they simply ventured north into the fertile wild rice marshes of Minnesota, rich with fowl, fish and game, then followed the many streams flowing into the Rainy River and Lake of the Woods.

BY 2,200 BP, WHEN they first arrived, they would have found caribou, clay to make pots and, in the river valleys and flood plains, organic soils for growing vegetables. During the next 1,000 years, the Laurel people spread east of Lake Superior, northwest to the Saskatchewan River and almost to Hudson Bay before suddenly retreating to the Lake of the Woods watershed. By a thousand years ago, they had virtually disappeared.

We know many places where these people camped because of the hearths, broken pottery, tools and animal bones they left behind. Both the earliest (circa 2,150 BP) and latest (circa 750 BP) known Laurel sites, excavated by Paddy Reid and Grace Rajnovich between 1975 and 1986, are on the western tip of Tunnel Island where Lake of the Woods empties into the Winnipeg River. Strategically located downstream from a convenient portage around the rapids – later known as Rat Portage – the campsites had a commanding view of the river. At both, as well as at other sites on the lake, Reid and Rajnovich found not only pottery sherds, stone flakes and bones, but rocks or post remnants arranged in the outline of a wigwam. At the later site, called Ballynacree, they uncovered a small village of three almost identical dwellings, large oval structures about eight by four metres with hearths and storage pits and hard-packed dirt floors.

From the evidence, they imagined a classic dome-shaped wigwam made of bowed poles covered with hides or birchbark, its entrance facing east towards the rising sun and away from the river. Each dwelling likely housed a family of ten to twelve people, and the camp, in an area abundant with game, fish and berries, may have been occupied year-round, with seasonal expeditions to spawning grounds and wild rice marshes.

Aboriginal people call wild rice a "gift from the Creator". Low in fat, high in carbohydrates, protein and vitamins, wild rice was their most nutritious natural food, more nutritious than cultivated vegetables and cereals, game or fish. Indeed it was a gift. It reseeded itself annually; seeds or plants could be transported to distant locations to create new beds; it was harvested by simply whacking the ripe grains into a canoe with a long stick, and, once dried, winnowed and parched,

Tipis, wigwams and longhouses continued to be used well into the nineteenth century.

Blackduck pots were widely used for storage and cooking, beginning about 1,300 years ago.

it kept indefinitely in dry bark, hide or clay containers. Boiled, the long black grains fluffing out to many times their size (they were also eaten as popcorn), wild rice had a delicious, nutty flavour that needed no seasonings. A meal in itself, it could be thinned into soup, mixed with fat, berries and sap, or thrown into a pot of boiling meat to thicken a stew. Stored wild rice saved people from famine if the winter hunt failed, and since it was lightweight, it allowed them to travel into strange territory with a secure supply of food. A population explosion caused by better

DENNIS FAST

One of the Manitou Mounds at Kay-Nah-Chi-Wah-Nung. Today, a lovely interpretive centre and guided tours along the Long Rapids of the Rainy River bring this fascinating site to life.

nutrition may have pushed Laurel people to fan out through the north; the cause of their retrenchment and disappearance is a puzzle.

Certainly by 1,000 BP, they appear to have been largely supplanted by a Late Woodland people recognized by an utterly different style of pottery called Blackduck. These pots, marked around the lip and neck with a cord-wrapped stick, have bulbous bottoms impressed with mesh-like markings. Unlike the conical Laurel pots, made, upside down, by coiling and smoothing ropes of clay, Blackduck vessels seem to have been made by pressing wet clay into mesh bags. Since there is no practical reason for the change – Laurel pots, easy to make, nestled comfortably within a ring of hearth stones – the change seems to represent cultural revolution. One theory is that mesh bag technology was brought by women captured from a distant tribe. This theory helps to explain why sites like Ballynacree, which contains an abundance of Laurel and Blackduck artifacts, may have been occupied by two cultural traditions at the same time, and why Blackduck people settled at Laurel locations throughout the Lake of the Woods area. Alternatively, immigrating Blackduck people might have driven the Laurel people from their camps or slaughtered them. Yet again, the new pots may reflect the evolution of fibre technology: potters find it faster and simpler to shape wet, coiled clay in a mesh bag than by smoothing it with their hands, and Blackduck pots, larger, rounder and thinner, held more. Their shape bears a striking resemblance to European iron cauldrons, but Blackduck pots date back to 1,300 BP, about 300 years before the Norse, according to their sagas, set foot in North America.

The mystery of the Woodland peoples' way of life is only deepened by the tumuli or burial mounds they built on the shores of the Rainy River. These mounds range in size from the Grand Mound on the river's south bank near International Falls, Minnesota, to small, low mounds in a grove of old oaks northeast of the river's mouth. On the north side of the river, the Manitou Mounds at Kay-Nah-Chi-Wah-Nung, "the place of the long rapids", cluster along a three-kilometre path along the Long Sault rapids. The largest of the mounds, eight metres high, rises on a bluff near an ancient campsite at a bend in the river above the rapids. It is, to this day, a place of serene beauty and spiritual power.

WE HAVE TO SURMISE that all of the Manitou Mounds are graves because only one, called the Armstrong Mound, has been excavated. The work was done in 1966 by Walter Kenyon, archaeologist with the Royal Ontario Museum, at the request of the Historic Sites and Monuments Board of Canada. Kenyon uncovered a rectangular log enclosure containing three burials. In one, the skeleton, a child of about five, was intact; the other two contained bundles of bones that had apparently been transported from their original graves. One bundle contained the bones of four adults, two of them about forty-five years old, and two children aged about six and thirteen. All the adults had arthritis. The third grave contained four bundles of bones, three adults and one teenager. Bones of two children were scattered about. The bundled bones had been liberally sprinkled with iron oxide and red ochre before burial.

There were no grave goods to give clues to the identity of the mound builders, but a lump of charcoal found on one of the logs established an approximate date of 1,030 BP. In the soil removed from the mound, Kenyon found tools, spear points and pottery sherds he identified as Laurel; he surmised that the mound builders had scraped up soil containing debris from an abandoned campsite and carried it to the mound in birchbark baskets. The mounds themselves established a traditional connection with the earlier Ohio River Valley mound builders, and the artifacts Kenyon unearthed included a pipe, or tube, hollowed from soft pink stone, its bowl carved with two exquisitely stylized frogs; the only comparable carving, a double serpent design on Ohio red pipestone, had been found in Illinois. How did this exotic tube, likely used by a medicine man to suck sickness out of a patient, come to be dumped on a burial mound on the

Rainy River? Had it been discarded there, and if so, by whom? Or had it been hidden in a sacred mound for safekeeping? The mystery will likely never be solved; Kenyon's team, excavating with shovels, neglected to record the location or context of the material they uncovered.

Two small, shallow mounds at the mouth of the Rainy River, excavated by Kenyon ten years earlier, reveal more astonishing evidence of the customs and beliefs of the Late Woodland people. Named Hungry Hall 1 and Hungry Hall 2 after a nickname given to a nineteenth-century Hudson's Bay Company post near the site, the mounds contained, in addition to numerous human bones, perfectly preserved Blackduck pots, awls made from the bones of loons, herons and eagles, and sea shells, including conch and scallop, used as beads, gorgets and spoons: shell spoons found in two pots indicate that the spirit was fed on its journey to the Afterworld.

Hungry Hall 1, Kenyon discovered, had long been used as a communal burying ground, but at Hungry Hall 2, he unearthed a pristine grave dug, with sharp sticks and antlers, about 800 years ago. The pit, containing the scattered remains of twenty people, eleven of them children, had been roofed over with spruce and tamarack logs. A fire had been built nearby, charring some of the logs, then the logs had been covered with earth. Scratches and cut marks on the bones showed that the bodies had been dismembered. The skulls of nine adults, all young men, and the two oldest children, were placed

ROYAL ONTARIO MUSEUM, TORONTO

A rare pipe or sucking tube, exquisitely carved of Ohio red pipestone, was found at Manitou Mounds.

Left, one of the skull masks that was excavated at Hungry Hall 2 by Walter Kenyon.

ROYAL ONTARIO MUSEUM, TORONTO / 961.236.98a-b

MAKING MEDICINE

THE FIRST PEOPLE TO PICK, sniff, taste and swallow the native plants were brave: many mushrooms are deadly, marsh marigolds are toxic, poison ivy, red baneberry and water hemlock aptly named. Determining whether the root, leaves, stem, flower or seeds of a plant were nourishing or medicinal required generations of experimentation and the skills of a chemist. Some plants advertised: the oozing sap of pine trees was used to close and heal wounds; sage and ginger had a delicious taste and smell. Except for yellow pond lilies, with their nourishing roots, gaudy flowers did not reveal a plant's value; Labrador tea, a popular brew with the Algonquians, is a homely evergreen shrub, and the rhizomes of the common cattail are as nourishing as potatoes.

Roots and bark, boiled as teas or poultices, were likely eaten only in times of hunger: sucking the sweet sap of the white birch or mountain maple in spring may have created a delicacy born of desperation. Local bees did not make honey, and there was no salt. Tobacco was not native to the area, and there is no evidence of pipe-smoking here prior to European contact. However, it is likely that sweet grass and the aromatic bark of trees and shrubs were thrown on fires for ceremonial purposes, and used for smoking meat and fish.

Long cold winters preserved dried berries stored in bark and clay containers, but they did not ferment into wine. These sober northern

DENNIS FAST

people used combinations of herbs as tonics, and boiling, by killing bacteria in food and water, made these brews good medicine. In many cases, the medicinal value may have been largely psychological – a hot "cuppa" is still highly valued around the world – but some were true miracle drugs.

Tea made of spruce needles, rich with vitamin C, prevented scurvy. Peat moss, antiseptic and absorbent, made excellent bandages and diapers. Herbalists would have been skilled at setting fractures and healing wounds – lung diseases, caused by inhaling smoke in wigwams, must have been common, as was arthritis – but the First People may have been healthier, better fed and more horticultural than we have imagined. The presence of bur oak, a fire-resistant tree, and prairie plants at ancient campsites is a signal that people may have periodically burned the undergrowth to regenerate the vegetation; blueberry heaths in particular thrive on burned-over ground, and the oak, with its annual crop of acorns, was itself worth cultivating. Knowledge of plants made herbalists experts on animal habitat: reindeer lichen, boiled as a poultice for arthritis or, in times of hunger, a soup, was named for the caribou who ate it; muskrats frequented cattail marshes, acorns and blueberries attracted bears. If people knew where to look, the Lake of the Woods watershed provided everything they needed.

Mushrooms, above, and highbush cranberries, right, were among dozens of wild foods gathered seasonally.

56

Autumn's glory is reflected on the still waters of the lake.

together in two clusters; all skulls had large, round holes through which, Kenyon concluded, the brain had been extracted. Seven of the skulls had been transformed into "masks". Fine clay had been pressed over the bone and into the facial orifices; white shells set into the eye sockets gave the skulls a wide-open stare. The finished masks, painted with red ochre, may have included hair and noses.

Were these masks used in community rituals to honour fallen warriors, or do they represent the work of a sorcerer, a legendary, flesh-eating windigo shunned for practicing human sacrifice? Kenyon did not attempt to solve this complex puzzle, and no one since has tried. But the Hungry Hall 2 grave may have survived because, unlike its neighbour, it was avoided. Why? Its pottery, decorated with plain, primitive stick patterns, is foreign to the local culture of the time, and the practice of severing heads is characteristic of a powerful people to the south and west, the Dakota.

The Algonquian-speaking Woodland people shared a southwestern border with a people who spoke Siouan, a language so different that the two were mutually unintelligible. The Siouan people, like their neighbours, had moved north, bringing with them remnants of prosperous, agricultural civilization that emerged in the Mississippi River Valley about 1,100 years ago. Like the earlier Algonquian chiefdoms, the Mississippi Siouans lived in villages and small cities characterized by mounds and monumental earthworks. However, their architecture, a flat-topped pyramid, resembles Mayan temples in Central America, and motifs in their artwork — the plumed serpent, the severed head — reflect the influence of Central and South American Aboriginal cultures. Shells, plentiful and varied on the Gulf of Mexico, were used to make beads, gorgets and spoons similar to those found at Hungry Hall. While their pots were similar in shape to Blackduck, their zig-zag decorations were distinctive.

A GRAVEL RIDGE SOUTHWEST of Lake of the Woods, Lake Agassiz's old shore, marked the informal eastern boundary of the Dakota. While they lived in conical tipis, not wigwams, their seasonal round of hunting, fishing, berry-picking and wild rice harvesting differed little from their Algonquian neighbours. Raids on one another's camps, a blood sport for the young men, were a form of cultural exchange: goods were stolen, prisoners adopted to replace dead and captured warriors and women abducted for their domestic talents. Mutual gift-giving was part of the peace process, and in both patriarchal societies the men delighted in feasts and ceremonies. So accommodating was the relationship that the most serious feud occurred among the Dakota themselves. At a time lost to memory, for reasons uncertain, a northern Dakota band, the Assiniboine, declared war on their kin and allied themselves with the Algonquians. By 1660, when the Dakota on the southwestern shore of Lake Superior greeted two strange, French-speaking white men, Pierre Esprit Radisson and Médard Chouart des Groseilliers, the Assiniboine dominated the territory from Red River to Rainy Lake. These, then, were the people watching from the shore when the first Europeans paddled past the Rainy River burial mounds and camped on Lake of the Woods.

ARTS & CRAFTS

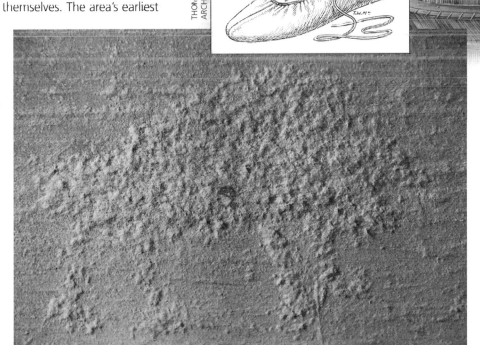

WITH A RICHNESS OF NATURAL RESOURCES, these early people might well have led lives of relative ease, with plenty of time for stories, arts and crafts. Algonquian oral tradition tells of weaving cattail mats with basswood twine, making dishes, toys, torches and shrouds out of birchbark, and boiling cedar, hemlock and alder barks with ashes to make colourful dyes. Porcupine quills were plentiful and easier to dye than shells or bone beads; birchbark provided a natural paper for drawing. If red ochre, mixed with oil, had been painted on the masked skulls for artistic or religious reasons, the living also likely painted their utensils, clothing and themselves. The area's earliest rock paintings may date to the Laurel period.

The petroglyphs at Mud Portage, now a channel into Clearwater Bay, are art. The oldest, believed to be between 5,000 and 9,000 years old, is a solid, realistic bison delicately pecked into the basalt with a sharp instrument. Nearby are smaller, cruder figures, some not more than ten centimetres long, representing several animals and a man. Curiously, the same rock outcrop has been carved with stylized outlines, including turtle shapes, that reflect a radically different iconography.

THOMAS W. McLEAN / NATIONAL ARCHIVES OF CANADA / C-069773

DENNIS FAST / LAKE OF THE WOODS MUSEUM, KENORA

A sampling of arts and crafts, clockwise from above: A finely decorated modern quillwork box, featuring Canada's symbols; an nineteenth-century Ojibwe moccasin, and a solidly-pecked bison petroglyph in the "early hunter style", dating to Plano times.

COURTESY OF JACK STEINBRING

59

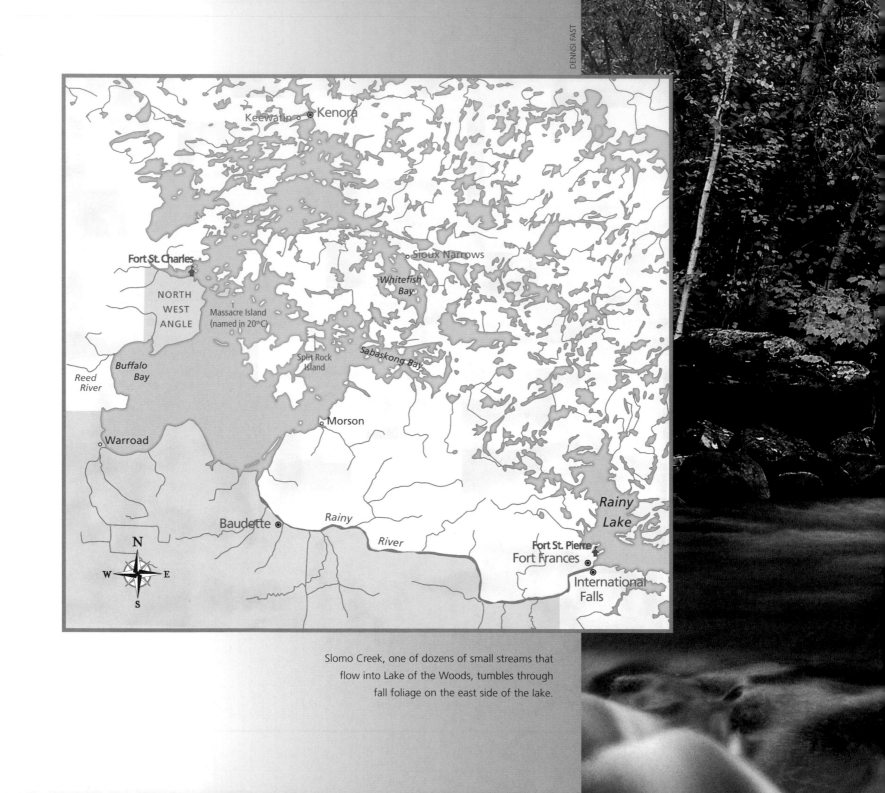

Kenora

Keewatin

Sioux Narrows

Fort St. Charles

Whitefish
Bay

NORTH
WEST
ANGLE

Massacre Island
(named in 20ᵗʰC)

Split Rock
Island

Sabaskong Bay

Buffalo
Bay

Reed
River

Morson

Warroad

Rainy
Lake

N

W   E

S

Baudette

Rainy

River

Fort St. Pierre
Fort Frances

International
Falls

Slomo Creek, one of dozens of small streams that
flow into Lake of the Woods, tumbles through
fall foliage on the east side of the lake.

THE MYTH OF THE WESTERN SEA

TRADING *EN DÉROUINE*, IN THE WINTER CAMPS OF NATIVE NORTH AMERICANS,
MADE SENSE TO THE FRENCH AND ALLOWED THEM TO RAPIDLY EXPAND THEIR TRADE INLAND.

this point, the Winnipeg River was not where his map placed it. Moreover, the Cree were eager to go to war against the Dakota, the Assiniboine had been scared away by rumours, no doubt spread by the English, that the French would eat them, and La Vérendrye's own men, fearful of dying of starvation, refused to go further until their winter's provisions had arrived. The need to feed so many men largely determined the location of Fort St. Charles. "There is good fishing and hunting," La Vérendrye reported to Beauharnois in May 1733, "quantities of wild oats, and excellent land cleared by fire which I am now putting in seed."

That spring, La Vérendrye sent Jean-Baptiste and La Jemerais down the Winnipeg River to locate a site for a fort on Lake Winnipeg. Stopped by an impassable rapid they named La Barrière, they used an easier Aboriginal route from Buffalo Bay up the Reed River and across a portage to the Roseau River, a tributary of the Red. The land was marshy, the rivers meandering, but the sluggish Red River had only one rapid to circumvent before it reached Lake Winnipeg. La Vérendrye's men seem to have used this route the following year when they built a fort on the west bank of the Red about twenty kilometres from its mouth. They named it Maurepas in honour of France's colonial minister, Jean Frederic Phelippaux, Comte de Maurepas.

The count himself, however, was unimpressed that the expedition had reached a huge, unexplored lake the English on the Bay had never seen; he was too irritated by La Vérendrye's slow progress and his request for 30,000 livres to cover his debts to the merchants. Maurepas suspected that the expedition's primary purpose was to divert North American commerce into the hands of the Quebec *bourgoisie*. All to the good, but let the profiteers take the risks. In a cynical note to Beauharnois, Maurepas wrote: "His Majesty is still indisposed to incur any expense in connection with this enterprise, in which it seems very likely the parties concerned will sustain no loss."

LA VÉRENDRYE may well have gone through the king's money as quickly as he did his own. Voyageurs charged premium prices to make the many arduous portages between Lake Superior and Lake of the Woods; they didn't work until they were paid, and then they had to be housed and fed over the long winter. Some wheat and peas were raised at Fort St.Charles, but fish, meat, fat and wild rice were bought from the Cree for goods that otherwise could have been traded for furs, and Cree guides, without whom the French were lost, were well rewarded. Although the Cree and Monsoni, delighted to have French traders among them, were hospitable, La Vérendrye maintained a garrison at Fort St. Charles. He loved a parade, and at every opportunity he had his drummers beat a call to a general assembly so he could address the throng; he marked saints' days with volleys of musket fire and the booming of the fort's cannon.

La Vérendrye's pleasure in ritual and long-winded speeches endeared him to the local chiefs; it was exactly their style of diplomacy. Though he used the conventional

Yet another map of the Lake of the Woods region, showing much more detail as the La Vérendryes became more familiar with the region.

which astonished them. I then made them a feast, after which they continued the war chant.

T EN DAYS LATER, La Vérendrye departed in haste for Québec. He had given away all his trade goods, and his merchants, without tobacco, guns and kettles, had nothing of value to offer for furs. The Cree and Assiniboine returned to the English; the furious French merchants, facing bank-ruptcy, quit. Beauharnois persuaded La Vérendrye to "farm out" his posts to free traders for an annual fee, but they had no obligation to supply him with provisions. When he returned, with his fourth son, Louis-Joseph, and a fearful, reluctant Jesuit, Father Jean Aulneau, to Lake of the Woods in October 1735, they believed that canoes laden with their winter provisions were close behind. As the lake froze over, they watched the horizon in vain.

The shores of the Rainy River, seen here near Rainy Lake, became familiar territory, as La Vérendrye made the arduous trek to Quebec and back.

Life at Fort St. Charles that winter was so harsh Father Aulneau wrote home to complain about his nauseating diet of mouldy fish, and, in remembrance, the Cree named a nearby island "Famine". At Fort Maurepas on the Red River, many lodges of Assiniboine died of smallpox. La Jemerais, commander at Maurepas, was mortally ill. In February 1736, Jean-Baptiste La Vérendrye, home safely from the Dakota wars, and his brother Pierre rushed to relieve Fort Maurepas. On June 2nd they returned to Lake of the Woods with the news that La Jemerais had died en route, and they had buried him at the junction of the Red and Roseau Rivers.

THE BROTHERS HAD TRAVELLED IN HASTE,

warned by the Cree that Dakota warriors were on the lake. Yet three days later, on June 5th, La Vérendrye sent three canoes manned by twenty Frenchmen, led by Jean-Baptiste, across the *grand traverse* to search for their missing supply brigade; Father Aulneau, having no stomach for a missionary's life, seized this opportunity to return east. "I advised them to be on their guard," La Vérendrye wrote in his journal. "With one accord they replied that I might make my mind easy, as they meant to keep a sharp look-out."

On June 12th, three Monsoni came to the fort to report that a trader, René Bourassa, had been captured and robbed by the Dakota on the morning of June 4th. Bourassa had been released unharmed, and he warned that the Dakota had a grievance against the French for giving arms to their enemies. On June 17th, two heavily-laden canoes from La Vérendrye's missing supply brigade arrived, but they had not met Jean-Baptiste's search party on the lake. La Vérendrye ordered a sergeant and eight men to follow the route his son had taken. "On the 22nd, he wrote, "the sergeant and his men arrived bringing the sad news of the massacre of the 21 men seven leagues from the fort on a little island. Most of the bodies were found, all decapitated, and lying in a circle against one another, which made me to conclude that they were killed while holding counsel; the heads were wrapped in beaver skins."

La Vérendrye did not go to the island, retrieve the bodies, investigate the circumstances, describe the island's location or confirm the identity of the culprits. He relied on the word of Monsoni, who reported finding two of the three French canoes tied up with about twenty Dakota canoes at the south end of the lake; the Dakota canoes were bloody, and men's limbs had been buried in the sand. La Vérendrye took heart that the Dakota had suffered some casualties, but when his men went to retrieve the bodies on September 17th, more than three months after the slaughter, it appeared that the limbs were French; the corpses of Jean-Baptiste and Father Aulneau were headless, and only the scalped heads of the other men remained. La Vérendrye buried the skulls in a common grave in the chapel; Jean-Baptiste and Father Aulneau shared a separate coffin.

Grisly stories made their way to Quebec and France. According to one report, "the missionary had one knee on the ground, his right hand raised. The Sieur de la Vérendrye was lying on his face, his back all scored with knife cuts, a stake thrust into his side, headless, his body ornamented with leggings and armpieces of porcupine." One popular story claimed that a great clap of thunder had frightened the Dakota away.

Two simple gravestones at Fort St. Charles serve as memorials to the 1736 ambush.

The coming of winter brought great trepidation. Though travelling was in many ways easier, and it generally meant a cessation of hostilities, the long months of cold also brought sickness and hunger.

BOURASSA'S STORIES OF HIS OWN ENCOUNTER with the Dakota, a force he estimated at thirty canoes carrying ninety to 130 men, differed from his letter to La Vérendrye. He reported now that he had distracted his captors by telling them that Cree were camped outside Fort St. Charles, and the Dakota had gone off pellmell after the Cree. Beauharnois, who kept himself well-informed, sent Maurepas a more dramatic version:

> They [Dakota] fastened the conductor of the canoe [Bourassa] to a stake, meaning to burn him. Happily for him, he had a female slave of that tribe who said to her people: 'My friends, what are you going to do? I owe my life to this Frenchman: he has done me nothing but good: if you want to be avenged for the attack made on

you, you have only to go further on and you will find twenty-four Frenchmen, amongst whom is the son of their chief, the one who slaughtered us.' There-upon they released Bourassa and his hired men and went to destroy the entire convoy.

Beauharnois believed that the Dakota avenged themselves on Jean-Baptiste for having gone to war against them in 1734: an eye-witness had reported that when the ambushed Dakota called out, "Who is killing us?" the Cree had replied: "It is the Frenchman." Jean-Baptiste claimed that he had left the war party early after a disagreement, but his whereabouts are unaccounted for and the Dakota attackers knew his appearance well enough to distinguish him from his canoemen: they carried his head away as a trophy. Beauharnois observed: "the first step taken counted for as much as if he had been then on the spot."

The Dakota, armed only with knives, hatchets and bows and arrows, seem to have surprised the French around their campfire, then vanished with the smoke. The coup nearly frightened off the French: "The disaster which overtook the convoy of the Sieur de la Vérendrye is most annoying," Maurepas wrote to Beauharnois in April 1737, "and gives rise to the apprehension that it may be necessary to abandon all the establishments made by that officer." The Jesuits lost enthusiasm for western missions, but La Vérendrye did not give up. In 1738, he and his sons built Fort La Reine far to the west on the Assiniboine River, then travelled overland to visit a prosperous agricultural nation they named the Mandan. The Mandan guided Louis-Joseph to the headwaters of the Missouri River, and four years later Louis-Joseph and his brothers travelled as far west as the Big Horn Mountains, an eastern range of the Rockies. Their

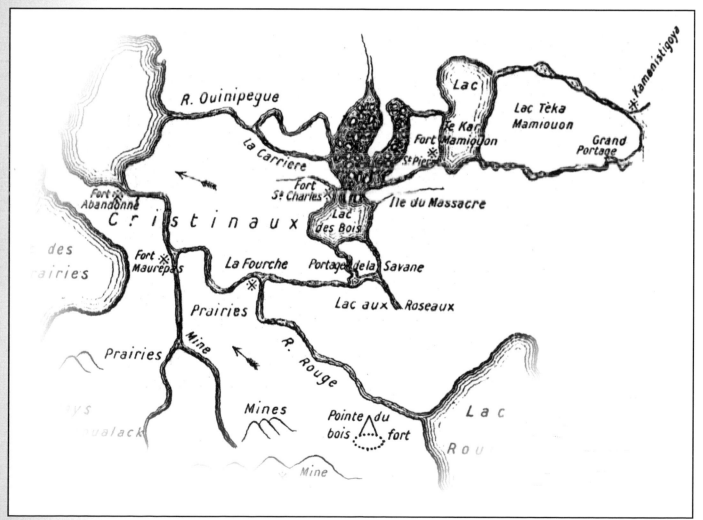

Drawn after 1736, this map shows not only the second incarnation of Fort Maurepas, but also indicates "Île du Massacre", where the Dakota overcame Jean-Baptiste La Vérendrye's party. Though it's possible that the mapmaker had no idea where the island was, some historians believe it may in fact be near the eastern shore of the lake. To avoid the dangerous crossing to the Rainy River, canoe brigades sometimes crossed the lake diagonally, heading north of Split Rock Island toward Sabaskong Bay.

DETAIL OF "CARTE CONTENANT" / BURPEE / CHAMPLAIN SOCIETY / TORONTO

Though Robert KaKayGeesick's painting, "Sacred Fire", has a bold and modern feel, its inspiration is timeless.

"SACRED FIRE" / ROBERT KAKAYGEESICK / COURTESY OF THE WAH-SA GALLERY

guides were too frightened to venture farther, and finding themselves led more south than west, the La Vérendryes realized, with dismay, that the mysterious white-skinned native people their Cree informants had described were Spaniards.

THE LA VÉRENDRYES MISSED THE COLUMBIA, the great west-flowing river that would have taken them to the ocean, but in 1739, Louis-Joseph scouted the western shore of Lake Winnipeg, explored Cedar Lake and found the Paskoyac River of the Cree, the Saskatchewan. Ascending the river it to its fork, where it branched north and south, Louis-Joseph learned that the river rose in towering mountains, and beyond the mountains was a vast lake not fit to drink. By 1742, the La Vérendrye sons, not yet thirty, had built three forts, Dauphin, Bourbon and, near the mouth of the Saskatchewan River, Paskoyac, strategically placed to intercept western Cree headed for Hudson Bay. They had pushed the western boundary of the French empire far beyond the middle of the continent, but Maurepas was convinced that the La Vérendryes were vulgar *coureurs de bois* growing rich from the fur trade.

True, Pierre de La Vérendrye, beguiled by fanciful stories, had wasted years wandering in the wrong direction. Forts Maurepas and Dauphin had to be abandoned for want of provisions; he had mismanaged his finances, been sued by his creditors and his reports were vague and self-serving. Louis XV may have feared that La Vérendrye intended to set himself up as monarch of his own wilderness colony, a scheme an earlier explorer, Robert René Cavalier, Sieur de la Salle, had tried, with ghastly consequences, on the Mississippi; La Salle's deserted colonists had disappeared and he had been murdered by his own men.

La Vérendrye's expedition too had been marred by murder, and he had failed to prevent the Cree and Monsoni from wreaking bloody vengenace on the Dakota. The chiefs

DENNIS FAST

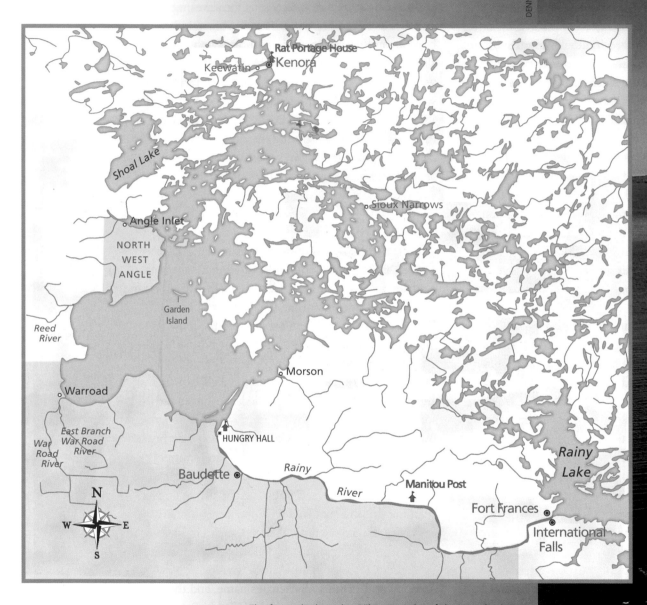

Rat Portage House
Keewatin Kenora
Shoal Lake
Sioux Narrows
Angle Inlet
NORTH WEST ANGLE
Garden Island
Reed River
Morson
Warroad
East Branch War Road River
War Road River
HUNGRY HALL
Baudette
Rainy
River
Manitou Post
Rainy Lake
Fort Frances
International Falls

N
W E
S

The fur trade drew the Ojibwe to Lake of the Woods; the beauty and bounty of the woods and the water allowed them to create a forest fastness for 150 years.

THE EMPIRE OF THE OJIBWE

THE EMPIRE
OF THE OJIBWE

THE RUIN OF THE LA VÉRENDRYES marked the beginning of nearly 150 years of lawlessness, cut-throat competition, murder, rebellion, revolution and warfare throughout North America. In 1759, the French garrison was defeated by the British at Quebec City; when the French surrendered their northern empire in 1763, British garrisons on the Great Lakes were sacked in a bloody resistance led by an Odawa warrior, Pontiac. In 1776, the revolt of the British colonies in New England cost Britain the southern half of the continent. Warfare between Britain and the United States erupted again in 1812, and, in the west, the establishment of an agricultural colony at the forks of the Red and Assiniboine Rivers by the Earl of Selkirk, a director of the Hudson's Bay Company, started a feud with the HBC's arch rival, the Montreal-based North West Company. In 1816, the colony's governor, Robert Semple, and twenty-one settlers were killed at Seven Oaks on the Red River by a group of Métis hunters associated with the Nor'Westers. The merger of the two companies in 1821 created an uneasy peace until 1869, when, without consulting the residents, the HBC sold its proprietary interest in all the Northwest to the Canadian government. This time, the French-speaking Métis, English mixed-bloods and some Scots settlers, led by Louis Riel and representing a majority of the population, prevented the new governor from entering the settlement, seized the HBC headquarters at Upper Fort Garry, and established a provisional government. When Canadian troops, commanded by Colonel Garnet Wolseley, arrived, Riel fled. In 1885, however, the western Cree and the displaced Métis, again led by Riel, fought pitched battles against British and Canadian soldiers on the plains of northwestern Saskatchewan; the Métis alliance was defeated and Riel was hanged.

Like the bitter Civil War to the south, and the stage-coach robberies, shoot-outs and massacres of the American "wild west", these conflicts are well known in folklore and history. Equally significant, however, was the growth of a political and economic power new to the Northwest, the empire of the Ojibwe. In 1732, by all accounts, the Ojibwe were still entrenched at their ancestral Great Lakes strongholds, Sault Ste. Marie and Michilimakinac, but by 1775, they had pushed west into Rainy Lake, Rainy River, Lake of the Woods and the Winnipeg River, as well as occupying all of the land between the western tip of Lake Superior and Red Lake, the headwaters of the Red River. By the 1820s, the Ojibwe had driven the Dakota out of the woodlands east of the Mississippi, and displaced the Cree and Assiniboine in the Lake Winnipeg watershed as far west as La Verendrye's old post at Portage la Prairie and along a northwest line to the present city of Saskatoon. Although the Ojibwe intermingled with their allies, and many of their campsites were visited only once or twice a year, their rapid domination of this vast new territory was a feat worthy of Alexander the Great.

To the northwest, their advance was unresisted. The Cree had moved north and west to areas where buffalo, fur and game were plentiful; the Assiniboine moved west, retreating to the river valleys of the western prairies as far west as today's Banff National Park, after a smallpox epidemic annihilated their Red River Valley camp in 1782. While the Ojibwe also suffered from smallpox, centuries of exposure in eastern Canada may have increased their immunity.

CONTINUED ON PAGE 85

FOR 150 YEARS, NO ONE KNEW LAKE OF THE WOODS,
WITH ITS MULTITUDE OF ISLANDS AND MYRIAD CHANNELS, BETTER THAN THE OJIBWE.

THE MEDICINE SOCIETY

DENNIS FAST

GLIMPSES OF THE OJIBWE EMPIRE in its twilight are provided by the records of two government expeditions that travelled to the western plains in 1857. The British expedition, which included a botanist, was led by an Irish gentleman, Captain John Palliser. Arriving at Fort Frances on July 1, Palliser noted: "A large camp of about 200 Chippeways or Ojibeways were pitched in the neighbourhood, and we are amused while passing through their tents on our way to the fort with the number that pressed forward to shake hands with us, but with such a manner as to leave it doubtful whether the honour was done to us or by us.

"Presently, a loud beating of the drums announced the signal of assembly to the tribe. Five long stools were placed in a pentagon, and five chairs were placed in the centre of this enclosure. Here and there, at a very respectful distance, sat groups of women and children awaiting the commencement of the ceremony. The sound of the drum came nearer and nearer, and shortly the men of the tribe marched into the fort, in Indian file, with faces painted of every colour, heads decked with eagles' feathers, necks and fingers with brass rings, and many wearing very elegantly beaded dresses. The men were all armed, with the exception of the old or principal chief, who bore the calumet or pipe of peace." The chief and elders seated themselves on the benches, the young men standing or sitting behind; Palliser and his colleagues sat on the chairs. After five minutes of profound silence the old chief spoke:

"'Perhaps,' said he, 'you wonder who I am that I should address you. My arms extend far back into time; my father and his father were the chiefs of this once mighty tribe. Their graves are in our lands, and not far from here. If you further question my authority for addressing you, look around me! These are my chiefs, my soldiers, my young men. It is by their wish and desire that I address you.' Here many voices grunted approbation. 'All around me,' continued he, 'I see the smoke of the pale faces to ascend; but my territories I will never part with; they shall be for my poor childrens' hunting fields when I am dead.'" After lamenting his children's present poverty and hunger, the chief came to the point: "You are our equals, so do not deceive us, but inform us of the true reason of your visit and whither you are about to procede to from here." Palliser hastily assured him that they were merely passing through, and moreover, "if any body of people should wrest their lands from them, our great Queen would send her soldiers to drive those people back and would restore their lands to them again."

An advisor to the old chief whispered in his ear: "Make him put that on paper, I say, make him put that on paper. I know how my people have been treated by the Kitje Mohomans." Kitje Mohoman, "Big Knife", was the Ojibwe word for Americans. But the old chief replied: "What he says he will act up to, for no one who came from the great Queen ever lied." The chief's only request was the the botanist "should take no plants out of the country for fear that people far off should think the lands valuable and seize them."

Evaluating the land with an eye to seizure was precisely Palliser's purpose, and when the Canadian expedition, led by Toronto geologist Henry Youle Hind and engineer Simon J. Dawson, arrived the next month, the Ojibwe were waiting for them on Lake of the Woods. Hind wrote: "We landed during the evening of the 24th August on a low, gravelly beach, at the north-west corner of Garden Island. We camped near a well-cultivated field of Indian corn, and a rapid exploration of the island revealed to us a large potato patch, and a small area devoted to squashes and pumpkins of various kinds. Our camp fire evidently soon attracted the attention of a number of Indians, for about midnight we were aroused by the sudden appearance at the door of the tent of two of these people, and in half an hour twenty more had arrived."

THE OJIBWE insisted that Hind visit their chief, camped four miles away, and when Hind refused, they curtly informed him that their chief would visit him the next day; at noon, a flotilla of thirteen canoes, with fifty-three men and boys, descended on Garden Island to find out why the Canadians intended to travel their private pathway, the Reed-Roseau River route, to Red River.

The chief likely knew that Dawson wanted to survey the route for a canal or a road, and Hind's evasiveness angered him. "You say that all the white men we have seen belong to one party, and yet they go by three different roads, why is that?" he asked. "Do they want to see the Indian's land? Remember, if the white man comes to the Indian's house, he must walk through the door, and not steal in by the window. You gathered corn in our gardens and put it away; did you never see corn before? Why did you not note it down in your book? Did your people want to see our corn? Would they not be satisfied with your noting it down? You cannot pass through those paths."

The chief rejected Hind's request for guides: "We see how the Indians are treated far away. The white man comes, looks at their flowers, their trees, and their rivers, others soon follow; the lands of the Indians pass from their hands, and they have nowhere a home." To the interpreter, the chief said: "Let them send us no presents; we do not want them. They have no right to pass that way. We have hearts, and love our lives and country. If twenty men came we would not let them pass to-day. We do not want the white man; when the white man comes, he brings disease and sickness, and our people perish; we do not wish to die. Many white men would bring death to us, and our people would pass away; we wish to love and hold the land our fathers won, and the Great Spirit has given to us. Tell the men this, and the talk is finished." Hind thankfully accepted the chief's offer to guide his expedition north to the "white man's road" at Rat Portage.

To the south of Lake of the Woods however, the Ojibwe and the Dakota waged a cruel and bloody guerrilla war. Both employed the same tactics: stealth and surprise. Stories of these raids, ambushes and pitched battles are told in William Warren's *History of the Ojibway Nation*, a manuscript completed in 1852 and published in 1885. Of Ojibwe ancestry on his mother's side, Warren spoke the language fluently enough to interview the elders, including proud old warriors with vivid memories of the warpath. Deceit and subterfuge could be more effective weapons than guns and knives; Warren tells of an Ojibwe war party who notified the Dakota they were coming to smoke the pipe of peace.

> The Dakotas, believing the reported peaceable disposition of their former enemies, became careless; they did not send scouts to watch on the surrounding hills, and the Ojibway arrived within a close vicinity of their camp without the least discovery. During the night, the leaders of the war party sent five young men, who could speak the Dakota language most fluently, to go and spy the lodges of the enemy, note their situation and find out their number. The five scouts entered the encampment at different points, and, drawing their robes closely over their heads, they walked about unsuspected by the young Dakota gallants, or night walkers, who were out watching the lodge fires to flicker away in embers in order to enter and in the darkness court their sweethearts.

The scouts having reported the locations of about three hundred lodges, the Ojibwe prepared themselves for battle:

> At the earliest dawn of morning, they marched on the sleeping encampment of the Dakotas. They made their approach by a deep ravine which led to the narrow prairie which skirts the waterside

on which was pitched the leathern lodges of the enemy. It is said that through the dim twilight the advancing warriors saw a woman step out of the nearest lodge to adjust the door covering; she stood as if a sound had caught her ear, and she listened anxiously, looking up the dark ravine, when she again entered her lodge. She must have heard the measured tread of the advancing warriors, but mistook it for the moaning of the rising wind and the dashing of the waves on the sandy beach.

As they neared the lodges of their sleeping enemies, and the dogs of the encampment began to snuff the air and utter their sharp, quick yelp, the shrill war whistle was sounded by the leaders, and suddenly the dread and fear-striking war-

whoop issued from the lips of hundreds of blood-thirsty warriors. Volley after volley of bullets and arrows were discharged into the frail and defence-less tepees, and the shrieking and yelling of the inmates ... suddenly startled from their sleep made the uproar of the attack truly deafening.

Completely taken by surprise, the warriors of the Dakota fought at a disadvantage; their women and children ran shrieking to the water's side, and hastily jumping into their narrow wooden canoes, they attempted to cross to the opposite shore of the lake. The wind, however, had increased in force. Sweeping down the lake in a fearful gale, it caused the waves to run high, and in many instances the crowded canoes filled with water or upset, launching the fleeing women and children into a watery grave.

After a long and unavailing defence, such of the Dakota warriors as had stood their ground were obliged to retreat. Thirty of their number are said to have fled under a ledge of rock, where, being entirely surrounded, they were shot down one after another.

This is one of the most successful war parties the Ojibway talk of. It is said that at each encampment on their return homeward, the scalps which they had taken, being each tied to the end of a stick three or four feet long, were planted close together in a single row, and an arrow shot by a strong arm from one end of this row of human scalps fell short of reaching the other extremity. One of their story tellers states explicitly that the Ojibway secured three hundred and thirty-five scalps, and many more than this are thought to have perished in the water. But one captive is mentioned as having been taken.

The eastern or woodland Dakota, such as this family photographed in the 1870s, were a branch of the larger Dakota Nation, including the Nakota and Lakota who lived farther west.

JACOBY / MINNESOTA HISTORICAL SOCIETY / e91.31/p21

LAKE OF THE WOODS MUSEUM, KENORA / 964 17.29

SUMMER WAS THE SEASON FOR WARFARE, and a winter truce was usually declared to allow the Ojibwe and Dakota to hunt in safety over the same territory. Isolated family groups, however, were vulnerable to enemy raiders. Warren tells of an old Ojibwe hunter, his wife, two sons and their families who camped in the land of the Dakota's allies, the O-dug-am-ees or Fox:

> One morning early, one of the sons, as usual, put on his moccasins, tied his blanket around his body, and, shouldering his gun, started on his day's hunt. It was snowing heavily, and the rest of the family remained at home. The hunter had been gone but a short time when he returned, and, without saying a word, commenced whittling his bullets so that they could be easily and quickly thrown into his gun. Then he sharpened his knife, and placed his war-club and spear ready at hand for immediate use.

Going out to investigate, the old man found an O-dug-am-ee footprint in the snow. He proposed flight, but his son replied: "All we can do is prepare for death, for I have seen the trail of the O-dug-am-ee warriors, and it is deep-beaten and wide." During the night, the imitated hootings of owls and howlings of wolves told the Ojibwe the O-dug-am-ee only waited until dawn to attack:

> The old hunter, being anxious to save a portion of his kindred, took two girls – his grandchildren – each by the hand and silently led them some distance into the surrounding woods, amid the darkness, and informing them the direction they were to go – to be judged by the wind and fast falling flakes of snow – he bade them save their lives by flight and inform their people of his fate. The old man then listened anxiously for

Rushing River tumbles toward Lake of the Woods.

87

the yell that would denote the discovery and death of 'the little birds he had let out to fly away'. That expected yell came not, and the old man became satisfied that his two grandchildren were safe.

At the first dawn of morning, the O-dug-am-ee commenced the attack with loud and thrilling war-whoops. The Ojibways defended themselves bravely, and, as long as their ammunition lasted, they kept their numerous assailants at bay, and sent many of their more hardy warriors to the land of Spirits; but as soon as their powder gave out, the O-dug-am-ees rushed into their camp and the work of death ... commenced. All perished but the old hunter, who, during the last brave struggle of his two sons, miraculously escaped through the dense ranks of his eager foes, entirely naked and covered with blood from numerous wounds.

He had not proceeded far before he met a small party of his friends, who had been informed of the desperate situation by the two girls whom he had caused to escape the previous night. Although almost dead with fatigue and loss of blood, the old man returned, and found his wigwam in ashes. The O-dug-am-ee wolves had already done their work and departed, and the bodies of his murdered kindred ... lay strewn about the blood-stained snow.

The old hunter lived to exact a terrible revenge on the Fox, but while revenge fueled the cycle of slaughter, the prime motive for war was control of the area's fertile rice lakes, with their beaver meadows, maple sugar bushes and forests filled with game. Added to the annual sturgeon and whitefish catches, these resources provided a stable year-round economy based on elementary horticulture and animal husbandry.

Cousins of the Cree, the Ojibwe had developed a close-knit social structure, rich with music, ritual, stories and art, that included an oral history and a complex mythology. Spiritual beliefs, embodied in the rituals of the Midewiwin, or Grand Medicine Society, were codified by hieroglyphs drawn on birchbark scrolls. The Ojibwe divided themselves into clans, each with a fish, bird or mammal totem – Crane, Loon, Bear, Marten and Great Fish were the original totems – inherited from their fathers. Kinship among clan members, wherever they lived, was so sacred they were, like brother and sister, forbidden to marry. Clan membership, a powerful network uniting the scattered Ojibwe community, was reinforced by their emphasis on geographic location: they described themselves as "the people of rainy lake, rice lake, bad winding river, long rapids, muskrat portage, war road, white fish lake and other recognized locations. The French called them Saulteaux or Saulteurs after their home at Sault Ste. Marie, a name later adopted by the English.

OJIBWE, SPELLED SEVERAL WAYS, historically Ojibway and Ojibwa in Canada and Chippewa in the United States, translates as "puckered". The name may be derived from their early moccasins, stitched on top with one puckered seam from toe to ankle, or, as Warren claims, from a practice of roasting enemy captives alive until their skin blistered and "puckered". It could also be derived from "the voice of the Crane", their chief totem. The Ojibwe call themselves Anishinabe, "the spontaneous people", children of two spirits, Sky Woman (Moon) and Thunder. They believed in a Great Spirit, Kitche Manitou, who had first created the elements, then plants, animals and, last, people.

All possessed spiritual powers, but only humans had the power to dream. Dreams, often achieved by fasting and meditation, enabled them to communicate with the spirits immanent in their universe and to share in their power. Young children were given a secret name dreamed by an elder, boys at puberty fasted in hope of finding a guiding spirit and when game was scarce, hunters dreamed of locating a moose or bear. Animals and plants, rocks, rivers, the winds, seasons and stars all were endowed with names and personalities, and fanciful stories were told to explain their behaviour.

Their favourite character was a half-man, half-spirit, Nanabush, who acted as Kitche Manitou's emissary and intervenor in the affairs of the world. Capable of transforming himself into anything from a tree to a toad, Nanabush expressed both the capriciousness and uncertainty of the natural environment, and the paradox of the human condition. "It was the human ideals of courage, generosity, resourcefulness, kindness that made him lovable," Ojibwe historian Basil Johnston writes in *Ojibway Heritage*, "as it was the human limitations of ineptitude, indecisiveness, inconstancy, cunning that made him a figure of fun."

Islands? Clouds? Ojibwe artist Robert KaKayGeesick, above, captures the dreamlike quality of Lake of the Woods at dawn in "Sacred Island."

Far left: Touched by the first frosts of fall, sumac brightens a rock outcropping along the Rainy River.

89

Like other Aboriginal people living off the land, the Ojibwe were acutely observant: a broken twig, a circling eagle or a whiff of smoke all carried a message, and on Lake of the Woods survival could depend on sensing a coming storm in a change in the wind. They avoided the dangerous waves of the Big Traverse. Instead, they paddled along the south shore to the War Road and Reed Rivers, and from there to Red River, or they portaged the narrow isthmus of the Aulneau Peninsula to reach the eastern channels that led to Rat Portage. A hunter's relationship with the animals he tracked and killed was so intimate he left a gift, usually tobacco, in exchange for the gift of his "elder brother's" life. Tobacco, along with sage, cedar and sweet grass, was smoked in a solemn ceremony as a sacred offering to the spirits; at some feasts, a dog was sacrificed. Community feasts were held in spring to celebrate the earth's rebirth, and in fall to give thanks for the summer harvest; throughout the year, individual families held feasts to honour visions, puberty, the end of mourning and death; the corpse was provided with enough food for its spirit's four-day westward journey to the sunny, bountiful Land of the Dead.

Ojibwe society was organized into five groups: leaders, warriors, hunters, teachers and healers. Excellence in any field was acquired by diligent study, and good behaviour – industriousness, quiet, generosity, respect – was taught by example and cautionary tales: there were plenty of cannibals, lake monsters, owls and other scary creatures in Ojibwe legends. Exorcising the evil spirit causing an illness was a medicine man's primary task, and sorcerers, believed to cause injury or death by poisons

Snug in a beautifully crafted cradleboard, a baby, or papoose, waits near the family tipi.

CARL GUSTAF LINDE / MINNESOTA
HISTORICAL SOCIETY / e 97.33/r.42

and charms, were greatly feared. Each band had a hereditary chief, but a chief had only as much power as he had supporters, and influential leaders were chosen, as needed, by consensus. Individual freedom was constrained by moral and social taboos; those who defied them suffered ridicule, harrassment and ostracism.

The Ojibwe lived a systematic life based on what American ethnologist Frances Densmore calls in *Chippewa Customs* "the industrial year". About 1910, a seventy-four-year-old Ojibwe woman, Nodinens, described for Densmore the seasonal cycle as it had been in her childhood. The year began with a new moon in late autumn when Nodinens, her mother and grandmother, using bone needles and basswood bark cord, wove dried bulrushes into mats for the winter wigwam.

WHEN THE ICE ON THE LAKE froze we started for the game field. I carried half the bulrush mats and my mother carried the other half. We rolled the blankets inside the mats, and if there was a little baby my mother put it inside the roll, cradle board and all. It was a warm place and safe for the baby. I carried a kettle. We took only food that was light in weight, such as rice and dried berries. There were six families in our party, and when we found a nice place in the deep woods we made our winter camp. The men shovelled away the snow in a big space, and the six wigwams were put in a circle and banked with evergreen boughs and snow. Inside the wigwam, plenty of cedar boughs were spread on the ground and covered with

PRAYER TO A DEER SLAIN BY A HUNTER

tranlated by Basil Johnston

I had need.
I have dispossessed you of beauty,
grace and life.
I have sundered your spirit from its
worldly frame.
No more will you run in freedom
Because of my need.

I had need.
You have in life served your kind in
goodness.
By your life, I will serve my brothers.
Without you I hunger and grow weak.
Without you I am helpless, nothing.

I had need.
Give me your flesh for strength.
Give me your casement for protection.
Give me your bones for my labours,
And I shall not want.

DENNIS FAST / LAKE
OF THE WOODS
MUSEUM, KENORA

Even utilitarian items such as winter
mitts became works of art in the
hands of an Ojibwe woman.

blankets for our beds, bright yarn bags with our belongings being set along the wall for use as pillows. In the center was a place for a fire, and between it and the floor mats there was a strip of hard, dry ground that was kept clean by sweeping it with a broom made of cedar boughs. The wigwam looked nice with the yellow birchbark top and the bright-colored things inside. Outside the door there was a little shed made of cedar bark where we kept the split wood for the fire, so it would not get wet. The men brought the logs and the women chopped the wood.

There was a big fire in the middle of the camp, and all the families did their cooking around this fire if the weather was not too cold, but we always had a fire in the wigwam in the evening so it would be warm for us to sleep. We slept barefoot, with our feet towards the fire, and loosened our clothing. I wore a dress of coarse broadcloth, with separate pieces of cloth to cover my arms, and broadcloth leggings that came to my knees, but I wore no other clothing except my moccasins and blanket. The big rack for drying meat was over the fire. During the day the women kept this fire burning low and evenly to dry the meat. When the men came home, the rack was taken off, for the men put in lots of light wood to dry their clothing. They sat around it, smoking and talking.

91

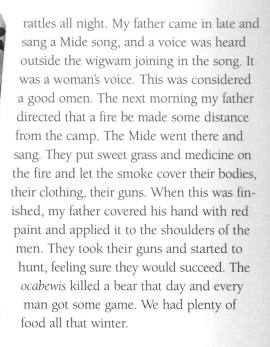

While the men hunted, the women mended the hunters' torn skin clothes and tended the drying meat – every part of the deer was saved, even the hoofs – and the whole family snared grouse and hares:

My father was a good hunter and sometimes killed two deer in a day. Some hunters took a sled to bring back the game, but more frequently the women went the next day and packed the meat on their backs. It was the custom for a man to give a feast with the first deer or other game he killed. The deer was cut up, boiled and seasoned nicely and all the other families were invited to the feast. I remember that once a hunter heard an owl following him. When he returned to camp, he said: 'You must preserve every bit of deer. This is a bad sign, and we will not get any more game for a long time.' The hunters went out every day, but could find nothing. We were so hungry that we had to dig roots and boil them. My father was a Mide [priest] and one day a young man entered our wigwam with a kettle of rice, some dried berries and some tobacco. He placed these before my father, saying: 'Our friend, we are in danger of starving, help us.' The man was the *ocabewis* who managed and directed things in the camp, and his arms were painted with vermillion.

My father called his Mide friends together and the men sang Mide songs and shook their rattles all night. My father came in late and sang a Mide song, and a voice was heard outside the wigwam joining in the song. It was a woman's voice. This was considered a good omen. The next morning my father directed that a fire be made some distance from the camp. The Mide went there and sang. They put sweet grass and medicine on the fire and let the smoke cover their bodies, their clothing, their guns. When this was finished, my father covered his hand with red paint and applied it to the shoulders of the men. They took their guns and started to hunt, feeling sure they would succeed. The *ocabewis* killed a bear that day and every man got some game. We had plenty of food all that winter.

IN EARLY SPRING, the families moved to the maple sugar bush, pulling bundles of furs, dried meat and tanned skins on sleds. They uncovered a cache of dried rice, fruits and vegetables they had stored in birchbark makuks in the fall, along with iron axes to tap the trees, tin pails and brass kettles to boil the sap. While the women made the sugar and collected cedar bark for summer mats, the men fished through the ice with spears and wire hooks. As soon as the river ice went out, fish were caught in nets made of nettle-stalk fibre and dried in the sun.

In the late spring, the families moved to a cluster of bark houses on the lake shore:

This was our summer home. Each family had its

own garden. We added to our garden every year, my father and brothers breaking the ground with old axes and bones. My father had wooden hoes that he had made, and sometimes we used the shoulder blade of a large deer or moose, holding it in the hand. We planted potatoes, corn and pumpkins. After the garden was planted, the Mide gathered together, made a feast and asked the Mide *manido* to bless the garden. The gardens were never watered. A scarecrow made of straw was always in a garden.

FOR NODINENS, summer was the time to pick berries, drying a supply to last the rest of the year, and to gather birchbark and bulrushes for the winter wigwam. Next came the rice season, followed by the vegetable harvest. Both were dried and cached for the next spring. "When colder weather came, the women began their fall fishing, often working at this until after the snow came. The men had gone away for the fall trapping. When the men returned, we started for the winter camp."

Nodinens' memoir of a convivial seasonal routine based on shared labour reveals that, after centuries of involvement with the European fur trade, these Ojibwe integrated trapping and foreign goods into their traditional economy. Goods were purchased only when, like guns, ammunition, knives, blankets and cloth, they were better than Mother Earth provided, or, in the case of coloured yarn and red paint, prettier. Far from being exploited by the fur trade, the Ojibwe, as producers, consumers and traders, controlled it.

The Ojibwe had prospered by establishing intimate, friendly relations with the Canadian and American traders. Alexander Henry, who traded out of Montreal between 1760 and 1776, was adopted by an Ojibwe as his brother. Henry's head was shaved, except for a topknot adorned with a feather

on the crown, his face painted red and black and his shirt coloured with vermillion. A collar of wampum was placed around his neck, silver bands and bracelets on his arms; his legs were covered with leggings of scarlet cloth, his naked torso wrapped in a scarlet blanket. Usually, Henry noted, Ojibwe men painted themselves with charcoal and white clay; the women wore their hair coiled in braids at the nape of the neck and rouged their cheeks with vermillion. Gifts customarily included a chief's offer of a daughter to be a trader's wife. The benefit was mutual: by feeding, clothing and protecting the trader, the daughter and her family acquired for their band a monopoly on his exotic goods. This practice became the "custom of the country" as well among the *gens du nord,* the men who made their homes in the Northwest. Pushing west in search of furs, traders and canoemen brought their Ojibwe families with them, and their relatives followed.

THE COVERDALE COLLECTION / NATIONAL ARCHIVES OF CANADA / C-040914

Ojibwe cradleboards were early forerunners of today's infant backcarriers.

After 1767, a British policy of free trade opened the Northwest to any freebooter who could raise enough money for a canoeload of beads and brandy; the biggest brigades were financed by Montreal's merchant princes. Unlike the HBC, which forced the native trappers to make the tedious trip to its forts on Hudson Bay, this new swarm of "pedlars from Quebec" took their goods directly to the

The Ojibwe recognized expertise in a number of areas. Some trained as traders, hunters, warriors or clan leaders, but only a select few were invited to join the Midewiwin.

THE MIDEWIWIN

THE SONGS, PRAYERS, RITUALS AND SCROLLS of the Midewiwin formed an encyclopedia of traditional knowledge, a history of the Anishinabe, a code of conduct and a religion; its most sacred symbol was a white seashell, the *megis*. According to legend, the Anishinabe, living on the Atlantic Ocean, had been dying from a terrible plague when a shining white shell rose out of the waves and led them on a westward migration to safety.

The journey had four stops: Montreal, Sault Ste. Marie, La Pointe, Wisconsin, and Red Lake, Minnesota. These were symbolized by four degrees of initiation into the Midewiwin mysteries and recorded as pictograph maps on rolled birchbark. (In many versons the trek's leader is a crane, otter or bear.)

On a deeper level, the journey represented the path of life, with its obstacles and temptations, a path often cut short by sickness and death; power over life and death could be acquired by knowledge of the properties of plants and animals, and by communication with the spirit world. Mide elders taught their lore to apprentices, and in the Midewiwin lodge initiates acted out a ritual journey from death to rebirth: seated by a Tree of Life, the candidate was "shot" by megis shells, fell unconsious and was revived, or reborn.

The Midewiwin codified ceremonies and beliefs – conjuring, herbalism, the feast, the megis shell, sweat lodge and medicine bundle – that dated from ancient cultural origins, but over centuries the idea of medicine seems to have incorporated elements of Christianity and Free Masonry. At Shoal Lake in the twentieth century, a Midewiwin lodge was adjacent to a Presbyterian church and the leading shaman, James Redsky, was a church elder. Mide teachings – kindness, courage, honesty, sobriety, respect for women and elders – had a strong moral tone; the best path to a long life was a good life. While both men and women could join the Midewiwin, usually by invitation, initiates had to bestow elaborate gifts on the lodge members, an expense few could afford, and Mide elders were often suspected of using poisons and casting spells.

trappers' camps. Fierce competition benefited the Ojibwe, who drove hard bargains, more than the pedlars, who were often cheated, robbed or murdered by unhappy customers – one Lake of the Woods band was called "Pillagers" by their rivals. By 1787, the Montreal merchants, realizing that profit could only be made from a monopoly, combined to form the North West Company.

The Nor'Westers revived and improved La Vérendrye's transportation network. In the fall, goods purchased in England were transported by freight canoe up the St. Lawrence to the Ottawa River, then, via the French River, to Lake Huron and Lake Superior. At Grand Portage or, later, at Kaministiquia, the baggage was repacked into smaller, lighter canoes bound, via Rainy River, Lake of the Woods and the Winnipeg River, for posts as far away as Athabasca; in spring, the canoe brigades, manned by the *gens du nord*, returned, loaded with furs, to Lake Superior. The North West Company was so efficient it soon controlled more than eighty per cent of the Canadian fur trade.

In August 1793, a tough, shrewd HBC trader, John McKay, left northern Manitoba with ten men and four boatloads of goods to break the Nor'Westers' monopoly on Lake of the Woods. At an Ojibwe camp on the Winnipeg River, he picked up an old, lame woman to guide them across the lake to Rainy River. On September 18th, McKay notes in his journal:

> Wind South blowing a strong gail. Set of[f] half past 5 oclock at 9 oclock A.M. fell in with the Chief of Lake du Bois. I give him two Gallons of Spirits and two pound of tobacco for which I received in return from him 16 Gallons of Rice. He seems to favour the Canadians much in his opinion of them. 11 oclock set of from his tent But the wind blowing so strong on our side we Was obligd to put up in sight of them. After we was campd the Chief and his Brother came to us

and several women. I traded 24 Gallons of rice and twelve Ducks from them and give debt to the Chiefs Brother and son.

TRAVELLING IN THE RAIN up the Rainy River, "one of the Beautifullest rivers I ever saw in this country," McKay reached the Nor'Westers fort, near today's Fort Frances, on September 26th. Though cordially greeted by the manager, Charles Boyer, McKay saw that there was no timber to build his own post, so headed downriver to Manitou Rapids. Here, the next day, he met the "great chief"

> He Wore a Silver Medalle with the Kings Empression on One side and Coat of arms on the other, likewise a Large gorget and arm band of the same mettle I give him a keg of Indian Brandy and two fathoms of tobacco, some flour and Sugar the two latter He asked for."

Flour was a luxury, but liquor had become a staple of the fur trade, demanded by both post employees – "Give the people a pint of Bumbo" is a regular entry in McKay's journal – and the Native trappers.

> September 29: Wind North cloudy weather 4 men squaring timbers for the house, Samuel Hervey making a Sturgeon net, the rest boating Home stones for the Chimney. nine oclock A.M. The Chief and twelve Canoes arrivd I traded 40 Gallons of rice from them. Sixe of these Canoes Contained the Chiefs family he has 5 wives and a Great number of Children, they are very troublesom wanting more Brandy than I can afford To give them.

McKay was trading brandy because he had nothing

better. "I doo not know what to doo for want of pointed Blankets," he laments in October. "The Brandy pays for all. The old Indian and son went off for the Settlement above To take articles in debt that I had not, such as Steel traps fish Darts Shirts Blankets and Gartering."

Once winter set in, McKay and his men, snug within their new stockade, found that the Ojibwe had gone away to their winter hunting grounds near Red River. The fish too had disappeared, and the men lived on rabbits until January 14, 1794: "Two Indians came in. Thay brought 24 beaver which was their Debt and a little Deer meat thay Shot a moose deer [elk?] on their way which I Bought." On January 18th, McKay writes: "9 oclock A.M. an Indian arrived brought nothing with him but a Cat He Shot on hisway he is the son of the lame woman That lives here. I find he is an imbassoder sent by some Indians of Lake Dubois to learn how I receive Indians."

The chief of Lake of the Woods, whose name McKay spells Naw Ekuzick, was displeased that McKay, by settling downriver from the Nor'Westers, was "shutting up the river." Says McKay:

> 4 Indians came in. Thay brought amongst them 20 Beaver. There is so Many Traders about this place that the Indians is at a Loss how to dispose of their furs to the best advantage. I am very sure these four Indians had upwards of an Hundred Beaver at their tents. And I have don all in my powr to get them. I Even offerd some goods under value and To send my men for the furs but they would not agree saying Thay wanted to give a little to Every Trader.

In the early years of the fur trade, the forests of Lake of the Woods were filled with a wealth of fur-bearing animals, but the demands of the trade soon depleted the region.

McKay returned to Hudson Bay in the spring with eighteen packs of fur, enough to encourage the HBC to finance him for another winter:

September 19, 1794: Wind N.W. a gentle breeze in the morning at 9 A.M. We arrived at the rat carrying place. Where we found Canadian Industry by their burning all the rollers in the path it rained just as we Carrying the Goods the men however got new rollers & launched the Battaux a little snow in the Evening.

September 22: Wind West foggy weather, small rain all day at noon fell in with the Indians 17 men besides Women & Children they made a long & Serious Speech to me the purport of which was for me to settle in Lake du Bois, at the River's mouth. They absolutely refuse to go up to Manitoo fall. It will however never do for me to stay here as I am certain the Canadians will be down as soon as they hear of my Arrival. I mean to leave men here and go up to Manitoo myself.

LEAVING HIS DEPUTY, Thomas Norn, with an interpreter and most of his goods at the river's mouth, McKay returned to his post at Manitou. It was a harsh winter. Fish and game were so scarce in "this barren place" that by March 24th McKay's men were living on flour. "This is the first time I have even seen men with me so reduced for want of victuals," McKay laments, "and I do not know where or when the first will come from." The Ojibwe too were starving, but five days later a hunter, Nawe-keeshickweb, brought in fresh venison. Although fish were plentiful at the river's mouth, Thomas Norn wrote to McKay: "I never passed such a disagreeable Winter in my life."

Norn had fought with five hunters who had threatened to break open his warehouse and take his brandy. Drunkenness plagued all the posts. "I get my share of abuse," McKay writes. "The Indians threaten loudly to kill some of the Canadians, and went so far as to say I would never see the rivers mouth. My only defence is brandy which has the best effect altho' expensive ... gave the men with me a pint of grog."

Young Dr. John McLoughlin, a Nor'Wester who would later run an empire of his own on the Columbia River, succeeded Boyer at Rainy River. He described the Ojibwe with grudging admiration: "They are full of pride, conceit and vanity which they hide in their intercourse with Europeans by gravity and distant formal behaviour resulting as much if not more from dissimulation than regard, as it is their opinion that no man is equal to an Indian, no accomplishment equal to skill in hunting, and they can pay no greater compliment to a European than to acknowledge he has as much sense and ability as an Indian."

McKay summed up his own credo in these words: "I like both Honor & money, money more than honor." Paying the Ojibwe in brandy, he scorned them for getting drunk, spied on them, berated them and accosted them in their tents, demanding their furs. He acquired the equivalent of 1200 Made Beaver, but they were "dearly bought on account of the enormous quantity of debt unpaid." Frustrated by the Nor'Westers, whose posts at Whitefish Bay, Shoal Lake and War Road River encircled Lake of the Woods, McKay left Manitou for the last time on May 6, 1795: "At 6 oclock A.M. set off from the falls after giving the Indians a little brandy; when we were pushing off Sha-sha-wish snapped his gun at the Batteaux I was in & was putting his gun on cock again when an old Indian woman laid hold of it and wrenched it out of his hand."

In 1797 after the Nor'Westers pillaged and burned Norn's old post at the river's mouth, the HBC abandoned the Lake of the Woods area until the two companies merged in 1821. The HBC rebuilt the post in 1825, and it was occupied sporadically until it closed in 1893.

THE VOYAGEURS

THE MEN WHO PADDLED AND PORTAGED the fur trade canoes were renowned for their strength, skill, singing and cheerful, uncomplaining ability to endure physical hardships. They included Iroquois, Métis and a few freed or escaped African slaves, but most were French Canadian. Trader Alexander Henry described their distinctive costume: "a cloth, passed about the middle, a shirt, hanging loose, a mouton [sheepskin] or blanket coat and a large red, milled worsted cap." They smeared their faces and hands with dirt and grease to ward off the insects.

"The voyageur's daily routine was a killing one," Eric Morse writes in *Fur Trade Canoe Routes of Canada*, "for the six-to-eight weeks he was on the road, he was roused as early as two or three a.m., and (provided that no rapids were just ahead) he set off breakfastless. Before eight o'clock a breakfast stop was made. A midday lunch was 'served'. However, fairly regularly, a stop was made for a few minutes to allow the men to have a pipe. This event was so important that distance came to be measured in pipes. Between eight and ten in the evening, depending on the light, camp was made. Supper, which might have been pre-cooked the night before, was warmed up and served. The men then dropped down on turf, moss, or beach, with their heads under the overturned canoe. A tarpaulin would be stretched from the canoe to give shelter from rain and dew."

From Montreal to Thunder Bay, the voyageurs lived on corn mush and salt pork; those who made the trip through the northwest ate corn mush, supplemented by wild rice, fish and waterfowl. At every campsite, they unloaded a ton or more of baggage from the canoe, then reloaded it for the next leg of the trip. At portages they carried a minimum of eighty kilos on their backs. They were not always cheerful. In 1847, traveller Frederick Graham describes men, "dead beat, bleeding at the nose", being whipped to carry on across a twelve-mile (or almost twenty kilometre) portage en route to Rainy Lake.

Entitled "The Pipe", this painting by Howard Sivertson captures a moment of tranquillity in the gruelling days of the voyageurs.

HOWARD SIVERTSON / FROM THE *ILLUSTRATED VOYAGEUR*

Despite the action on its riverfront, right, Hungry Hall was, like the post at Manitou, "a barren place", and deserving of its name.

Trader George Macpherson, seated below with his wife and family in 1872, had discovered the delights of Lake of the Woods by the time Colonel Garnet Wolseley.passed through.

Wolseley's scout, William F. Butler, describes a visit in 1870: About five miles from the mouth of Rainy River there was a small out-station of the Hudson Bay Company kept by a brother of my boatman, Morrisseau. As we approached this little post it was announced to us by an Indian that Morrisseau had that morning lost a child. It was a place so wretched-looking that its name – Hungry Hall – seemed well adapted to it.

When the boat touched the shore the father of the dead child came out of the hut and shook hands with everyone in solemn silence; when he came to his brother he kissed him, and the brother in his turn went up the bank and kissed a number of Indian women who were standing around. There was not a word spoken by anyone; after awhile they remained some time inside. In its way, I don't ever recollect seeing a more solemn exhibition of grief that this complete silence in the presence of death.

IN 1836, THE HBC BUILT A NEW POST, Rat Portage House, on an island in the Winnipeg River below the rapids at the eastern outlet of Lake of the Woods. On September 9, 1845, HBC inspector Robert Ballantyne visited the post's manager, Donald McKenzie: "We were hospitably entertained for a few hours by Mr. M'Kenzie. On the portage, over which we had to carry our canoe and baggage, a large party of Indians of both sexes and all ages were collected to witness our departure; Mr. M'Kenzie advised us to keep a sharp look-out, as they were much addicted to appropriating the property of others to their own private use. Everything, however, was got safely across; the Indians merely stood looking on, apparently much amused with our proceedings, and nothing seemed farther from their thoughts than stealing. We rounded an abrupt point of rocks, and floated out upon the glorious expanse of the Lake of the Woods."

McKenzie, called "The Major" because he boasted of his service in the Napoleonic Wars, appears to have irritated everyone. In 1847, his supervisor, Nicol Finlayson, wrote: "The poor Major's men complain much, not of himself, but the wife; and I believe if she did not meddle so much in his affairs he would be more popular than he is." But a Scottish tourist, Frederick Ulric Graham, scornful at first of The Major, his "half-breed" wife and "this miserable looking place," wrote: "He appeared very proud of his dogs and cattle, and gave us a capital breakfast, in which cream and whitefish predominated, or rather formed the whole. His daughters were very pretty."

In 1870, trader George Macpherson welcomed Colonel Wolseley to Rat Portage House, which had been moved to the mainland. In his "Narrative of the Red River Expedition", Wolseley writes:

> The post at Rat Portage consists of a few log houses surrounded by a high wooden palisading. It stands on a bank some fifteen feet high, and, when viewed from the river, bears a strong resemblance to a Burmese village. As you ascend the bank to enter the post, you are surrounded by a pack of the leanest-looking and most cur-like dogs, who are always quarreling among themselves, and have starvation written on their countenances. They are to the Indians, or the dwellers in the backwoods, during winter, what canoes are to them in summer. These dogs drag their traineaux or toboggins and are capable of lengthened exertions over snow-tracks where no horse could travel. In summer they are turned loose, and pick up enough to eat as best they can among the Indians encamped around; but in winter they are regularly fed upon fish.

Initially contemptuous of Macpherson, "a half-breed married to a squaw", Wolseley changed his mind when he found a hearty breakfast of broiled fish, potatoes and tea neatly laid out on a clean tablecloth. "There is a nice little farm," he wrote, "and a good garden, the vegtables of which were a great treat after our journey of so many days through a wilderness."

Captain G.L. Huyshe, who accompanied Wolseley, left this memoir:

> Mr. Macpherson, the official in charge, is a Scotch half-breed, a quiet, gentlemanly, elderly man who has received a good education in Montreal. He has been for thirteen years buried alive at this post! Is it not a most extraordinary thing, that men of any education can be found to stand a life like that, utterly cut off from the rest of mankind, receiving news of the outside world only once or twice a year, to all intents or purposes dead or sleeping? Mr. Macpherson replied simply that he had long since ceased to feel anything of the kind; he had his little farm and his wife and family and was quite happy and contented. Mr. Macpherson has a few acres of wheat, barley and potatoes, some pigs and cows and any number of mangy-looking pariah dogs.

Rat Portage House, pictured here in 1888 after the railway took much of its business, was still shipping goods to more remote posts

796. HUDSON BAY Co.'s POST—RAT PORTAGE.

THE DAWSON ROUTE

THE DAWSON ROUTE was inspired by politics, patriotism and greed. By 1868, Red River free traders were doing a brisk business with the Americans via a wagon trail linking the colony to the railroad at St. Paul, Minnesota. Eastern Canadian merchants were resentful, and Ottawa feared that the Americans might annex the Northwest. Simon J. Dawson was assigned to map a transportation route across the Canadian shield from Thunder Bay to Red River. Dismissing a railroad as "premature", Dawson chose a combination of wagons, steamboats and barges stationed along the old Rainy River canoe route. Dawson's route, estimated at $166,500, cost a tiny fraction of a railroad, but passengers, baggage and boats had to be hauled over ten portages, and the western leg of the road, from Angle Inlet on Lake of the Woods to Red River, crossed a morass of muskeg.

The Dawson Route was nothing but trouble. In 1869, surveyors prematurely staking the road across Métis farms in southeastern Manitoba provoked the Red River Rebellion; when Wolseley and his 1,200 troops tried to travel the road west from Thunder Bay to quell the resistance, they found it impassable. The route, operated by Canada's Department of Public Works, opened for business in 1871, but prices, $25 a head, were so steep they had to be cut to $15. By 1873, the Dawson Route had carried only 2,739 people, 805 of them settlers, at a cost to the taxpayers of $400,000 a year. Reverend George Grant, who travelled the route in 1872, described the Angle Inlet stopping place as "the dirtiest, most desolate-looking, mosquito-haunted of all our camp grounds," and the log corduroy road to Red River as "abominable".

In 1874, the operation was contracted out to the Dawson Route Transportation Company at a fixed subsidy; to make a profit, the company cheated the passengers. William Taylor, a homesteader from Ontario, denounced the company in a letter published by the *Brampton Times* as "the worst managed piece of business I ever saw or heard of anywhere. Their connections are bad and horrid, instead of good, as agreed on. Their stopping places that were to be clean and good are not fit for a pig-pen, let alone Ontario farmers." Taylor's family was delayed six days at Thunder Bay; on the first lake his boat became lost in fog, on the next, high waves swamped a barge carrying his horses, wagons and household goods. His son nearly drowned, his cookstove sank to the bottom and the trip took twice as long as the twelve days advertised.

Three hundred cold, weary passengers crowded into a makeshift post at Angle Inlet nearly rioted when they found there was no food. All the stopping places on Rainy River had been out of provisions, and many people had not eaten for days. The travellers' complaints were reported by the *Manitoba Free Press*: "Many of the station houses were in a filthy condition and passengers had to sleep on the ground or in stables. They had been forced to work on the way, carrying their own luggage on and off boats; women and children as well as men had been forced to walk over many of the portages; there had been a scarcity of men and teams to carry the luggage. The employees, with a few exceptions, were termed 'impudent, profane, obscene and lazy, whose best energies were employed in smashing luggage and swearing at passengers.' The boats were leaky and often unsafe and much property was destroyed when trunks in the bottoms of the boats were found nearly half-covered with water. Baggage was left on docks exposed to rain. The 300 passengers at the Angle found they either had to remain there without provisions, or walk 175 kilometres to Winnipeg without food. Many preferred the latter and boldly set out." Dawson, finding the complaints justified, advised abandoning the route; the government stopped work on the locks around the falls at Fort Frances and cut off financial support in 1876. The total investment had been $1.3 million. Simon Dawson

CARL GUSTAF LINDE / MINNESOTA HISTORICAL SOCIETY e97.35/84

entered politics as a Conservative member of the Ontario and, later, Canadian parliament until 1901. His route continued to be used until 1878, when a railway linked Winnipeg with American cities to the south and work began on the Canadian Pacific Railway. In August 1877, Lady Dufferin, wife of Canada's governor general, described in her journal their trip on the Dawson Road from Winnipeg to Angle Inlet:

Thursday, 30th – A hot day and the road dusty and extremely rough. During the afternoon we passed through a bush fire. We did not get to our camping ground until six ... there was no water and no food for the horses. We had to dig for the former.

Friday, 31st – Before lunch we did about 1/ miles, and as the road was rough we were glad of the rest in the middle of the day. When we started again, we were told that we had only nine miles to go. We had five miles of swamp and a road made with rough-hewn trunks of trees. When first made, this sort of perpetual bridge is not disagreeable, but when time has worn furrows in it, the jogging of the wagon upon it is not to be described! When we had been knocked about as much as we could bear, we got out and walked a couple of miles. In consequence of our slow progress, it was quite dark when we reached our camping ground.

The Dufferins, who were travelling first class, took four days to cover just under 150 kilometres. Remnants of the Dawson Route remain: the #102 bypass on the TransCanada highway east of Thunder Bay; signs east of Winnipeg marking where the TransCanada crosses the "Old Dawson Road"; a cairn at Ste. Anne, Manitoba, and a faint trace of wheel tracks, overgrown with moss, at Angle Inlet.

IN FACT, far from being in the middle of nowhere, Rat Portage House, a bed and breakfast for a constant stream of travellers, was strategically situated on the only Canadian transportation route that linked the new Dominion from east to west. The Canadian government was eager to open the western plains to agriculture, and Wolseley's soldiers had travelled part of the way from Thunder Bay over the Dawson Road, a primitive trail they largely built themselves.

Between Rainy Lake and Angle Inlet on the western shore of Lake of the Woods, the road, named after its surveyor, Simon J. Dawson, became a water route serviced by steamboats; wharves and warehouses had been built on the riverbank and trees felled for fuel. To the local Ojibwe, this was trespass; they had not given permission or received recompense. Dawson himself reported: "They are very intelligent and extremely jealous as to their authority over the country they occupy." As Chief Ma-we-do-pe-nais expressed it: "This is what we think, that the Great Spirit has planted us on this ground where we are, as you were where you came from. We think where we are is our property."

Unlike the Minnesota Ojibwe, who signed treaties and took reserves in 1854, the northern chiefs resisted until September 25, 1873, when they assembled at the HBC outpost at Angle Inlet to negotiate Treaty #3 with the Canadian government. It was an impressive sight. To the east, 100 birchbark wigwams and tipis, housing some 800

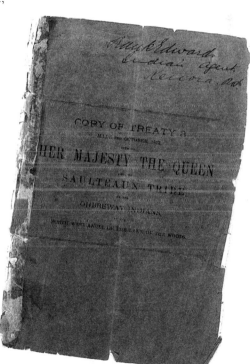

LAKE OF THE WOODS MUSEUM / KENORA

This rare copy of Treaty #3 belonged to Frank Edwards, the Indian Agent at Kenora.

people, stretched along the riverbank, the smoke from their camp fires rising into the crisp air, the birches and aspens behind them flaming gold against the black spruce. The men, dressed in their finery, faces gaudily painted, their long black hair adorned with feathers, were as colourful as the military honour guard, in blue coats and chalked white helmets, that accompanied the chief commissioner, Alexander Morris, lieutenant governor of Manitoba.

The day began well. Wrote Morris: "The Indians came up to the house I occupied, in procession, headed by braves bearing a banner and a Union Jack, and accompanied by others beating drums. They asked leave to perform a dance in my honour, after which they presented to me the pipe of peace. They were then supplied with provisions and returned to their camp."

AN OPEN CANVAS MARQUEE had been set up for the negotiations, which Morris expected to begin the next morning, but the Ojibwe as yet had to select their spokesmen from among the chiefs – twenty-four eventually signed the treaty – and to decide on a common position. The Ojibwe knew a railway would be coming one day, and they had heard the talk of precious metals in the rocks. "The sound of the rustling of the gold is under my feet where I stand," said one chief. "We have a rich country." The surrender of sovereignty over 55,000 square miles (nearly 140,000 square kilometres) was not to be done lightly, and the paltry terms the Manitoba bands had accepted in Treaties #1 and #2 were unacceptable.

Left to cool his heels in cold rain for five days, Morris threatened to leave; on October 1st, the Ojibwe, with Ma-we-do-pe-nais assisted by Chief Pow-wa-sang of North West Angle, as their spokesmen, laid out their terms: $15 for every Ojibwe present, $10 annually per capita thereafter, $50 a year for every chief, and an annual payment of $125,000.

Morris, expressing sorrow and regret, refused to discuss the chiefs' offer. Ma-we-do-pe-nais stood firm: "Our chiefs have the same opinion; they will not change their decision." Morris replied: "Then the council is at an end."

After 1873, hundreds of Ojibwe gathered annually at Rat Portage for Treaty Days.

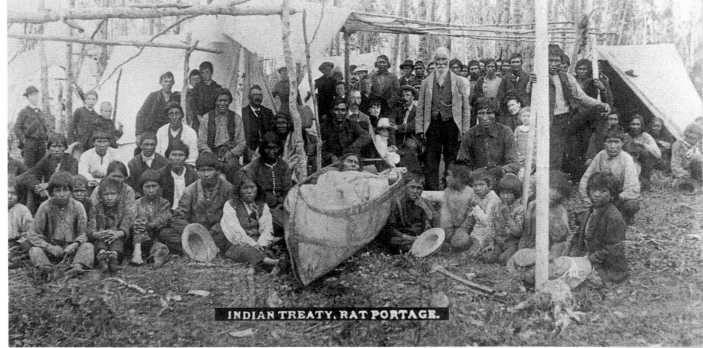

INDIAN TREATY, RAT PORTAGE.

But Sah-katch-eway, chief of the northern Lac Seul band, was unwilling to walk away empty-handed. Rising, he spoke for his own people: "We would ask you to assist us with every kind of implement to enable us to perform our work, a little of everything and money. We would borrow your cattle; the waters out of which you sometimes take food we will lend you in return. The time may come when I will ask you to lend me one of your daughters and one of your sons to live with us, and in return I will lend you one of my daughters and one of my sons for you to teach what is good, and after they have learned, to teach us." Sah-katch-eway may have glanced at Morris' militia guard, with its rifles and bayonets, when he added: "If I should try to stop you, it is not in my power to do so."

Morris had privately recommended that if Treaty #3 were not concluded this year, troops should be stationed at Lake of the Woods. Sah-katch-eway was expressing a bitter truth: Riel's flight and Wolseley's occupation of Fort Garry three years earlier meant that the alternative to a treaty would be war. The fur trade economy had collapsed; Chinese silk had replaced fur in Europe's luxury garment trade. Imported flour had destroyed the Ojibwe's market for local corn and wild rice, and they had little else to trade for guns, ammunition and cloth. They were at the tender mercy of their Great Mother, the Queen.

Ma-we-do-pe-nais admitted now that the Ojibwe had staked out their reserves; Morris sweetened the pot, offering, on signing, gifts of cash, clothing, ammunition and food. But Ma-we-do-pe-nais held out for better terms. After three days and nights of acrimonious bargaining, Treaty #3 was agreed to on October 3, 1873. It included, in addition to one square mile (2.5 square kilometres) for every family of five, or the equivalent according to family size, $5 per capita annually ($25 for each chief) as well as $1,500 worth of ammunition and twine. Each band requesting a school would receive one, and bands would be set up with tools, agricultural implements and cattle. They would be able to hunt and fish throughout their surrendered lands as long as the land was not occupied. Morris verbally guaranteed the Ojibwe's right to minerals found on reserve lands, and protection for their off-reserve gardens. The chiefs' request for a prohibition on alcohol was granted, and reserves would be policed.

THE TREATY WAS WRITTEN IN ENGLISH and read to the people in their own language. A Métis interpreter, Joseph Nolin, kept a written record of Morris' verbal promises, and an Ojibwe scholar memorized everything that was said. But Morris, a lawyer, had included a phrase that passed unnoticed: "Her Majesty the Queen hereby agrees and undertakes to lay aside reserves of land to be administered and dealt with for them by Her Majesty's government." Even Sah-katch-eway, who had spoken in terms of complete equality, had not envisioned the surrender of their right to govern themselves.

Accepting the treaty, Ma-we-do-pe-nais turned to Morris and said: "I take off my glove, and in giving you my hand, I deliver over my birth-right and lands; and in taking your hand, I hold fast all the promises you have made, and I hope they will last as long as the sun goes round and the water flows, as you have said."

Morris replied: "I accept your hand and with it the lands, and will keep all my promises, in the firm belief that the treaty now to be signed will bind the red man and the white together as friends forever."

Throughout the long history of the Ojibwe, the one constant has been change. The signing of Treaty #3 guaranteed yet more change for the future.

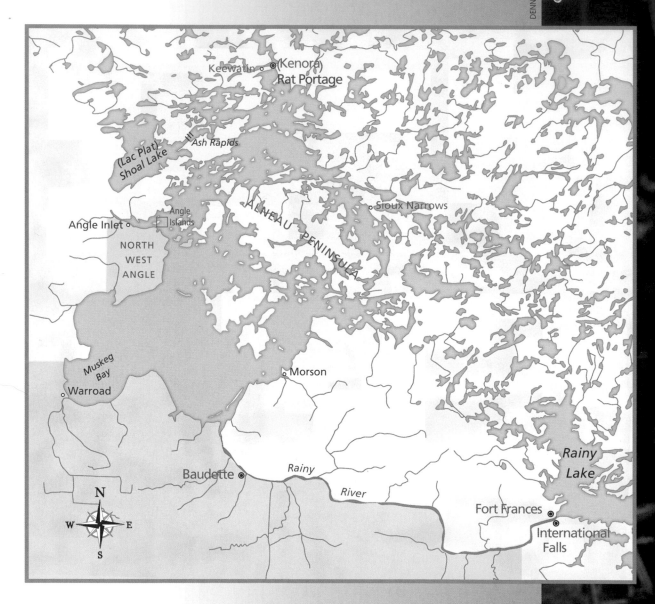

Keewatin ○ ○ (Kenora)
Rat Portage

Ash Rapids

(Lac Plat)
Shoal Lake

ALNEAU PENINSULA

○ Sioux Narrows

Angle
Islands

Angle Inlet ○

NORTH
WEST
ANGLE

Muskeg
Bay

○ Morson

Warroad ○

Rainy
Lake

N
W   E
S

Baudette ◉

Rainy

River

Fort Frances ◉

International
Falls ◉

Marsh marigolds brighten the wetlands
in late May and early June.

THE NORTH WEST ANGLE

ITS TREES STARK AGAINST A SUMMER SKY,
ONE OF THE ANGLE ISLANDS PROVIDES A FAVORED REST SPOT FOR GULLS, PELICANS AND CORMORANTS.

from a very large and shallow lake of the same name." Thompson seems to have decided that Lac Plat, as its name suggests, was a separate lake, and the Ash Rapids channel a river. The Americans had no incentive to question him: a boundary at Rat Portage would give them control over the Hudson's Bay Company's fur trade route.

THE HBC WAS ALREADY ALARMED. That spring it had reluctantly evacuated its Pembina post on the upper Red River because it appeared to be in American territory, then in August, with the surveyors still well east on Lake of the Woods, a United States Army expedition, arriving overland on horseback, occupied the village of Pembina. Commander Stephen Long drove an oak post, marked G.B. on the north and U.S. on the south, into what he claimed was the 49th parallel, hoisted the Stars and Stripes, fired a salute and proclaimed all of the territory to the south of the post to be in the United States. With the exception of one family, the residents, all HBC employees and pensioners, became American citizens. Then Major Long, against his written orders, travelled down the Red River to Fort Garry to ask the HBC's chief factor, Donald Mackenzie, to transport his troops back east through Lake of the Woods.

Mackenzie, curious and suspicious, complied. Long protested that his mission was purely scientific, but while his party included an astronomer, a naturalist, a geologist and an artist, his intent, to spy out the border with a show of military strength, was transparent. The Canadian canoemen watched their Yankee passengers closely, and when they camped at Rat Portage on August 25, 1823, relentless rain made it impossible for Long's astronomer to take the measurements required to drive a second U.S. stake into the imaginary border.

The HBC curtly informed the British government that retention of Rat Portage was "essential" to the trade of the

NATIONAL ARCHIVES OF CANADA / PA 074669

A recreation of David Thompson's monument at Angle Inlet, with geologist George M. Dawson standing in front, was photographed in 1873.

company and to British interests. The following summer, the boundary commission sent David Thompson back to Lake of the Woods, alone, to find an alternative. Thompson marked two points on the western shore with stone cairns, but the most promising site was in Angle Inlet. "Sent Belleau & 6 men up the lead of water to search for Stones but they found none," Thompson wrote in his notebook on July 26th. "All is alluvial & we have seen no Stones or Rock for the last 6 miles, searched & found a Tree of Red Oak." The next day, working in heavy rain and gale-force winds, he "sent the men with 26 oak Logs to build a Monument of 6 1/2´ feet by 6 1/2´ feet & 12 feet high. The Logs notched into each other & covered on the top with Aspin Logs, of which also the upper part of this Monument is built." A tin plate identified it as "North West corner of Lake of the Woods No. 1." Thompson mapped four potential points, including Rat Portage, and left it up to the commissioners to decide.

For the British, a simple solution was to run the boundary from Rainy River due west to join the 49th parallel in Muskeg Bay. But although the treaty had been based on an error, renegotiating it risked opening up other contentious boundary disputes, and if Britain tried to push

The boundary cutline, below, was created by Ojibwe axemen in October and early November 1872.

the border south, the United States could dig in its heels at Rat Portage. Angle Inlet would be a satisfactory compromise, but it was impossible to determine from Thompson's rough map whether his monument No.1 was the most northwesterly point. In the summer of 1825, the British sent an independent astronomer, Dr. J.L. Tiarks, on a secret mission to re-examine the lake's western bays.

TIARKS CONFIRMED THAT MONUMENT NO.1 appeared to be northwest of Rat Portage, but the difference, not much more than a kilometre, could be challenged as a mathematical error. Noticing that the inlet ended in a marsh, Tiarks pushed his canoe through a channel in the reeds for about a kilometre and a half until he came to a small pond. This, he declared, was the most northwesterly point of Lake of the Woods. The Americans, furious at being caught by surprise, had no choice but to agree: they had not examined Thompson's markers, and Tiarks had made irreproachable calculations with modern instruments.

Now that the boundary point had been moved to a remote and worthless swamp, joining it to the 49th parallel ceased to be important. The scientists had found no mines of precious metals, no mountains of sparkling jewels; the American surveyors described the country as "rocky wastes of no possible value in an agricultural sense," and David Thompson noted that even the Natives eked out a bare subsistence: "The country could never have been rich in animals and has long since been exhausted. The deer is almost unknown, and but few fur bearing animals remain."

The gap in the boundary remained in abeyance until 1842, when the British and Americans agreed to draw a line due south from Angle Inlet to the 49th parallel. There was no rush. Both Britain and United States saw the midwest as "Indian territory" inhabited by barbaric heathens

debauched with rum by licentious fur traders. Thirty years passed before a second joint commission was appointed in 1872 to survey the 49th parallel between Lake of the Woods and the Rockies. Its members included a third nation, Canada.

The young Dominion of Canada had bought out the HBC's interests in the west, and Louis Riel's abortive attempt to establish self-government at Red River in 1869 had led to the creation of the province of Manitoba in 1870. American settlers were spilling north across the unmarked border, and Minnesota's politicians clamoured to annex the Northwest. With feelings running high on both sides, the Anglo-Canadian commissioner, Captain Donald R. Cameron, was secretly instructed to reclaim, if possible, the North West Angle.

Cameron, a cocky artillery officer who didn't know a sextant from a compass, was a political appointment: his father-in-law, Sir Charles Tupper, a Father of Confederation, was Prime Minister Sir John A. Macdonald's closest crony. Cameron travelled west to Pembina in September 1872, with twenty-two tonnes of baggage, forty-four non-commissioned officers and men of the Royal Engineers, and an entourage of forty-two civilians; their ranks included, in addition to astronomers and surveyors, a blacksmith, carpenter, mason, baker, shoemaker, tailor, photographer, two medical doctors and geologist George M. Dawson. Since the expedition would winter at Pembina, Cameron packed a library of several hundred books. A few, with titles like *At Home in the Wilderness* and *Shifts of Camp Life,* were practical, but he brought books on fishing and shooting, mountaineering, Arctic exploration and the Battle of Waterloo. "Most numerous," writes historian John Parsons in West on the 49th Parallel, "were the works of fiction, history, essays, plays and poetry by such authors as Dickens, Dumas, Fielding, Scott, Trollope, Sterne, Smollett, Swift, Carlyle, Thackeray, Macaulay, Milton, Shakespeare, Byron,

Woodsworth, Hood and Pope." Perhaps the poetry was selected by Cameron's young wife, Emma, who came along with their infant child.

The impropriety of one woman sharing quarters with eighty-six men in a frontier military camp struck the Camerons as soon as they arrived at Pembina; they departed immediately for Government House at Fort Garry. But the comfort and extravagance of the British commission's Pembina headquarters, a compound of frame buildings named Fort Dufferin, aroused the jealousy of the veteran American commissioner, Archibald Campbell, whose men, expecting to stay only a month or two, were camped in tents about 350 metres to the south. Campbell had only half as many men, his astronomers' old instruments were inferior to those of the British, and the British had beaten him to Lake of the Woods.

A Canadian surveyor, A.G. Forrest, had gone to the North West Angle in August to search for David Thompson's monument No.1. Forrest scoured Angle Inlet, but he found no trace of the log pyramid Thompson had erected forty-eight years earlier. The local Ojibwe told him that it had burned in a forest fire, and because the lake level was presently five to eight feet higher than in 1824, the location was under water. To confirm their story, they brought him a charred, decayed oak log and offered to take him to the site. But Forrest suspected a hoax; vast tracts of surrounding forest had recently been burned over, and he rejected the Ojibwe's request for payment as "preposterous". Elderly Ojibwe who had watched Thompson's crew build the monument carried the log back to their camp.

Forrest was still stubbornly searching when the rest of the British and American surveyors marched from Fort Garry to the North West Angle via the Dawson Road on October 9, 1872. The Canadian road ended at a steamboat dock on the north shore of a shallow creek, but, by all calculations, the dock appeared to be in the United States.

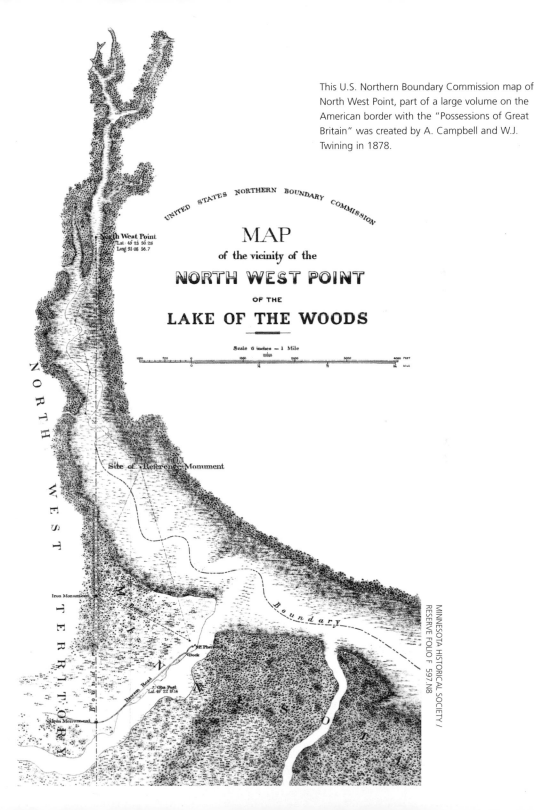

This U.S. Northern Boundary Commission map of North West Point, part of a large volume on the American border with the "Possessions of Great Britain" was created by A. Campbell and W.J. Twining in 1878.

MINNESOTA HISTORICAL SOCIETY / RESERVE FOLIO F 597.N8

111

The site was likely a convenience, or Simon Dawson's oversight, but it became another bone of contention. Thompson and Tiarks had left meticulous records, but Tiarks had built nothing in the swamp, and without monuments as reference points, astronomers could not confirm the earlier measurements. Fed up with Forrest's

MINNESOTA HISTORICAL SOCIETY / HD 1594.A2 1916 fb Map

By 1916, the Lake of the Woods watershed had largely been mapped. Though significant in size, it clearly had nothing to do with the Mississippi.

From a vantage point still proudly claimed, these Angle Islands gulls survey their much-contested domain.

DENNIS FAST

FARQUHAR WAS STOPPED IN HIS TRACKS by a huge, black-bearded, beetle-browed member of the Manitoba legislature, James McKay. McKay, a multilingual guide, interpreter, trader and the most powerful Métis in the Northwest, had brokered a deal with the Ojibwe: an old chief led the astronomers to an overgrown spot on the shore where, under more than two feet of water, they found the remains of a crib of hand-hewn, charred oak logs. Farquhar, examining their squared indentations in the mud, accepted the site as Thompson's monument No.1, and his British counterpart, Captain Samuel Anderson, agreed. Measurements taken at the site indicated that the most northwesterly point was almost exactly where Tiarks had located it at end of the inlet.

Canadian commissioner Cameron, however, refused to accept the evidence as conclusive. To the irritation of Anderson and the Americans, he insisted on referring the boundary question back to Ottawa and the British foreign office in London. "Our Commissioner has so far neither turned out brilliant nor successful," Anderson wrote to his mother. "He has a most unfortunate habit of rubbing everybody the wrong way."

futile wanderings, Major F.U. Farquhar, chief astronomer for the United States, arbitrarily chose a likely-looking piece of dry land, put up a marker and ordered his surveyors to cut a line due south to the 49th parallel.

BUT CAMERON HAD INFORMATION he kept hidden from the Americans. Surveying Angle Inlet in August, Forrest had discovered an idiosyncracy in the proposed boundary: a line drawn down the middle of the inlet's channel, as required by the treaty, meandered across the north-south boundary line at two places, stranding about 2.5 acres (or one hectare) of the United States in Canada. Cameron gleefully reported to Ottawa and London that these "irregularities may afford a convenient opportunity for inviting the government of the United States to reconsider the course of the boundary." He consented, however, to cut a "preliminary" line due south from the astronomers'

identified point on the inlet.

Anderson, employing Ojibwe as axemen, began work almost immediately and finished at Muskeg Bay on November 21st. "The British chief astronomer supervised the last few miles and erected a flagpole in the ice at the lake shore during a gale," writes Parsons. "Sounding the spot in the lake where the due south line intersected the parallel, he noted a depth of almost ten metres. He wrote home with marked restraint: 'I should like the old Plenipotentiaries who decided this Boundary Line by Treaty in 1818 to be resuscitated for a short time, in order to come and live at this spot. They would probably have

Among the North West Angle's attractions are its magnificent sunsets.

113

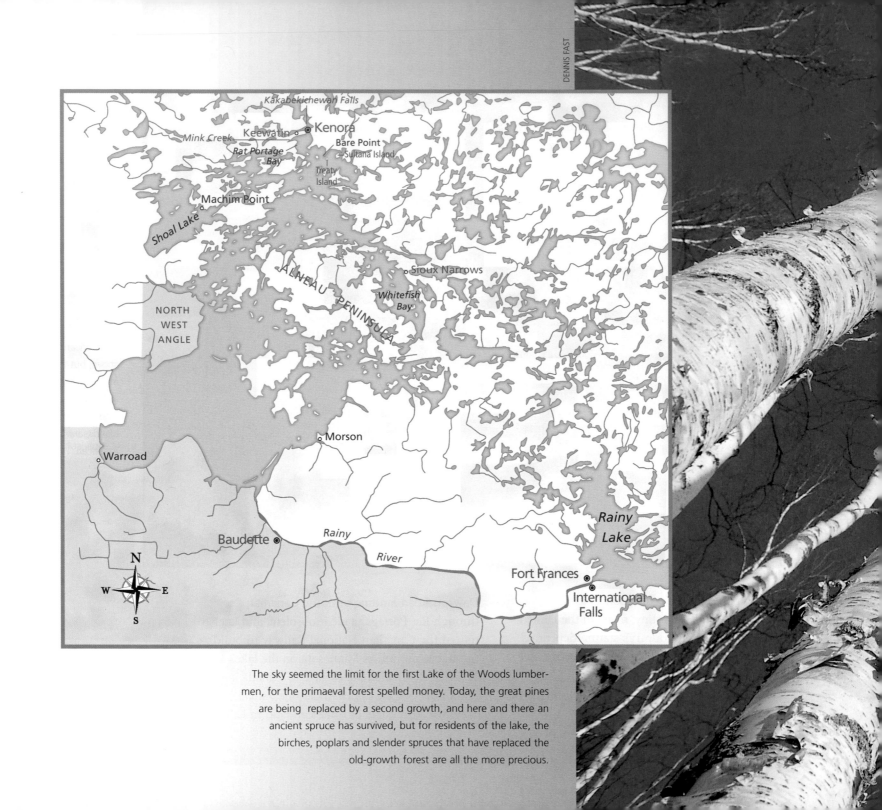

DENNIS FAST

Kakabekichewan Falls
Kenora
Keewatin
Mink Creek
Bare Point
Rat Portage Bay
Sultana Island
Treaty Island
Machim Point
Shoal Lake
Sioux Narrows
ALNEAU PENINSULA
Whitefish Bay
NORTH WEST ANGLE
Morson
Warroad
Rainy Lake
Baudette
Rainy
River
Fort Frances
International Falls

N
W E
S

The sky seemed the limit for the first Lake of the Woods lumbermen, for the primaeval forest spelled money. Today, the great pines
are being replaced by a second growth, and here and there an
ancient spruce has survived, but for residents of the lake, the
birches, poplars and slender spruces that have replaced the
old-growth forest are all the more precious.

116

MILLTOWN

MILLTOWN

The mills that grew up along the shore of the lake heralded a new era in Rat Portage – or Kenora, as it would be known after 1905.

IN AUGUST 1879, Captain Wiley of the steamboat *Speedwell* had two strangers from Ottawa as passengers on his run from the North West Angle to Rat Portage. The older man, his hair and beard flecked with gray, was a Scottish-born sawmill manager, John Mather, the younger, his twenty-five-year-old son, David. As the inaptly-named *Speedwell,* a homemade scow with no reverse gear, chugged slowly through the channels, John Mather scanned the stands of pine on the islands,

estimating, down to the last penny, the value of each tree once sawn into board feet. Mather, vice-president and general manager of the Keewatin Lumbering and Manufacturing Company, was scouting a site for a sawmill: his company had acquired timber rights covering on the northern half of Lake of the Woods, and a contract with the Canadian Pacific Railway to supply railway ties and other construction lumber as the line was being built between Winnipeg and Thunder Bay.

After eight years of political scandal and controversy, during which it was denounced as "preposterous", and an act of "insane recklessness", the CPR was inching its way east out of Winnipeg: the end of steel, stalled by a bottomless peat bog, had reached Cross Lake, sixty-four kilometres west of Rat Portage. Fortunes were to be made by investors and speculators who, through luck, acumen or influence, established themselves at key points along the proposed railway. John Mather, manager of Gilmour & Company's Ottawa Valley sawmills from 1857 to 1876, was one of the most experienced lumbermen in Canada; his shareholders included a senator, W.H. Brouse, and Mather, a director of the Bank of Ottawa, had friends and contacts among Canada's most powerful politicians and financiers.

The *Speedwell* docked at the bottom of Rat Portage Bay, and the Mathers entered the muddy little frontier town springing up around the HBC's new trading post. The hamlet's first hotel, the three-storey Rideout House, gleamed on a granite promontory. Owned by E.M. Rideout and his wife, the cook, it was the biggest building in Rat Portage and the first to have a coat of white paint. Other buildings, humble, squared-log structures, were occupied by free traders: young Frank Gardner and Jacob Hose, a hardware merchant, on the bay, and Robert Laurenson at the mouth of the creek that bears his name. Having managed HBC posts on the lake for years, Laurenson had quit when the company refused him a raise; to the company's chagrin, he built his popular post just outside the HBC's 276 hectares of property.

K AKABEKICHEWAN FALLS, just over a kilometre downriver from the village of Rat Portage, was a perfect site for a sawmill, but since the railway would first reach Lake of the Woods from the west, and timber would be needed to build monumental bridges across the lake's outlets before Rat Portage could be reached, Mather opted for the lake's shallow, sluggish western outlet, Mink Creek. Here he purchased eighty hectares of land adjacent to the CPR's right of way. During the winter, he deepened the creek and built his mill.

Logs were close at hand. Crews were cutting the railway's path through the primeval forest north of the lake; in its first year of operation, the Keewatin Lumber Mill produced 1.5 million board feet of lumber, as well as lathe and shingles. The sawn wood was used to build bunkhouses for the loggers, and homes, offices and stores for the hundreds of people who poured into Rat Portage to profit from the boom. The *Winnipeg Times* described the scene in the summer of 1880: "For some time now the railway works in the vicinity of Rat Portage have been besieged by a lot of scoundrels whose only avocation seems to be gambling and trading in illicit whiskey and the state of degradation was, if anything, intensified by the appearance, in the wake of these blacklegs, of a number of the demi-monde with whom these desperadoes held high carnival at all hours of the day or night."

In *The National Dream*, the first volume of his history

of the CPR, Pierre Berton gives this portrait of Rat Portage in 1880: "The town itself, in the words of one observer, seemed to have been 'laid out by a colony of muskrats'." Tents were pitched and shacks were built with no apparent plan in mind; the result was "a lot of crooked, winding trails that appeared to go nowhere in particular."

As headquarters for the CPR's Section B, Rat Portage

Main Street, Rat Portage, looking south in 1880.

was administered by contractors for the Dominion government; they built the jail and hired the police. Between April and November of that year, the court in Rat Portage collected $6,000 in fines for offences including highway robbery, larceny, burglary, assault, selling illicit whiskey and prostitution; drunkenness, fist fights, stabbings and murders were commonplace, and fines collected would have been higher were officials not routinely bribed. "It was the roughest town in Canada," writes Berton, "the headquarters of the illegal liquor industry with eight hundred gallons pouring into town every month, hidden in oatmeal and bean sacks or disguised as barrels of coal oil." The islands on the lake boasted a plethora of saloons, and whiskey peddlers sold "forty-rod" spirits at the same price that champagne sold in Winnipeg.

The saloons and storehouses were not illegal if they were outside the CPR's "seven-mile dry" zone; the proprietors of a brothel and saloon on Whiskey Island boldly carried goods and customers to and from Rat Portage on the steamer *Clipper*, the fastest boat on the lake. The revered Catholic missionary, Father Albert Lacombe, persuaded by the CPR to leave his work among the plains Cree and Blackfoot to minister to the sinners of Rat Portage, was scandalized. "What disorderly life of all kinds goes on in this place," he wrote in his diary. "Drunkenness, debauchery, and the infamous houses! The defiance of not keeping the Lord's Day! My God, inspire me!" In his biography, *Father Lacombe,* James MacGregor writes:

A day or so later, while a dance was going on two or three doors away, he was kept awake by the loud ribaldry of drunken men and women. Next day, he called on Mrs. G, the madam, to reprimand her for the evil she was doing and to demand that she shut up her bawdy house. With insults and jeers, Mrs. G flared back at him and ordered him out of her house. Never had he been so surprised, insulted or humiliated. Two days later, he happened to drop into the telegraph office where the operator

Hotels and rooming houses sprang up; some, such as Bismarck House, even had an air of propriety about them.

showed him a copy of a message he had just sent to Winnipeg. The good father was so exasperated that he wrote his diary entry in English: 'Always the same at Rat Portage. That G. woman is a very bad character. It seems by a telegraphic communication that she called for more women. Business is good, she says!'

SINCE 1818, ROMAN CATHOLIC PRIESTS had conducted sporadic missions among the Lake of the Woods Ojibwe, including a failed farm at Wabaseemoong (White Dog) downstream on the Winnipeg River. The Ojibwe had refused to accept Catholicism, but before returning west in 1882, Father Lacombe built, with his own hands, a small, frame Catholic church on the waterfront at Rat Portage. In this tarpaper shanty, he said mass, heard confessions, performed marriages and baptisms and taught school; he preached to the Ojibwe at their camps on the lakeshore. His mission became the parish of Notre Dame du Portage in 1882, Father Jean-Baptiste Baudin, O.M.I. the first parish priest. In that year, Anglicans, Presbyterians and Methodists all began holding services in Rat Portage, and John Mather built a Presbyterian church in Keewatin.

Prayer did not quell the chaos that erupted into pitched battles in 1883, and politics, not morals, was at the root of the lawlessness. With the signing of Treaty #3 in 1873, the territory surrendered by the Ojibwe, now called the District of Keewatin, had become the prize in a three-way power struggle between Manitoba, Ontario and the Dominion of Canada. Manitoba, given the authority to administer justice in the district, was determined to extend its own boundary east to Thunder Bay; Ontario retaliated by staking its boundary west of Lake of the Woods. The Dominion government, meanwhile, owned the land, with its riches, and administered the Indian reserves. The District of Keewatin had no elected government.

MAIN STREET, RAT PORTAGE, IN 1882.

In 1881, the Dominion government awarded the "Disputed Territory" to Manitoba, which set up a court in Rat Portage, with a magistrate, registrar, coroner and two constables. Manitoba replaced prohibition with a liquor permit system, but the Dominion government, with its own magistrate and constables, continued to enforce the "dry" zone around the CPR.

The first business district in Keewatin, circa 1888.

LAKE OF THE WOODS MUSEUM, KENORA / 1998.2.1

Conflict broke out when a Manitoba constable, Patrick O'Keefe, seized four barrels of illegal liquor and took them to his room; he was promptly arrested by a Dominion constable, brought before a Dominion magistrate and fined for the unlawful possession of intoxicating liquor. O'Keefe paid his fine, waited for the magistrate to leave the bench, then arrested him for having the same liquor in his possession without a Manitoba permit. The Dominion magistrate was taken before a Manitoba magistrate and fined $100.

ONTARIO JOINED THE FRAY IN JULY 1883, when the Manitoba government called an election for a Rat Portage seat in the Manitoba legislature. Within days, Ontario premier Oliver Mowat, promising "not to rest until every mile of the awarded territory is surrendered to us", appointed an Ontario magistrate, a chief of police and twenty constables for Rat Portage. Rat Portage had been incorporated as a Manitoba town in 1882, but Ontario now built its own jail and issued building permits and liquor licences; Rat Portage was incorporated as an Ontario town in August, and Ontario called a provincial election for September 28, 1883, the same day as the Manitoba election.

The Manitoba government was Conservative, Ontario Liberal; battle lines were drawn according to political loyalty, and the fracas involved most of the rough little town's floating population of 2,000 to 3,000 men (Ontario also allowed the owners of mining stocks to vote). Crime was ignored as the three police forces, totalling forty men, arrested each other.

"Prisoners arrested on the orders of one magistrate were liberated by the orders of another," John Burchill writes in "The Rat Portage War of 1883". "Prisoners committed to jail by the authorities of one government were taken out by parties of men who claimed they were merely upholding the rights of the other. This dull routine would be enlivened by an assault on a newspaper correspondent, or the apprehension of one of the magistrates on some trumped-up charge, to be followed a general swearing out of information and wholesale arrests all around the official circle."

The constables were assisted by unruly crowds of vigilantes. An Ontario mob set fire to the stables behind a hotel owned by a Manitoba magistrate; later they liberated prisoners from the Manitoba jail by breaking in the door with a battering ram. On July 18th, the jail burned down.

As election day approached, Manitoba dispatched sixty armed soldiers from the Winnipeg Field Battery to keep order at Rat Portage, a move Ontario's Mowat denounced as "a declaration of war." The elections went smoothly – J.A. Miller was elected in Manitoba, R.D. Lyon in Ontario – but it took a free-for-all scuffle between their two police forces in November to persuade the provinces to call a truce. After ten years of legal wrangling, the boundary dispute was decided by the highest court, Great Britain's Privy Council, in August 1884; Ontario won.

Keewatin, by comparison, was a sober little "company town". The Keewatin Lumber Company built duplexes for its managers in an area called the "Terrace", and workers built cottages in "Slabtown", named for the scrap ends of sawn logs that they burned for fuel. David Mather and his brother Robert, who managed the mill together, lived in identical homes on the main street; the upper balcony of David's house had such a panoramic view of the mill he was rumoured to observe the activities of his workers through a telescope.

He could spy out the competition too; the Dick & Banning Company's mill was next door. There were two mills, the Western Lumber Company and Ross, Hall & Brown, in Rat Portage, and three more, Cameron & Kennedy, H. Bulmer & Co. and the Minnesota & Ontario Lumber Company, at Norman between the two. The rival companies had acquired timber leases encircling Lake of the Woods, so now the Mather brothers began to buy their logs in Minnesota and hire contractors to cut timber stands on the Minnesota tributaries of the Rainy River. The logs were floated downstream, assembled into immense booms, some more than a kilometre long, and towed across the lake by the company tugs to the Keewatin Mill. Minnesota logs made up more than half the mill's annual production of 10.6 million board feet.

Competition was so ferocious that trespassing and theft were chronic problems; David Mather spent his winters patrolling the company's timber limits and inspecting the camps. Logging began as soon as the ice on the lakes and rivers was strong enough to support horse-drawn sleighs carrying men and supplies to the bush camps; on Lake of the Woods, mail and supplies were carried by cutter and dog teams over a winter road, marked by spruce trees frozen into the ice, between Rat Portage and Rainy River.

CONTINUED ON PAGE 120

Teamsters, led by Dan Nelson (in hat at centre), gather with their horses, in front of Short's Tie Mill.

LAKE OF THE WOODS MUSEUM / KENORA / 976.29.97

123

MATHER WALLS HOUSE

THE COMMUNITY OF KEEWATIN OWES its very existence to the Mather family. In addition to its lumber and flour mills, the Mathers were instrumental in the formation of the Presbyterian Church, the telephone system and the construction of the town's original housing. Today, the house of David L. Mather serves as a reminder of the family's influence. Constructed in 1889 in the Queen Anne style at the west end of Ottawa Street, the house has had only three owners in its long history. Purchased in 1906 by the family of John Walls, it is now owned by the Ontario Heritage Foundation, which was responsible for the restoration of the house. Managed by the Lake of the Woods Historical Society, it's open to visitors on a weekday schedule during the summer months, as well as for special events at Christmas, on Valentine's Day and during the May long weekend.

IMAGES THIS PAGE: DENNIS FAST

Competition may have been fierce on the streets of Kenora, but there were islands of civility in this rough and tumble atmosphere. For nearly 20 years at the turn of the century, David Mather's house was such a haven.

124

FIFE'S HARDWARE: A LEGEND

FOR NINETY-SIX YEARS, a shopping trip to Kenora was never quite complete without a stop at Fife's hardware on the water-front. "Go to Fife's!" was the advice given everyone looking for a scarce, peculiar, obsolete but absolutely essential piece of hardware. "Fife's will have it." And they always did.

In 1905, A.T. Fife's new store was a model of modern efficiency; in 2001, when Bill and Joan Fife retired and closed the store, it was a wistful reminder of a vanished age. Three generations of Fifes – Bill is A.T.'s great-nephew – changed their merchandise with the times, but they hated to throw things out. "Doing our inventory we'd come across something and say, 'Oh, did we have that?'" Bill laughs. "When I started in 1957, it took me a year to learn where everything was." The store's interior was designed like a Victorian carpenter's toolbox. Big items were displayed out front, screws and other small things were stowed away in tiers of drawers that lined the walls from floor to ceiling; clerks reached the top drawers by scrambling up ladders. Customers were waited on, preferably by a Fife, from 8 a.m. to 10 p.m. except on Wednesdays, when the store closed, as had been the custom in the early years of the twentieth century.

"At first, Fife's sold guns and ammunition, axes, water pails, stoves, ice boxes, chains, rope and horse harness," Bill recalls. "There was a tin

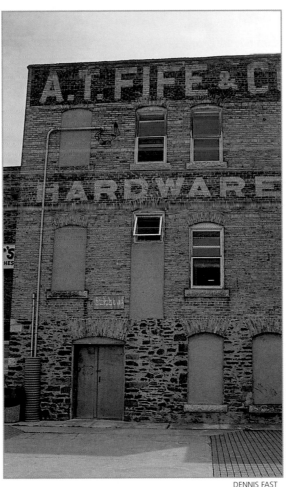

DENNIS FAST

shop upstairs where we made stove pipes and heating and plumbing fixtures. Paint was made by mixing white lead with boiled linseed oil and adding colour; it was indestructible paint! Kerosene was stored in a tank in the basement; people came in with wine bottles, whiskey jugs, whatever they had and we pumped it up to fill them. Dynamite was stored in a stone warehouse up on the hill. In those days, anyone could walk into the store and say, 'I want two sticks of dynamite.' We'd wrap it up in a parcel, and away you go. The caps were kept on a shelf."

A.T. Fife, or Colonel Fife as he was known after his service in the First World War, enjoyed waiting on his customers until his death in 1957. A conservative bachelor famous for his parsimony, Fife never forgot that when he'd opened his first Kenora store in 1897, business was done in pennies.

One day a small boy with a fistful of coins came in to buy a treasure. Fife, ringing up the sale, sighed, "Dear, dear that's an awful price!" The boy shoved his left-over pennies across the counter, replying: "Keep the change, sir, it's no good to me."

CANADA'S FIRST GOLD RUSH

THE OJIBWE CHIEF WHO SAID IN 1873, "The sound of the rustling of the gold is under my feet where I stand," knew more than geologists. "Minerals of economic importance, though carefully looked for, were not observed to occur in any quantity," George M. Dawson, geologist with the British North American Boundary Commission, had reported. But Dawson added: "Rocks of similar age and character which occupy the whole of Clearwater Lake [as the northern half of Lake of the Woods was called] are known to be metalliferous in other regions, and more especially in the country north and west of Lake Superior. They are there found to yield silver and gold in paying quantities, and it is not improbable that systematic investigation of the rocks of Lake of the Woods may lead to similar discoveries."

Traders had reported Ojibwe bringing in bits of gold-bearing ore, and when the Rat Portage band chose its reserve, 38B, on the northeast shore of Lake of the Woods, their land included a promontory with a rich vein of gold. Mineral rights were not included in Treaty #3, but Governor Alexander Morris had promised: "If any important minerals are discovered on any of their reserves the minerals will be sold for their benefit with their consent."

Construction of the CPR brought in swarms of surveyors and men skilled at blasting rock with dynamite. In 1879, a grizzled prospector from the

United States, Jacob Henesy, staked the first claim: the gold deposit on the Rat Portage reserve. Henesy named it Sultana. Within two years, surveyors found at least 100 gold ore sites.

But who owned the gold? Ontario's western border was not ratified until 1889, so Ontario and the Dominion of Canada both claimed mineral rights, and the Department of Indian Affairs strongly

LAKE OF THE WOODS MUSEUM / KENORA / 972.52.1

THE SULTANA CLAIM.

Many of our readers will remember the case of a dispute in ownership of the Sultana mining claim. Mr. Henesay claimed it, and about the time he expected to receive his patent, Mr. Capistran put in a counter claim, on the grounds of a former discovery. Evidence was taken last fall, and as a result, a decision was given last week in favor of Mr Hennesy.

Messrs. T. Blackwood, H. G. McMicken, A. C. McMicken, J. G. Bennett, and J. A. Kerk, of Winnipeg, arrived here on Thursday and let ha a mining claim they have near th Sultana mine. They intend going over the survey, in order to make formal application for the patent. The claim is the balance of the island on which the Sultana is located

defended the Ojibwes' right to gold on their reserves. But miners went ahead anyway, without licences, and thieves and claim jumpers found Rat Portage a good place to do business: Jacob

Henesy had to sell all but 1/16 of Sultana to pay the legal costs of defending it.

In the gold fever, smart speculators flipped a few acres of rock for hundreds of thousands of dollars; most mining companies who tried to extract gold from it, failed. Gold-bearing hardrock had to be shipped by barge to Keewatin or Kenora, where primitive "reduction works" pounded the rock into fragments: up to seventy-five per cent of the gold was lost in tailings dumped into the lake. Some mines produced gold bricks, but the process was ruinously expensive. By the end of the 1890s, when Klondike panhandlers were scooping gold nuggets out of Yukon's shallow streams, mine shafts at Lake of the Woods were filling with water. The Sultana mine drowned in 1906.

The early Lake of the Woods mines produced gold worth millions of dollars, but gold made no one a millionaire. The best money was made by the hotel and tavern keepers, merchants and freighters who supplied the mines: at its peak, Sultana alone employed up to eighty men. Henesy went into business as a real estate agent, liquor merchant and captain of two steamers, *Rambler* and *Sir William Van Horne*. Captain Henesy was Treasure Island's Long John Silver come to life. Thin, bearded, with sunken eyes, he had a wooden leg and shattered left hand – both had been blown away by dynamite – a salty tongue, especially when his pegleg got caught in a knothole on deck, a fierce temper, fondness for whisky and a reputation for marooning unwelcome passengers on reefs.

The only wealthy miner on the lake was a woman, Ida Knight Machin, the daughter of an Englishman, William Knight, who had made a fortune mining diamonds and gold in South Africa. In England, Ida had lived in luxury, but she had grown up in South Africa and inherited her father's passion for prospecting. The Lake of the Woods gold rush had petered out by the time Ida and her lawyer husband, Harold Machin, arrived in Kenora in 1906, but Ida dreamed of El Dorado. The Machins invested in ten mines, most of them on Shoal Lake, and Ida spent every summer exploring and staking claims; during the winter, Ida, Harold and their two daughters lived in a Kenora mansion furnished with the contents of her late father's English estate.

It seemed appropriate that the Machins' best-known mines, Mikado, Yum-Yum and Nankipoo, had been named for characters in a Gilbert and Sullivan operetta, but their somber story might have been told by Klondike poet Robert Service: "There are strange things done in the midnight sun / By the men who moil for gold."

In 1916, the wife and daughter of Emil Hubner, caretaker of the Machins' Shoal Lake properties, were murdered in their home at the Olympia Mine. The mine, little more than a network of surface trenches, was not operating; almost all of the lake's mines were derelict. CPR baggage handlers gossiped that Mrs. Machin's heavy trunks were lined with gold bricks, but she operated her camp on Gold Point as a farm. Harold Machin died there at fifty-six in 1931. Machin had commanded a battalion during the First World War, returning with the rank of lieutenant-colonel, and had served for decades as a member of the Ontario provincial parliament, but he suffered from the stigma of being a "kept man", or as one local wag put it, "an elegant cigarette lighter".

SIX YEARS LATER, the Machins' eldest daughter died in childbirth. Ida brought her newborn granddaughter, Carol, to Kenora, and in 1938 moved her family permanently to Shoal Lake. The Kenora house, with its furnishings, was left in charge of a housekeeper.

The three women, Ida, her daughter Barbara and Carol, lived in a log cabin at Gold Point Farm in almost total isolation until Ida's death in 1950. Their only neighbours were the Ojibwe. Kenora was more than forty-five kilometres east, by water, and boats had to navigate two sets of rough rapids. Barbara Machin became a prospector, one of the few women in Canada to have a miner's licence, but El Dorado eluded her; she sold the decrepit "haunted house" in Kenora, loaded her mother's silver, china and Victorian furniture on to a barge and towed it up the rapids to Gold Point. There, in the tractless wilderness, Barbara lived like an exiled monarch; guests told of her scattering diamonds on the table as if they were dice. After Barbara's death in 1978, Gold Point was eventually sold; Ida's English furnishings were given away or auctioned for a song.

THE LOGGING CREW, usually numbering forty to fifty men, cut a road from a lake or river into the stand of trees to be felled, then built a log shanty where the men would spend the winter. The most primitive logging camp shanties were one big room, thirteen metres by ten, with a peaked roof and windowless walls barely two metres high; in the centre, an open fire burned in a sand pit, the smoke escaping through a hole in the roof. The cook baked the men's meals – salt pork and beans, bread, potatoes, pie and tea – in iron pots, kettles and ovens he swung over the fire or buried in the hot sand. The cook's work table and pantry occupied one wall, with the clerk's desk and a small store with pipes, tobacco and clothing tucked into a corner. Two tiers of bunks, called "muzzle-loaders" because the men crawled in head first, were built at right-angles to the walls; wrapped in two heavy wool blankets, the men slept on mattresses of cedar boughs or hay. Sometimes they woke to find their hair frozen to the logs.

Early logging camps didn't bother with outhouses; the men used the bush and washed their faces and hands in tin basins placed inside the shanty's only door. They ate from tin plates and cups, sitting on the ends of their bunks. Unless the camp had some Finns to build a sauna, no one bathed or washed his clothes; wet socks and shirts were hung to dry on lines above the firepit. Shanties became infested with mice and lice; the stench was so foul the men

joked the shanty could get up and walk away by itself. Vermin and filth spread disease, but it was 1900 before the law required companies to provide medical care, and then the expense was deducted from the men's wages.

Later, companies built a separate cookhouse, with a stove, dining tables and benches. Loggers were picky about their food. "In the hierarchy of the bush camp, the cook was almost as important as the foreman," Louis Dion writes in a research paper on the history of Sioux Narrows. "The cook's control over his cookhouse was practically without question. He enforced the 'silence rule' with few exceptions. It was important for the men to eat and leave as quickly as possible (approximately 25 minutes) in order for him and his staff to clean up and prepare the next meal. It was not uncommon for the cook to 'patrol' the rows of tables brandishing a large butcher's knife to enforce the rule of silence."

The hallmark of a good cook was his ability to bake bread and pies. Says Dion: "Pie was served at the same time as the meat dish or the soup. Breakfast would see eggs, pancakes, bacon, oatmeal, fried potatoes, beans, prunes, pies and cookies. Lunch would be made from the morning leftovers, supplemented with sausage, salt pork, molasses, cheese, soup and bread. In most cases the loggers would make their own bag lunch if they were too far from the camp. Supper would include items such as steak,

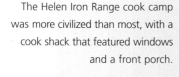

The Helen Iron Range cook camp was more civilized than most, with a cook shack that featured windows and a front porch.

LAKE OF THE WOODS MUSEUM / KENORA / 983.1.596

128

mutton, stew, soup, bread, potatoes, rice, cheese, beans, prunes, cookies and, of course, pie."

Loggers burned it off working –30°C to –40°C, from dawn to sunset. Cutting crews worked in three-man teams: an axeman and two sawyers. The axeman notched the tree to be cut; after it was felled, he stripped the branches and marked the trunk to be sawn into twelve, fourteen or sixteen-foot lengths. Depending on the size of the trees, and the density of the stand, a crew could cut from 100 to 250 logs per day. The logs, chained in bundles, were dragged out by horses to "skidways" along the bush road. Here, teamsters loaded the logs onto sleighs and hauled them over a road, packed with snow, that had been flooded to form a sheet of ice; only grooves gouged in the surface kept the heavy sleighs from sliding off. The logs, dumped on frozen lakes and rivers, were rounded up when the ice went out in the spring and towed to the sawmills.

Teamsters, who usually supplied their own horses, were, at $35 a month, amongst the highest paid bush workers. Cutters averaged $30; "swampers", old men and greenhorns who did brush clearing and roadwork, earned as little as $26 a month. Cooks were paid up to $75, foremen $100. Wages included room and board, such as they were, and for young men who had moved west building the CPR, bush work may have been all they could find.

As immigrants poured into the prairies, lumber from Lake of the Woods mills built their houses and shops, sidewalks, fences, telephone lines, barns and grain elevators. A far-sighted Montreal grain merchant, James Ogilvie, had explored Lake of the Woods as a site for a flour mill, and

when Ogilvie chose Winnipeg, John Mather seized his opportunity; by 1887 he had persuaded his friend and former employer, Allan Gilmour, and the CPR syndicate, led by Sir Donald A. Smith, Sir George Stephen, R.B. Angus and Sir J.C. Abbott, to build a flour mill at Keewatin Mills. Grain merchant Alexander Mitchell was president, Mather vice-president and a major shareholder.

Building a mill capable of producing

1,000 barrels of flour a day required blasting a millrace across the narrow neck of rock adjacent to the Keewatin Lumber Company, and raising the level of Lake of the Woods to increase waterpower; low water levels had been a chronic problem for the sawmill. The Dominion government was so enthusiastic about the flour mill – the prairies

Breathtakingly high, left, this CPR trestle is testament to human ingenuity and determination.

Viewed from high on a hill, Short's Tie Mill had a certain beauty that was perhaps lost on its employees.

129

With power aplenty, and grain pouring in from the newly-plowed prairies to the west, flour mills sprang up in Kenora. Among the largest, the Lake of the Woods Milling Company (seen at the end of Keewatin's Main Street, behind a gathering crowd), and the Maple Leaf Milling Company, shown below with employees at a display for an agricultural fair.

were being touted as "the bread-basket of the world" – that it financed the construction of a crude weir, called a rollerway dam, across the central outlet of Lake of the Woods.

The lake rose three feet. Sand beaches and rocky shore-lines disappeared; marshes spread inland. Flooding damaged the Ojibwe's wild rice beds, hay meadows and fish spawning grounds; they had not been consulted and, not surprisingly, they were outraged. Nonetheless, in 1892, Mather, intending to generate hydro electricity to run a pulp and paper mill, was allowed to build a larger dam downstream at Norman. To the south, Minnesota settlers, finding that their lakeshore homesteads were largely under water, raised a hue and cry, but both the Canadian and American governments believed that higher water improved harbours and navigation. The simmering dispute, which caused intense anti-Canadian feeling among both Americans and Ojibwe, was referred to the International Joint Commission in 1912; after an exhaustive, four-year investigation, the commission ruled in favour of the higher water. In the meantime, the controversy, and

opposition from rivals in Manitoba wanting to dam the Winnipeg River, made it impossible for the Mathers to finance their hydro project. In 1898, the Ontario government took over responsibility for regulating the lake's out-flow at the Norman dam.

The Lake of the Woods Milling Company, a flour mill built of granite quarried from a nearby island, began production in 1888. By 1903, when it was sold for $2.8 million, the company owned sixty-seven grain elevators across Western Canada and a second mill in Portage la Prairie; its product, Five Roses flour, was a household word. John Mather, having sold his shares for nearly $100,000, immediately invested his profits in a rival mill, the Keewatin Flour Milling Company, to be built on land he owned next door. Furious, the Lake of the Woods Milling Company sued, claiming the new company's name infringed on its right to use "Keewatin" on its flour bags and in advertising. Construction went ahead, but in January 1906, Mather sold his uncompleted mill to Lake of the Woods Milling for $950,000. It became known as Mill C (the mill in Portage la Prairie was Mill B).

John Mather was now seventy-eight. His health was frail, but he continued to do business from his bedroom in Ottawa. Soft-spoken and self-effacing, he took as much

delight in collecting scholarly books and cultivating his prize-winning flower garden as he did in commerce. He was a millionaire, but not everything had gone well. His ventures into gold mining, including a rock-crushing plant, had been unprofitable, the pulp mill was in limbo and his rivals in the lumber industry had merged to form the Rat Portage Lumber Company. Its president, Douglas C. Cameron, formerly of Cameron & Kennedy, was also president of Maple Leaf Mills, a new flour mill in Rat Portage powered by the town's hydro electric plant at Kakabekichewan Falls. Since "Rat" was not a good address for a flour mill, in 1905 Maple Leaf Mills had persuaded the town to amalgamate KEewatin, NOrman and RAt into an euphonious new name.

KENORA, A FRONTIER TOWN OF ABOUT 5,000,

had not, as predicted, become the Minneapolis of the north, but in April 1906, Minneapolis came to Keewatin: the Mathers sold their lumber company to the Minneapolis-based giant, Backus Brooks, for $350,000. Their sawmill had burned down in October 1905, but the company's remaining assets included its tie and planing mills, steam boats, twelve million feet of saw logs and timber leases in Ontario and Minnesota with an estimated 117 million feet of standing pine. John Mather died the next year, Robert retired and David, who had established his own Kenora-based contracting company, moved to Winnipeg. The only Canadian on the new company's board was its general manager, young Donald "Dan" McLeod. Hired by the Keewatin mill in 1884 at age sixteen, McLeod had worked his way up through the ranks; he had the respect of the men and of the company's new owners.

Backus Brooks rebuilt the Keewatin sawmill, but as the company bought up sawmills at Rainy River and Spooner, Minnesota, logs were no longer boomed north to Keewatin. By the 1920s the pine in the Canadian limits was so depleted the Keewatin mill ran only sporadically. It was shut down and destroyed by fire on June 17, 1942. The life of the Rat Portage Lumber Company was shorter. Running the company from Winnipeg, Douglas C. Cameron opened lumber yards across the prairies, expanded into the British Columbia timber business and invested in the grain trade. Cited as one of Winnipeg's nineteen millionaires in 1910, Cameron served as lieutenant governor of Manitoba from 1911 to 1916; he was knighted in 1913.

The Lake of the Woods Milling Company, left, quickly dominated the industry, and its Five Roses flour became a household word nation wide.

Long years of wrangling stalled the construction of the Backus Brooks paper mill, but the sod turning finally took place on June 8, 1922.

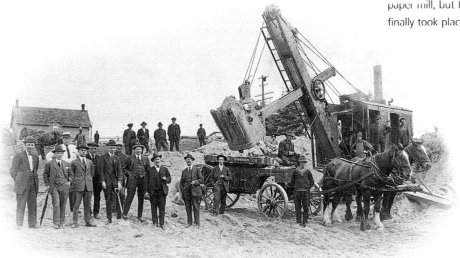

The Norman Dam today, and Norman Park, on the shore of Lake of the Woods.

IR DOUGLAS, HOWEVER, had guaranteed bank loans with lumber company stock. When a recession hit the prairies in 1912, followed by the collapse of grain prices with the outbreak of World War I on August 4, 1914, the banks seized the Rat Portage Lumber Company, liquidated its stockpile of lumber and sold its assets to Backus Brooks for a token $35,000; the mill was idle until it burned in the 1930s.

American ownership of pioneer Ontario companies grated on a lot of Canadian nerves, but Edward Wellington Backus, the rough-hewn president of Backus Brooks, grated on American nerves too. Raised on a homestead in northern Minnesota, Backus had begun with a desk job with a lumber company in 1877; four years later, at twenty-one, he owned the company. Cast in the ruthless capitalist mould of John D. Rockefeller, Backus was known for bulling ahead and asking permission later. Using borrowed money and political connections, Backus gained a monopoly on the timber of northern Minnesota; once the pine was gone, he intended to cut the spruce for his paper mills.

Backus' cross-border pulp and paper mills at Fort Frances and International Falls on Rainy River had already embroiled him in controversy; having dammed the Canadian side of the river, Backus was building his Fort Frances mill without a licence to cut Canadian timber. The Ontario

132

government refused to be stampeded into granting a licence after the fact, and Backus was having difficulty financing construction. It was 1913 before Backus, his Rainy River mills up and running, turned his attention to building a pulp and paper mill at Kenora.

First he seized control of Lake of the Woods hydro power by buying the Norman dam, and, from the town of Kenora, its antiquated, nearly bankrupt power plant at Kakabekichewan Falls. Backus next demanded from Ontario the right to build a dam at White Dog Falls sixty-four kilometres down the Winnipeg River, and a licence to cut nearly 5,000 square miles of timber on the English River system east of White Dog. His audacity infuriated Canadian lumber companies, but in 1920, after years of pro-mill lobbying by Kenora politicians, the contract was signed. In February 1923, the Kenora Paper Mill Company started operating in a drained swamp that been the town's circus ground and lacrosse field.

Eight years later, the mill was forced into receivership. The Backus Brooks empire had crashed, an early victim of the Great Depression; Backus, a humbled man, died suddenly in 1934. The Kenora mill, taken over by the Minnesota and Ontario Pulp and Paper Company, survived to become the cornerstone of the twentieth-century Kenora economy.

Milltown, as the workers proudly called Kenora, was a noisy place in the early years of the century. "Every steam operation had a whistle," John Currie, a former town clerk, recalls. "At 6 a.m. each gave a good blast as a reveille and for some reason the town fire bell and the Catholic church bell clanged away. At 7 a.m. each company whistle blew to announce starting to work and the bells rang to compete. The CPR locomotives whistled when starting to chug; the roundhouse whistled at work starting

and stopping time as well as a lengthy howling when a wrecking crew was being summoned. This whistling was repeated at 12 noon, 1 p.m. and 6 p.m., and at 7 p.m. if night shifts were running, always with the bells accom-

LAKE OF THE WOODS MUSEUM / KENORA / 989.53.8

panying. On the lake, every boat whistled two or three times before setting out, coming in or passing each other. Even the ferry did this each trip." Fans at hockey games blew whistles and clanged cow bells, and every evening the Salvation Army band held a brief concert in front of one of the hotels. "They would sing a hymn or two and offer a short prayer," says Currie, "while one or two of the ladies would go into the bars and take up a collection on their tambourines. Then, with the band playing, they would return to a service in their barracks. In fine weather, the Sunday service might be held on the street."

Sawmills screeched twenty hours a day from May until November, and the racket from the trains was constant.

Picturesque but noisy, trains were a crucial fact of life in Kenora.

133

The track ran right through the centre of town, and every train stopped to load and unload passengers and baggage and to take on coal and water. The Kenora station, the divisional point between Winnipeg and Ignace, had hectares of sidings and marshalling yards where, day and night, locomotives slammed wooden boxcars together to make new trains. The railway was such an important presence in the town its activities were reported in the newspapers. On September 26, 1905: "CPR yards busy on Sunday last, something like 28 freights pulled in and out of here, totalling 720 cars transferred and attached," on March 23, 1910: "CPR westbound traffic unusually heavy. Since Saturday upwards of 400 cars of settlers' effects have passed through here," and on November 6, 1912: "800 cars of grain passing through daily – largest in history."

The first CPR Station, right, dated from the late 1880s.

Railway construction in the Canadian Shield was arduous and dangerous.

Train traffic meant prosperity: Lake of the Woods lumber, flour, paper and fish were shipped out by rail, and until the CPR began to convert to diesel engines in the 1950s, eventually shutting down its Kenora yards, it employed about 800 men. In early days, jobs were seasonal. Trainmen were paid fifteen cents an hour for a ten-hour shift, and they were on call twenty-four hours a day. "They could call you any time," recalls William McKinnon. "A call boy came to the house before they had the phones, then you had two hours to get ready and go down to work."

THE MEN NEVER KNEW when they would get home; the run to Ignace was only 233 kilometres, but the freights, slow at best, were often stalled by mechanical failure and washed-out tracks. Few lives were lost in wrecks, but many men were killed and maimed on the job. For a freight crew, the run could be cold, tedious and dirty. Trainmen cooked their meals on a stove in the caboose; the fireman became black with soot from shovelling coal. "You put it in all the time, 20 tons of it from Kenora to Ignace in six or six-and-a half hours," remembers Tommy Thorpe. "The fire boxes were seven feet wide and 10 feet long. You had a fire in there eight or nine inches thick. You had to keep it covered with fresh coal and be sure it was scattered evenly to keep steam pressure up; it used quite a lot more coal going uphill."

THORPE LIVED IN A YMCA BOARDING HOUSE across from the station: "There were 66 beds, single rooms and double rooms, a 24-hour-a-day restaurant, billiard tables and reading rooms with all the latest magazines, two bowling alleys in the basement, lots of washbowls, toilets and baths. The desk clerk would call you, and while you were getting your clothes on, he'd give your order in the restaurant and it would be hot and ready for you on the table."

The YMCA was more sanitary than the rest of the town. Says John Currie: "Today, one does not see sheets of yellow tanglefoot covered with dying and dead flies, or coils of similar stuff hanging from the ceilings, nor is it necessary to cover exposed food with cheesecloth. Summer meant flies. All the traffic was horse-drawn, the streets were not paved and were cleaned mostly by sparrows, wind and rain. Stables for horses and cows were everywhere, and manure was moved only when the pile was too big. Garbage piled up behind stores until enough for a drayload, and most residences burned it in their backyards as occasion required. We accepted epidemics of scarlet fever, diphtheria, typhoid, measles etc. as part of living. Milk was not bottled or pasteurized; when the milk delivery arrived one presented a container and a pail or a quart at a time would be poured. When we began to test milk for cleanliness in 1913, the shock from what was found made corrective measures imperative. It was at this time we checked the water and began to chlorinate. The typhoid ceased. As a small boy,

I often would ride the waterwagon as it went about delivering water by the pail to homes where the town water did not reach. Every winter, the ice houses on the lake front would be filled with large blocks of ice covered with sawdust. During the rest of the year, these would be cut into blocks of about 1.5 cubic feet and peddled around town to fill the iceboxes." Sewage was pumped untreated into the Winnipeg River.

With prosperity, Kenora, its solid new buildings made of local brick and stone, began to look like a town in Old Ontario; the church of Notre Dame du Portage could have been in Quebec. Old Rat Portage had been swept away by fire. Rideout House had burned in 1888; its grandiose successor, the Hilliard Opera House and Hotel, burned in 1898. The fire engulfed a nearby liquor warehouse; casks and bottles burst, sending a river of flaming booze across the street. Louis Hilliard rebuilt, but the

The town was still called Rat Portage in 1899, but increasingly the community did not suit the name. Now the main street boasted churches with classical lines and a hotel with a sweeping verandah.

NATIONAL ARCHIVES OF CANADA / PA–017828

135

C. P. R. Station, Kenora, Ont.

KENORA WAS NOW A PLACE TO SEE AND BE SEEN AND THE CPR STATION,
WITH ITS BROAD WALKWAY AND ADJACENT PARK, WAS PERFECT FOR A SUMMER OUTING.

hotel/opera house burned again in 1902, 1906 and for the last time in 1910. It was replaced by the Tourist Hotel, taken over by the town when it went bankrupt, and later the Kenricia. The Anglican Cathedral Church of St. Alban was destroyed by fire in 1892; the church of Notre Dame du Portage went up in flames on Christmas Eve 1914, and the Methodist church burned in 1916. The Anglicans and Catholics rebuilt, but the Methodists joined the Presbyterians to form Knox United Church (the Presbyterians' first church had burned in 1892).

Every lumber yard in Norman burned. In 1915, fire gutted Kenora's skating rink, the Orange Hall, a pop bottling plant, movie theatre, billiard parlor, carpentry shop and several warehouses. Arson was always suspected, but the fires were not investigated. The Kenora fire hall and police station burned down three times; the last fire, in 1912, destroyed the horses and pump wagon and killed a prisoner locked in his cell.

With the building of a courthouse and two hospitals, Kenora developed a professional class of judges, lawyers and doctors whose solid brick homes, along with those of wealthy merchants, dotted the bays and promontories. For most families, social life centred around the church – Bethesda Lutheran for Scandinavians, St. Vladimir's Greek Orthodox for Ukrainians – and Sundays were strictly observed.

Apart from the board of trade, the Royal Canadian Legion and the Ukrainian Literary Society, religion determined the clubs men belonged to and the friends their wives invited for tea or cards. Ojibwe elders retained their own traditional beliefs and customs in secrecy, and unlike the Christians, they did not attempt to convert the unbelievers.

LAKE OF THE WOODS MUSEUM / KENORA / 956.3.60

The destruction of Notre Dame du Portage on Christmas Eve of 1914, above left, drew a somber crowd and provided a sad ending to a difficult year.

St. Alban's Anglican Church, left, replaced the Anglican Cathedral that burned in 1892.

LAKE OF THE WOODS MUSEUM / KENORA / 984.33.14

CONTINUED ON PAGE 136

137

STONE BOATS

N 1897, TWENTY-TWO-YEAR-OLD JOHN W. STONE arrived in Rat Portage from Barrie, Ontario with a couple of rowboats. He rented a shed next to the rowing club and hung out his sign, "Boats for Hire". Stone did so well he returned the next year with a boxcar of Lake Simcoe skiffs, then began building his own canoes and boats to rent and sell. By 1906, when the J.W. Stone Boat Manufacturing

Company moved to a new factory at the foot of Main Street, its inventory included duck boats, sailboats and sailing canoes, ice boats, barges and rowing shells. Stone boats, custom made by skilled crafts-men, rivalled imports in both quality and design: sailboats *Freya* and *Bubbles* were frequent winners at yacht club regattas, and in 1909

Stone built for George Galt, using Galt's own drawings, the fastest motor launch on the lake.

Inboard gasoline launches arrived on Lake of the Woods with the twentieth century. On August 22, 1905, a reporter for the *Miner and News* described "a big bunch of gasolines" gathered in the bay to watch a sailing race. Identifying seven by name, including Galt's *Whatyouwill*, Jim Ashdown's *Atheldune* and Stone's own *Nameless,* the reporter estimated that this fleet represented fewer than a third of the "chuk-chuk crafts" on the lake. The Stone factory built fifteen motor launches the following year. The standard size, about ten metres, carried sixteen passengers sitting in wicker chairs or on uphol-stered benches under a fringed canopy. In fair weather, with a light load, a launch might make almost twenty kilometres per hour. Stone built five "motor skiffs", a poor man's launch powered by a cranky new contraption, the outboard motor.

The art of boat and motor maintenance did not come easily to most men, so in addition to his carpentry, machinery and paint shops, Stone built dry docks and sheds for repairs and storage. He sold gas and oil, oars, sails, paddles, boat furnishings and cars. In the 1920s, he rented houseboats to hunters and fishermen and towed them, with guides, cooks, food and liquor, to the best bays. With its docks, campers' message boxes and grocery deliveries, Stone's operated a marina long before the word entered the Canadian vocabulary.

Above left: John Stone, still in his mid-twenties,
at work on one of his many creations.

The J.W. Stone Boat Company headquarters, about 1901.

Inset, by 1924, Stone's boats could no longer be termed "skiffs"; now they were launches, even yachts.

J.W. STONE / LAKE OF THE WOODS MUSEUM, KENORA / 988.21.8

J.W. STONELAKE OF THE WOODS MUSEUM, KENORA / 982.3.1

139

The Ojibwe, who had taken reserves at Shoal Lake, North West Angle, Whitefish Bay, the Aulneau Peninsula and all around the town, linked old ways with the new; birchbark gave way to canvas, blankets were replaced by jackets and shawls, but they camped, as always, on the beaches, carried their babies in cradle boards and brought moccasins, baskets, rice and blueberries to sell. "We can recall the yearly migrations of groups of Indians crossing the Keewatin Portage during the blueberry season," Ed Sweet writes in his "History of Keewatin". "Flotillas of up to 100 birchbark canoes were not uncommon. One had to admire the clock-like precision of such a large movement of people and canoes, the speed of its execution, the voluntary self-discipline and the almost total absence of fuss and bother." On July 1st, the Ojibwe celebrated Canada's birthday by dancing, drumming and smoking the peace pipe at Kenora's main intersection.

AFTER 1918, the Ojibwe no longer traded at the Hudson's Bay post; the HBC had closed its store and converted its warehouse from fur to liquor. Prohibition, a provincial law which forbade the retail sale of liquor, shut down Kenora's bars, but a Dominion law allowed a company like the HBC, based in Manitoba, to import

As Kenora grew, the Ojibwe combined their traditional ways with those of European society. Women still used *tikinagans* to carry their babies, and encampments of tipis, below, could still be found on a rocky point during the summer months.

Indian Encampment, Ontario, Canada.

wholesale liquor from Europe, then export it across provincial and international borders. Kenora, one of ten HBC "mail order" warehouses spotted across western Canada, did the lion's share of the business: in 1917, the Kenora branch earned a net profit of $161,412 on sales of $891,530.49. Profits would have been higher had "pilfering" not been a problem in transit.

Cases of scotch, rye, gin and rum were shipped from the warehouse; customers purchased bottles from bootleggers, or, for medicinal purposes, from druggists. Liquor flowed as freely as ever, only not in public, and Kenora's high consumption indicates that much of the liquor found its way to an equally thirsty United States. The Americans had no licence to import, but neither did they have customs agents to patrol miles of uninhabited shoreline, or to inspect border islands, with their sheltered coves, where heavy boats met in the dark of night. The Ontario Provincial Police had only one officer based in Kenora, and he had no boat. The complete absence of liquor violation reports in the OPP archives suggests that he turned a blind eye to the blind pigs.

As the repeal of Prohibition in the United States ended bootlegging, building the Trans-Canada highway, which reached Kenora from Winnipeg in 1932, boosted the town's economy. During the hard times of the 1930s, people in Kenora and Keewatin were able to fish, hunt, pick berries and live off the lake's bounty. They made pickles and canned vegetables from their gardens, and in winter an outdoor shed served as a freezer.

The humblest bungalows, perched on the cliffs, had spectacular views, and residents, unless they worked the boats, or prospected for gold, were content to remain within the harbours and the bays. In summer, the *Argyle* ferried swimmers and sunbathers to Sandy Beach on Coney Island, and in the evenings, an orchestra played in the beach's dance pavilion. The *Keenora* and smaller boats offered moonlight cruises among the islands, and day trips for picnickers; a beach with a reputation for skinny dipping was named Bare Point. Civic holidays, from the Queen's birthday on May 24th, when everyone took off their long underwear, to Labour Day in September, were celebrated with flags and fireworks, a parade down Main Street, led by the Legion band, baseball tournaments, games and races.

Racing on the calm water of Kenora's sheltered harbour, the oarsmen of the Kenora Rowing Club were inspired

Coney Island, Kenora, Ont.

by Jake Gaudaur, a sculler from Orillia, Ontario, who had defended his world championship here in 1901. Gaudaur, winner of the American Championship Cup from 1888 to 1891, had defeated an Australian, James Stansbury, in England to become world champion in 1896; the next year Gaudaur moved to Rat Portage as proprietor of the Russell House hotel.

Undefeated over the next five years, Gaudaur challenged any rower in the world to race him at Rat Portage.

Coney Island was the place to be during the long, lazy summer days, even in the rather restrictive clothing that persisted through the summer just prior to World War I.

The new English champion, Australian George Towns, took him up. The date for the race, three miles around Coney Island, was set for September 4, 1901. Rat Portage hotels were booked a month ahead; the CPR offered $2 day trip tickets from Winnipeg and steamboats brought fans from Minnesota. With Gaudaur a 2-1 favourite, money bet on the outcome far surpassed the winner's prize of $2,500.

CARL GUSTAF LINDE / MINNESOTA HISTORICAL SOCIETY / GV3.61B/r63

American rowing teams regularly came north to compete; rowers from the Minnesota Boat Club are seen here in 1910.

Towns looked like a lightweight, but when the race, postponed by rough water, got underway on September 7th, Towns sprinted into the lead, and rowing with slow, powerful strokes, left Gaudaur struggling in his wake; Gaudaur finished more than two boat-lengths behind. It was Gaudaur's last international race; Towns reigned as world champion until 1906.

In winter, the harbour became a skating rink. Horse races were held on the ice, and skiers groomed a trail to Sultana Island. Boys lived for hockey. Players on the Kenora Thistles, a club formed in 1894 to compete against amateur teams in Winnipeg, Brandon and Portage la Prairie, were so young the Thistles had to compete at the junior and intermediate levels. The teenage Thistles

won by such lop-sided scores they were allowed to join the senior Manitoba and Northwestern Hockey Association in 1903. They won the championship, then challenged the eastern division winners, the Ottawa Senators, for the Stanley Cup. They lost, and lost again in 1905, but fans loved this David and Goliath drama, and when the Thistles challenged the Montreal Wanderers for the 1907 Stanley Cup, their sold-out two-game series in Montreal made headlines across Canada.

The Thistles won the first game, 4-2. Excitement was running so high in Kenora on January 21st, the night of the second game, arrangements were made to "broadcast" the action. A Kenora high school student described the scene:

All the sports minded townfolk gathered at the Victoria rink to hear first hand the reports of the game. This was long before radio. A telegraph receiver was installed in the band room, and a running report was read by Mr. Joseph Johnson, one of the executive. The first 30 minutes of the game was all Kenora. Our team led 5-2. Our hopes were high, especially when we scored the first goal on resumption of play, making it 6-2. Then the roof fell in. Montreal scored the next four goals. It was 6-6 with two minutes to play. Mr. Johnson's face was getting longer and longer with each bulletin. It looked as though it was all over. The next telegram came in, and Joe came bounding out yelling and waving the wire over his head. Bedlam broke loose, but it was some time before we knew the score as in all the excitement Joe lost his voice and there were too many goals to show them on his fingers. Finally things quieted down and we were able to learn that with time running out Kenora had scored two quick goals to win 8-6 and become the only small town in Canada ever to win the Stanley Cup.

THE DROWNING OF LAVINIA RILEY PERRY

ONLY THE WEALTHY COULD AFFORD A MOTOR LAUNCH and a boatman to run and repair the engine. Boat fires were frequent, yet nobody bothered to wear the clumsy cork life-jackets. On the evening of August 19, 1920, the launch *Wabisa* was returning to Treaty Island with a party of sixteen women and children when the engine blew up. The launch caught fire, and the passengers leaped into the lake. Their screams and shouts were heard on shore and men set out in rowboats, but with *Wabisa* drifting in flames, the passengers struggled to swim to shore or stay afloat. Lavinia Riley Perry, within sight of her own camp, saw her husband Guthrie rowing to the rescue. Lavinia, a strong swimmer, spread out her long linen skirt to support her six-year-old daughter Harriet. As the rowboat came near, she cried to Harriet: "Race to your father!" Harriet made it, but Lavinia's skirt, weighted with water, dragged her under.

The *Arrow II*, a motor launch similar to the doomed *Wabisa*, with its owner, H.E. Hook in the captain's seat.

LAKE OF THE WOODS MUSEUM / KENORA / 974.41.20

DENNIS FAST

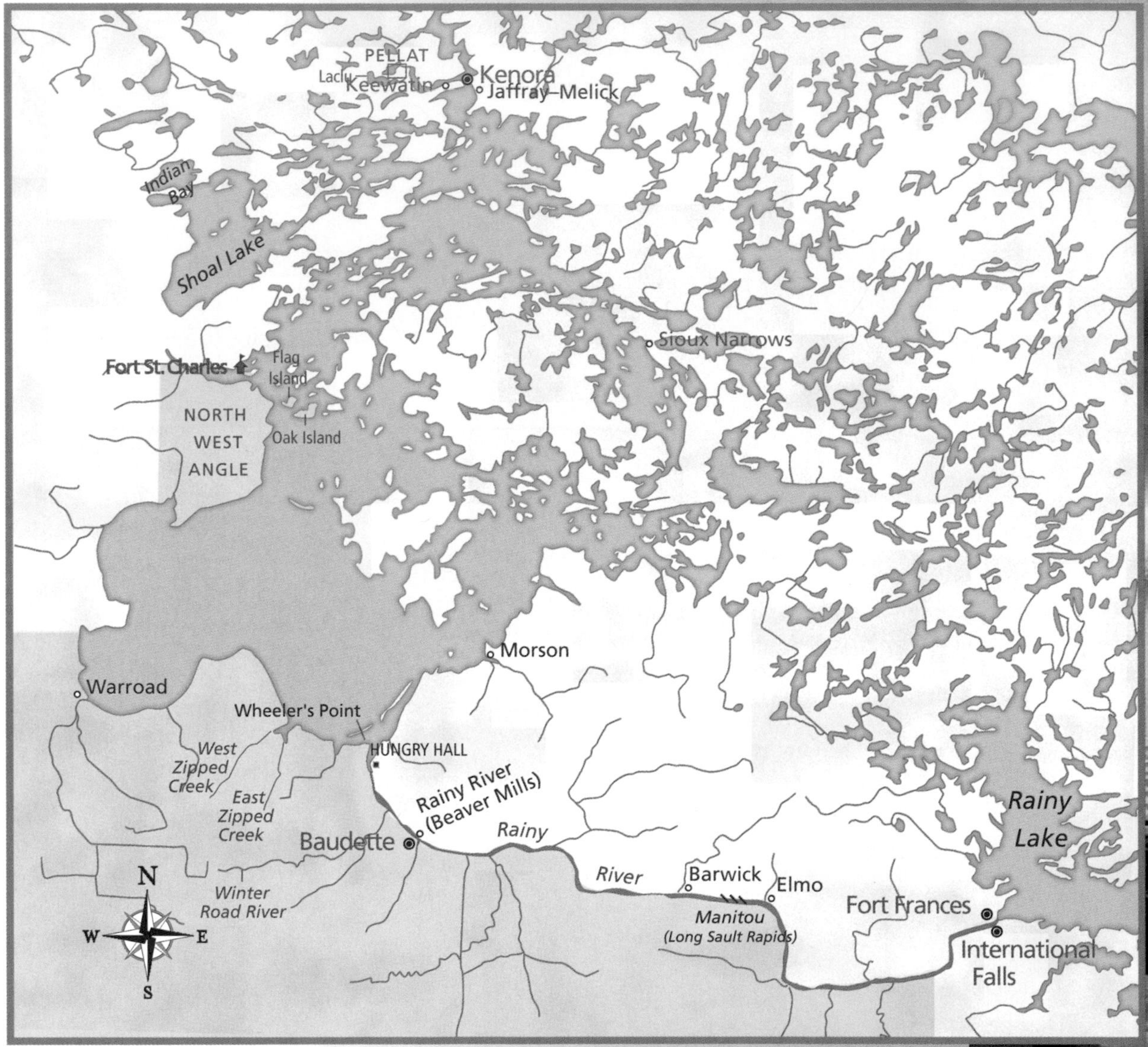

PELLAT
Kenora
Lac du
Keewatin
Jaffray–Melick

Indian
Bay

Shoal Lake

Sioux Narrows

Fort St. Charles
Flag
Island

NORTH
WEST
ANGLE

Oak Island

Morson

Warroad

Wheeler's Point

West
Zipped
Creek
HUNGRY HALL

East
Zipped
Creek

Rainy River
(Beaver Mills)

Rainy
Baudette

Rainy
Lake

River
Barwick
Elmo

Winter
Road River
Fort Frances

Manitou
(Long Sault Rapids)

International
Falls

N
W   E
S

Morning fog swirls past a dock on
the lake's southern shore.

144

SQUATTERS & SETTLERS

Monarch was lost amidst a log drive as the ship plowed into a jam of logs which crushed the hull. The *Swallow* was lost in a storm on Lake of the Woods near Bigsby Island. A passenger could board a boat easily enough, but there was never any guarantee that the craft would arrive at its destination.

SMALL BOATS WERE WRECKED BY DEADHEADS,

half-sunken logs floating just below the water's surface; harbours and channels became choked with stray logs from broken booms. As sawmills sprang up along the CNR, the Rainy River became a carpet of logs. In 1895, the Beaver Mills Lumber Company had located a small sawmill on the Canadian side of the international border upstream from

Hungry Hall; in 1901, when the shanty town of Beaver Mills was reborn as Rainy River, the Rat Portage Lumber Company of Kenora bought and enlarged Beaver Mills. An American company, Shevlin-Mathieu, built a rival mill in Rainy River, and, across the river, a twin mill in the Minnesota hamlet of Spooner.

Three little frontier towns, Spooner (named for district judge Marshall Spooner), Baudette and Rainy River grew up around the sawmills at both ends of the railway bridge across the Rainy River. Fires were frequent in milltowns built of wood, but the fire that in October 1910 burned Spooner and Baudette to the ground, laid waste the countryside and took at least forty-two lives, started in the bush. Elnora Bixby and Florence Ferrier describe the fire's beginning:

The *Swallow*, with Captain Lewis atop the upper deck, was photographed in 1896, before the lake claimed her.

AN AMERICAN FLAG FLIES PROUDLY NEAR BAUDETTE, OVER A LAKE THAT LOOKS DECEPTIVELY INNOCENT

The railways greatly improved access and thus railway stations were generally at the heart of a community. This one, in Rainy River, has been carefully maintained.

Thomas Cathcart had lost "squatters rights" to their land. Cathcart sued when Mackenzie and Mann, now Sir William and Sir Donald, claimed his Baudette property on behalf of the Canadian Northern Railway; before the case was resolved, in favour of the railway, Cathcart had died and Mackenzie and Mann were bankrupt. Their rail lines, taken over by the Canadian government in 1918, became part of the Canadian National Railway.

FEW OF THE HOMESTEADERS who survived the fire could afford to start over, and those who remained most often found that the rich farmland they had been promised was nothing more than sterile peat bog, gravel or clay. Canadians who settled on the Rainy River's fertile flood plain were luckier, but even they must have laughed cynically at government pamphlets boasting about "the comparative ease with which the virgin land can be cleared and tilled," the healthful and equable climate, constant sunshine, moist summers and dry winters, with "November about the best month of the year". The advertising didn't mention bugs, floods, blizzards and temperatures that reached –40°; besides, the land was free. Ontario offered a quarter section to each head of family, male or female, who "cleared and cultivated at least 15 acres, built a house 16' by 20' and lived on the property six months of the year."

There was no easy way to clear the land. Once the huge trees were cut and the slash burned, hay and grain were seeded among the stumps and cut by hand with a scythe; it took up to ten years for big stumps to rot to the point where they could be pulled out or blown up. Then the ground was ploughed and cleared of stones. For Canadian settlers who followed the logging or "tote" roads deep into the bush, life was much as it had been for their pioneer grandparents in the east; they kept chickens, cows and horses, and grew enough potatoes and turnips to fill a root cellar. Women made bread, butter and soap, boiled water for the laundry, sewed clothes, quilts and feather comforters and canned enough berries, vegetables and venison to last the winter. Since the men usually spent the winter in the logging camps, much of the labour fell to the children. Hugh Luttrell recalls going to school in Alysworth township in 1906:

> One got up in time to do the chores, milk two or three cows, fill the woodbox, carry the day's water from the river, have breakfast and walk over clay roads for three and one quarter miles, rain or sunshine, and if you were the first one there it was your duty to sweep out the school and, if a fire was needed, you made the fire. That's what it was like in the summer. In the winter there were the same chores and you waded through any snow that might have fallen over-night. It took half a day to warm the old log school. The desks were all handmade and mobile, so we would ring the stove with the desks until the place warmed.

FAMILIES WERE LARGE, and in remote areas neighbouring women assisted each other in childbirth. In the town of Emo, an enterprising widow, Mary O'Keefe, opened a maternity home for expectant mothers and served as anaesthetist for the doctors. In the years before the First World War, the Rainy River area was fortunate to have a highly educated and dedicated doctor, Frederick H. Bethune. Dr. Bethune visited his patients at all hours of the day and night, summer and winter, by railway handcar, canoe, sleigh, horse and buggy, on horseback and on foot; if a road was swampy, he'd take off his shoes and socks and wade through the water. Dr. Bethune attended to wounds and fractures and did emergency surgeries on the kitchen table; serious cases were sent to hospital in Winnipeg. When the telephone arrived in the area in 1907, the doctor could be reached more quickly, if only the gossips would get off the "party" line. Anyone could listen in, and after waiting an hour for two women to hang up, Bethune commented dryly, "I think they'll soon be done as they are starting to cook the beans." The area's first telephone operator, Ida Davis, was also on call as a nurse and midwife.

At the time, doctors could do little to treat pneumonia, tuberculosis or childhood diseases; one Emo family buried six of eleven children. Dave Loney, the owner of the furniture store, was the undertaker. "He had a team of black horses," his daughter-in-law Grace recalls. "The horses were covered with black net, from which black tassels dangled.

CONTINUED ON PAGE 156

Life was difficult and it was often only sheer determination, as can be seen on the faces of this unidentified mother and children, that stood between survival and disaster.

For some, dreams went beyond survival. The Muncer family shared their living quarters (at right) with the original Minaki Lodge (left-hand section of the building).

153

The Shoal Lake Aqueduct

AS EARLY AS 1883, the young prairie city of Winnipeg was thirsting for clean water: the rivers were contaminated with sewage and the area's few wells could not supply a population expected soon to reach a million. "A sufficient supply of wholesome, potable water is a fundamental sanitary necessity," Dr. N. Agnew wrote to the *Manitoba Free Press* on March 8th. "I unhesitatingly say that we must look to the Lake of the Woods." The lake's granite catch-basin guaranteed pure, soft, sparkling water free of sediment, he said, and while the lake's nearest point, Indian Bay on Shoal Lake, was a hundred kilometres from Winnipeg, a 220-metre drop in elevation meant that lake water could flow through a system of canals and pipes by force of gravity with no need for pumping.

Dr. Agnew's proposal was ignored – another doctor objected to the "deposits of green vegetable matter" in the lake's bays during the summer. Then, on October 11, 1904 fire raged through Winnipeg's commercial core. Firefighters' hoses were ineffectual because the city's depleted wells and reservoirs could not provide sufficient pressure. River water was pumped into the watermains; pressure was restored and the fire extinguished, but the next year the city experienced the worst typhoid epidemic in its history. The dual crisis prompted the city to set up a Water Supply Commission to investigate alternative sources, including Shoal Lake, Lake Manitoba and the Winnipeg River. Among the committee members were two Lake of the Woods campers, civil engineer Thomas R. Deacon, owner of the Manitoba Bridge and Iron Works, and the committee's chairman, hardware wholesaler James H. Ashdown, whose seven-storey warehouse had been destroyed in the fire. But

Shoal Lake was not the choice of the consulting engineers: they recommended a pipe from the Winnipeg River as the "best and cheapest" solution.

City council hesitated. It was already investing in hydro-electric dams on the Winnipeg River; should it depend on the same source for water? Penny-pinchers argued in favour of drilling more wells, but the well water tasted vile and left scaly deposits. In 1912, when a new engineer's report recommended Shoal Lake, T.R. Deacon ran successfully for mayor on a single issue: "an ample and permanent supply of pure, soft water that will forever remove the menace now hanging over Winnipeg of a water famine and the consequent danger of conflagration and sickness."

As soon as the ice was out of Shoal Lake the next spring, Deacon took city councillors and a team of engineers on a personally-guided steamboat tour. Deacon knew the lake well: from 1892 to 1901 he had prospected for gold. The Ojibwe had dubbed Deacon "Chief No-Gold", but he found a bonanza for Winnipeg in the lake's clean water.

The engineers reported that even in the driest years Shoal Lake, with Lake of the Woods acting as a reservoir, could supply "a practical inexhaustible supply of water of excellent quality, soft, practically free from contamination, without noticeable colour, free from odours and of an agreeable taste." The water would be delivered by gravity flow via a horseshoe-shaped, arch-and-invert aqueduct: cost of construction $13 million.

The province of Ontario and the International Joint Commission gave the Greater Winnipeg Water District permission to take up to 100 million gallons of water a day from Shoal

Lake. No one thought to ask Shoal Lake's only permanent residents, the Ojibwe. Nevertheless, two concrete dikes were built on Indian Bay to deepen the water at the intake, and a swampy stream was diverted into their wild rice beds. A railroad was built along the aqueduct's route to haul in trainloads of sand, gravel, lumber and the workmen needed to dig the trench and mix the cement. Canada was at war by the time construction began in 1915, but the work continued uninterrupted until the tap was turned on in Winnipeg on March 20, 1919.

A MARVEL OF ENGINEERING IN ITS DAY, the Shoal Lake aqueduct lived up to expectations, although since the water has been chlorinated the taste can't be said to be "agreeable." The countryside around the aqueduct was logged and homesteaded, and hamlets with names like McMunn and Hadashville sprang up along the rail line; the intake site was named Waugh in honour of R.D. Waugh, Deacon's successor as mayor of Winnipeg. However, the Shoal Lake First Nation, Skate-saaga'igan, had to bear the brunt of responsibility for the water's purity. In 1912, Dr. C.S. Slichter cautioned: "The country roundabout must remain in its present wild state indefinitely." Slichter saw "no fear of the growth of cities or towns," but the 530 people who live now on Skate-saaga'igan land cannot develop cottage sites, campgrounds, golf courses, motels, marinas or anything else that threatens to pollute Winnipeg's water.

Once First Nations were encouraged to become economically self-sustaining, Skate-saaga'igan felt doomed to a future of backwoods poverty. However, Ontario's permission to build the aqueduct had required from the GWWD compensation for "all private parties whose lands and properties may be taken, injuriously affected or in any way interfered with." The First Nation, Ontario, Manitoba and the Canadian government have drafted a Shoal Lake Watershed Management Plan that awaits approval from all jurisdictions.

The resident engineers of the Greater Winnipeg Water District, pictured here on August 26, 1915, at Mile 33, must have taken a good deal of pride in their feat.

Summer amusements came in many forms, among them a horsedrawn bandwagon, a county fair ...

DENNIS FAST

CARL GUSTAF LINDE / MINNESOTA HISTORICAL SOCIETY / D1.3/r14

MANY FUNERALS WERE HELD IN HOMES, and this often necessitated a long drive to the cemetery. No matter how cold or wet, the committal service was always held at the graveside. Even on bitter cold winter days, it was not allowed to trot the horses."

Homesteaders trudged long distances to church services, and the women organized dinners, picnics and concerts. The Women's Institute held classes in cooking and canning, child care, home decorating, sanitation and nutrition, and getting together was a boost for women cooped up in the bush. For men, there were lodge meetings and sports clubs. Musical families sang hymns and popular songs, accompanied by bagpipes, organ, piano, fiddle, washtub or whatever else came to hand. A wedding party lasted for days. In Emo, Ed Tompkins converted the second floor of his hardware store into a dance hall and theatre: Recalls Nellie Booren:

Many square danced to the tunes of 'Turkey in the Straw' and 'The Irish Washerwoman', on the polished hardwood floor. During the dance craze of the twenties the young crowd did the Charleston and danced the flea-hop to 'Yes, sir, that's my baby.'

... and of course swimming, from Minnesota's sweeping sand beaches to Coney Island, adjacent to Kenora, above.

When silent movies came along Ed put in a projector and folding, red plush seats. The town and country people viewed Tom Mix, Will Rogers, Rin Tin Tin, Charlie Chaplin and Rudolph Valentino on Thursday and Saturday nights. It was a treat when Ed brought in vaudeville shows such as the Winnipeg Kiddies, the Bell Ringers, magicians, minstrel shows and cartoon artists. There were local talent shows held there and the town's young people practiced all winter to stage a play in the spring. The school Christmas concert was held there, and Ed in his coonskin coat, draped with harness bells and wearing the traditional mask and beard, acted as Santa Claus many times.

CEMETERIES DO NOT BEAR WITNESS to those who came, and, for many reasons, left. Yet one lonely man, James Allan McQuat, known as "Jimmy Hightop," built his own monument in the wilderness. In 1887, McQuat, a bachelor homesteading at Emo River, expressed his frustration in a letter to a Mr. Locking:

I want you to get me a woman. Rather a wife if you Can get me one. Now I want you to get me a good one. I am not Without falt, but deserve a good girl for a wife. I have kept myself purty decent lived decent all my life. I have good family Connections. I do not want to disgrace them. I want my wife to have good Connections too. I do not want to deceive any girl. Myself at 31 a little bald from sickness that I had at about 16. I yous no ligaur nor tobaco no do I make yous of profane language. I have not much larning but I have morality and Caracter to make up. I would like a girl under 27 years, brought up on a farm and she would be the better of a little means to take Care of herself as I have no money Except any stock I

Until the end of the Second World War, horses played an indispensable role in moving people and goods. In summer and winter, for business and pleasure, horsepower meant just that for the Kendall family, below, and many others.

have 5 head not bad for this place. My desire is to have a home. What is a home without a wife I don't wish to work myself to deth nor my wife either. her hair may be any colour Except firey red. Not too thunderen big you no what kind of girl alright. I will meet her in Rat Portage any time. She Can Come as soon as she likes let me no what you Can do.

LOCKING RECOMMENDED JANE GIBSON, a Scots-born servant. Ten years later, McQuat, still unmarried, sold his Emo property and built an immense log house, with glass windows and a sixty-five-metre tower, at White Otter Lake sixty-five kilometres to the east. According to legend, "Jimmy Hightop" was building a castle for his Scottish bride-to-be. McQuat, still single, drowned in the lake in 1918.

By 1911, a colony of Finns was becoming established north of Manitou Rapids. Rachel Blom Gallinger describes how her father, Victor Blom, William Lampi and Malakias Matson arrived from Fort Frances: "The three men built a raft below the falls and set sail. They each carried building tools, a saw blade rolled up, a hammer and an axe, a shirt or two, some food, mostly flour, tea, salt and oatmeal, and a gun. With $1.25 left over from buying their supplies, they purchased a gallon jug of whiskey to cheer them up during the long journey downriver. While Victor steered the raft, the others sang. Spirits were pretty high when they reached the Manitou Rapids. As they passed, natives waved and shouted to them. They waved back,

NATIONAL ARCHIVES OF CANADA / PA–113301

thinking them very friendly people. They soon found out why all the shouting as they rounded the bend and found themselves in the rapids. They sobered up in a hurry and made it safely to Barwick. Heaving their packsacks on their backs, they started down the tote road to their homesteads."

Life in Finland, as the community was called, was a struggle. Rachel recalls the winter when the Bloms could not pay their taxes – $8 – and nearly lost their farm; in the winter of 1923, when Victor was too sick to work, the family finances were down to three pennies. Her mother Hanna raised hens and sold eggs, or traded eggs at the store for coffee, salt and sugar. Rachel remembers: "We had one school dress, wool in the winter and cotton in summer. We changed into our home dress as soon as we got home. In summer we ran barefoot but had to wear shoes to school." The family's living was mostly earned from the woods. "My father had a .22 rifle that supplied many a rabbit for the pot. Bear meat was good to eat. Meat was shared so it would not spoil. The lakes had plenty of fish. Some of the settlers were good at making nets, having been fishermen in Finland. A lot of salt was used to preserve meat and fish. In September or early October the young

Left: Life was, if not simpler, certainly less accessoried. Even today, many rural families still live in two- or three-room homes, or trailers.

LAKE OF THE WOODS MUSEUM, KENORA / 972.43.5

Hunting, whether for waterfowl or big game, was more often a matter of putting food on the table than simply sport.

159

AS THE YEARS PASSED, PRIORITIES CHANGED; RESORTS LIKE WARROAD'S STONE HARBOUR
WERE BUILT FOR THOSE WHO CAME TO PLAY, RATHER THAN WORK.

men went trapping. They had their own traplines about a day's walking from one another. They all came home for Christmas."

Christmas Eve was celebrated with a play, a concert and a dance in the Finland Hall. Since the community had no church, the hall was used for weddings, funerals and visits by missionaries; in the hall, children were taught to read and write the Finnish language, men held gym classes and politicians gave speeches during election campaigns. Many in the audience didn't understand a word of English, but the women enjoyed visiting and the men could get a bottle of beer outside.

Smoking was forbidden at dances – chewing tobacco was fine and no one was allowed in drunk. Homebrew was as plentiful and potent, as it was everywhere else on Lake of the Woods, but it caused so much violence that outsiders quipped that no Finn ever died a natural death. In 1921, a Finnish bootlegger was sentenced to ten years for killing a man who criticized his mash; in 1928 Laurie Niel beat his father to death in a drunken rage. Niel was the first man in the Rainy River district to be hanged.

"Can You Beat it"
Muskallonge 4½ ft. long
Weight 43 lbs.
Caught in Baudette Bay
By J.W. Collins

Far right: A fabulous catch. While residents fished for a livelihood, visitors fished for pleasure.

Right: A family of four, dressed for posterity.

161

Though far from the big cities of the East, the young women of Lake of the Woods were quick to jump on the female emancipation bandwagon that followed World War I. By the late '20s, girls were playing not only softball (and in short pants), below, but hockey too.

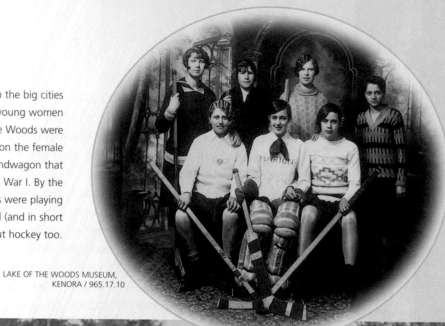

LAKE OF THE WOODS MUSEUM,
KENORA / 965.17.10

THE SWEDES WHO HOMESTEADED at LacLu, a cluster of sheltered lakes in Pellatt township northwest of Keewatin, had the advantage of being close to Keewatin's Swedish community. Their children and grandchildren found jobs in town, and sometimes a town girl like Elsie Christianson would fall for a LacLu boy:

Having grown up in Keewatin, a bustling town in the 1920s and '30s, I thought we had it all. After all, my mom and dad had fur coats and were the first in Keewatin to own a washing machine. I played baseball, broomball, football and hockey. And, of course, all of them in a dress. On Saturday nights our ladies hockey team, the Keewatin Millionaires, would play at the big outdoor rink in Beatty Park. After the game we used to go on a tally-ho to the Sundins in Pellatt. We would get a 5 cent doughnut and 5 cent cup of coffee for the ride.

Because I helped at home, my dad would treat me to a special gift once in awhile. My favourite gift was my very first pair of pants, jintz [chintz] pants. They were made of a flowered material with very, very, very wide legs. One day, with a basket of blueberries in each hand, I was walking down the big town hall hill to sell my berries to the campers on Beach Road. I had my favourite jintz pants on and was keeping an eagle eye open to see if the mail truck would go by – Arthur Hager drove the mail truck and would give this good-looking Swede a ride home. His name was Algot Schroder and he had caught my eye. So, nonchalantly trying to catch his attention, I tripped on my favourite jintz pants and rolled down the town hall hill covered in blueberries! Oh yeah, I got Algot's attention all right!

LAKE OF THE WOODS MUSEUM, KENORA / 990.31.10

For the first settlers, paths winding into the woods meant backbreaking work, fields to clear and stumps to pull. Those that followed found the romance.

Though many of the original summer "camps", such as this one owned by the Ashdowns, can still be seen, and hundreds of simple cabins are still to be found, many cottages have been replaced by million-dollar mansions. And many other summer homes are becoming full-time residences.

168

THE SUMMER PEOPLE

THE SANDY BEACH AT McCARTHY'S ISLAND PROVED IRRESISTIBLE;
BY 1893 IT HAD BECOME A PUBLIC PARK, WITH A NEW NAME – CONEY ISLAND.

opposite Rat Portage. The McCarthys built the area's first island camp – a frame cabin near the beach where they provided sunbathers with overnight room and board. By 1893, when McCarthy sold his interest for private lots – the name was changed to Coney Island – Sandy Beach had become so popular it was taken over by Rat Portage as a park.

The town may have acted more from prudery than public interest. "As the number of our summer visitors has increased, the greater has become the demand for better regulations respecting the dresses and conduct of bathers," huffed the local newspaper. "There is more reason to give them legal protection and to surround them with restrictions as if Sandy Beach were one side of our Main Street. Improper exposure of person should no more be permitted there than in the heart of town." If town by-laws were enforced, the editorial said, "ladies who passed to and from their baths would not be subject to the indecencies of bathers openly undressing and dressing on the beach or bathing in an almost nude condition." A change house was the first building erected at the beach.

Women bathers were not expected to swim: an old-fashioned bathing costume, as voluminous and cumbersome as an ankle-length street dress, would have drowned them. Men's woollen swimsuits drooped to their knees and covered their chests. Even this modesty did not satisfy the indignant writer of a July 20, 1912 editorial:

Yesterday while the ferry was calling at Coney Island beach to allow some passengers to get off, some smart alick deliberately walked from the beach out to the wharf in his bathing suit, passing some ten or twelve ladies and some children in his stroll.

Now we would like to say to this young man and others if this paper has to go to the trouble to obtain your name and address we will consider it our duty to mark you through our columns as one who is not fit for human society. Your figure does not figure very large in the making up of the world's really big personalities. We would state further that if the lessee of the beach does not attempt to keep men from exposing themselves in this manner, then the town should put an official on the beach to see it is done.

THIS KENORA SCOLD must have been sweating it out in his starched collar in an airless office: muscular men had been competing for years in water sports – diving, rowing, canoe jousting, log rolling – and these contests drew ferry loads of smartly dressed spectators who could, if they wished, rent a bathing costume, towel, rubber cap and water wings. Children loved the shallow water, see-saws, swings and "toboggan" water slide; ice-cream, tea, coffee, cold drinks and other refreshments could be purchased at the bath house.

Boating competitions of all kinds have been popular on the lake since the early years of the twentieth century. In 1910, members of the Minnesota Boat Club participated in several classes of races, including rowing, sailing and skulling.

CARL GUSTAF LINDE / MINNESOTA HISTORICAL SOCIETY / GV3.61B/r62

It was in the evening, however, that the Coney Island dance pavilion began to swing, and the live music, provided by local orchestras, was fresh, fast and sexy. Dancing started

We have not been overkind to our visitors. We should permit the stranger within our gates to realize that we do not always regard him as an intruder and a nuisance. Young people who have been tied up in an office for an entire year are easily liable to become a little exuberant in their display of gratitude for an opportunity to enjoy the pleasures of our beautiful lake. This may find expression in a style of dress somewhat too flamboyant for our ideals, or a costume of reckless bohemianism, but for goodness sake let us wink the other eye and pass on."

ANXIOUS TO ATTRACT a more respectable clientele, tourism promoters advertised the lake as a spa for "the overworked businessman of the city who can spare but a few weeks, or perhaps only a few days, to build up annually the weakened health caused by the strain of city business life."

Since vacations were almost unheard of, illness was a respectable reason to take a holiday and great emphasis was placed on bathing and fresh air. "Clean living" became part of a muscular Christian ethic expressed by one of the lake's earliest summer campers, Reverend Charles Gordon. Under the pen name "Ralph Connor", Gordon wrote popular novels extolling "all that is virile, straight, honourable and, withal, tender and gentle in true men and women."

At Lake of the Woods, Gordon found a landscape similar to his beloved childhood home in the dense forest of Glengarry county in eastern Ontario; a vanished pioneer past, with its virtues of hard work and self-reliance, could be recreated at Lake of the Woods as Henry David Thoreau had done at Walden Pond. Canadian poets romanticized

That formality was a way of life among a certain class of people, is evident in these early twentieth-century photographs of picnicking (above) and lounging in front of the cottage.

at 8:30 p.m. and ended at midnight when the Argyle made its last trip back to the mainland; on a hot summer night, with a soft breeze off the lake, dancers cooled their tired feet in the water and walked hand-in-hand along the beach, the pavilion a pulsing golden orb against the trees. Sleepy and sunburned, maybe a little drunk, they might cuddle up or slip out of their clothes for a skinny dip.

The City People, sometimes called the Manitoba People, were not greatly loved by the Locals, even the children. "The camper girls walked through the streets, their overalls cut short above the knee," one girl complained. "How bold, we thought. The best we could do was to go around without shoes or stockings." In 1899 the *Miner* admonished:

by his son, King Gordon

RALPH CONNOR'S BIRKENCRAIG

THE LAKE STRETCHES FOR 12 MILES. The nearest island is called Lone Tree Island. Ten or fifteen years ago the solitary dead tree fell down but the name persists. Beyond it is the Island with the Leaning Pine Tree. Then beyond farther is Bare Point and past the point the channel taken by the boats going to Blindfold Lake or Yellow Girl Bay.

This is the view from the Birkencraig Lookout. My father did most of his writing there in the last few years. In the morning the lake would sparkle in the sunshine. Across the lake in the boat channel the motorboats would crawl along – stubby gray fishing boats with a slow pop-pop-pop, Chris-Craft with an airplane roar racing to meet the Winnipeg train, livery boats from the Devil's Gap Camp, with a long string of canoes and rowboats cruising up the lake for a day's fishing. Sometimes a canoe would come silently close to shore immediately below the Lookout, in and out of the bays of Birkencraig. Then he would stop writing and watch the flash of the paddle and study critically the stroke of the man in the stern. At night, when the full moon rose over the Indian Reservation and climbed up into the southeastern sky, the lake would be turned into molten silver. On these nights the birches near the Lookout would appear ghostly and they whispered among themselves. There he would sit writing in the circle of yellow light from the oil lamp and over his shoulder and beyond him you could see the silver lake stretching for miles, silver to the horizon.

He slept up there. When he first came down from the city in July he would tell us how he lay awake listening to the lapping of the waters on the rocks below him, how the crows wakened him in the morning holding council in the spruce trees, how, when he got up and looked out in the early morning, he saw a mother duck and her six little ducks in the water just beside the Pump House.

For more than thirty years we have been coming down to Lake of the Woods. First he came alone and pitched a tent on an island close to the mainland. He was working on a book. The publishers were calling for manuscript and it was impossible to get on with it in the midst of all the calls upon him in Winnipeg. He would cook his breakfast over an open fire, work all morning and paddle across to the boarding house at Norman for lunch. The next summer he took me down with him and I slept for the first time on a balsam bough bed and heard the sound of the wind in the pine trees at night. He gave me my first lessons in swimming and woodcraft and in handling a canoe.

The next year we acquired Birkencraig – my highland grandfather gave it its name – and built the cottage and the Lookout. We all grew up to feel more at home in the woods and in and on the water than in cities. Our friends would come down to visit us and there would be sixteen to eighteen around the dinner table on the veranda. When the numbers got down to eight or nine we had a 'small camp'. In those carefree days before the war, it was tennis and swimming and sailing, even woodchopping and splitting was made a game of skill, and in the evening singing around a fire. Sometimes it would be a big bonfire on the point, to which our friends would come from other islands. More often, especially as the autumn chill was felt, we would gather around a fire of pine knots in the living room. Then, beginning with plantation songs, he would gradually lead us into the rousing French-Canadian river songs – "Alouette" and "En Roulent". But when he sang Drummond's pathetic habitant ballad – "The Wreck of the Julie Plant" – we would sit hushed, looking at his face in the firelight.

Rat Portage, May 4th, 1893
R.J. Whitla Esq.

Dear Sir,
We the undersigned builders hereby
agree to build your summer residence
on Coney Island as per plans,
specifications and memos for the
sum of $670.00 and finish same in
a thorough workmanlike manner.
Yours respectfully,
Scott & Horswell

All exterior walls to have two coats
of paint. Wainscot to be oiled and
varnished, every other piece to be
stained, others natural colour.
$10.00 extra allowed for extra paint
– building to be strongly braced.
House building to be completed
by the 15th day of June.

Like Charles Gordon, Walter J. Phillips was endlessly inspired by the lake – a pine twisting in the wind, moonlight on the rocks, the sparkle of the sun on the water.

the wilderness. Pauline Johnson, emphasizing her Mohawk ancestry, wore a deerskin dress and bear-claw necklace when she recited poems titled "The Portage", "The Camper" and "Under Canvas":

> Lichens of green and grey on every side;
> And green and grey the rocks beneath our feet;
> Above our heads the canvas stretching wide;
> And over all, enchantment rare and sweet.

Enchanted islands were in vogue. Irish poet W.B. Yeats published *The Lake Isle of Innisfree* in 1893, the year Irish-born dry goods merchant R.J. Whitla of Winnipeg built one of the first island camps at Lake of the Woods for $670.

For this modest price, the contractors built "Erin Castle", a fortress-like frame replica of an Irish aristocrat's

country estate. D.K. Elliott, Whitla's business partner, built more modestly next door. For neighbours they had Captain George Young, a veteran, like Whitla, of the Northwest Rebellion, and pioneer hardware merchant James Ashdown; another colony of Winnipeg financiers built summer homes on the mainland at Keewatin Beach. These men played as hard as they worked, and they were as competitive in sports as in business.

Lake of the Woods weekends were an escape from the constraints of a hot, dusty puritanical city; sailing on a Sunday morning was a lot more fun than listening to a sermon, and children didn't have to go to Sunday school. Some wealthy families brought the comforts of home with them, including the nanny, a housemaid or two and the cook, though the Galts' Scottish-born cook flatly refused, saying she'd had enough of the damp.

The Gordons, who bought an 11.6-hectare island in 1906, brought a railway boxcar full of household goods, including a rented piano, every spring, but Gordon, like many other campers, encouraged his son and five daughters to swim, paddle, row and play in the woods. Other wives and children found camping backbreaking work. Anna O'Grady, one of banker J.L. deCourcy O'Grady's ten children, was fourteen when her father bought an island in 1910. "We had a twenty-one-room home in Winnipeg," Anna writes in her memoir.

We practically stripped that house of excess furniture to furnish the island home. This was shipped to Keewatin, loaded on an open scow and dumped on the rocks at the water's edge quite a distance from the house. We youngsters – I was the oldest of the four young ones [the older boys were employed in the city] – put our shoulders to the task of getting the furniture up the hill and away from the water in case of a storm. Refrigerators, double bedsteads, sofas and large chairs presented quite a problem. No underbrushing had ever been attempted; there was not a sign of a path anywhere.

CHILDREN BECAME ACCUSTOMED to hauling pails of water from the lake – the pump rarely worked – and toilet facilities were two "two-holer" outhouses in the bush. Laundry was a particularly burdensome task, Anna recalls:

After a weekend when there were 20-25 beds occupied, my aunt and I stripped the beds on Sunday evening after the weekend guests had returned to the city on the Campers' Special. We trudged down to the boathouse armed with several large galvanized tubs, a generous supply of Fels Naptha soap and a pail with which to dip the water into the tubs. There we did a commercial-sized wash, soaking all night and returning in the morning to rinse and carry it up to the lines at the back of the house. The men and boys had camp cots in the rooms over the boathouse, while the girls and women had a row of cots on the sick veranda, where in the night we often heard the heavy tread and breathing of large animals.

Saturday and Sunday were gala days – sailing races at the yacht club and everyone went if possible. Those of us who remained at home kept watch from the front veranda and in stormy weather watched for upsets, in which case someone would hasten to start out in the launch to rescue. Saturday evening there was a dance at the yacht club, and sometimes we could hear the music as we sat on the veranda.

Anna, her mother and aunt cooked all the meals on a small woodstove: "Some meals there had to be two sittings, but when the meal was over, and the boys and men lined up in a chain, passing the dishes to the kitchen, all was completed in record time. How happy they all were! Work? Yes, very definitely, lots of it, but did anyone consider it to be punishment? No, No, No, and such glorious happiness!"

Spartan living was a matter of pride for many campers. "Summer shacks", as the local newspaper called them, were uninsulated single-storey frame boxes surrounded on two or three sides by wide, screened verandas. Some verandas had rolled-up canvas blinds to lower in case of rain; at the T.R. Deacon camp, sloped floors allowed the water to run off. The interior room was heated by a fireplace in cold weather; on hot days it offered a shady retreat from the sun. Bedrooms were such stuffy little cubbies nobody spent much time there; a camp bed was by definition uncomfortable, a mattress lumpy. Furniture was homemade – plank tables, chairs of bent branches – worn out, or cast-offs from the city. Threadbare old clothes were worn until they turned into paint rags.

Dressed in the formal wear that the era demanded, Ethel Aldous (on the bow) and friends take a spin on Frank Matthews *Chiquita* in July 1909.

CAMPERS PAINTED, HAMMERED, TARRED, varnished; they felled trees, chopped firewood and cleaned soot and ashes out of the stove. As soon as children could walk, they were expected to pick berries, fill the woodbox and fetch water. Campers spent their summers brooding about where the mice were getting in, how to get the otters' nest out of the boat and what in the bloody hell was wrong with the motor. Then by the end of August came the exhausting, anxious ritual of closing up for the winter.

In the early years, campers rowed heavy flat-bottomed scows or paddled canoes. Cautious about pitting their strength against the lake's strong winds and powerful current, they stayed close to the mainland. By 1904, however, Winnipeggers were buying automobiles; a gasoline engine worked as well in a boat, and a chauffeur would certainly know how to drive a motor launch. Anna O'Grady recalls: "Wealthy people were building what were considered mansions on islands farther out on the Lake. Water and electricity were being installed, but we had none of that – our respect for the purity of the lake would never have allowed it."

One of the biggest and most beautiful of these new summer homes belonged to Arthur and Edith Rogers, owners of Winnipeg's Crescent Creamery ("You can whip our cream, but you can't beat our milk!") Its three wings and octagonal sunroom covered 5,000 square feet or about 1,500 square metres; the octagon alone was a fifth of that

with a ceiling more than six metres high. Uninsulated, with huge windows, exposed ceilings and simple wood or wicker furniture, the style of the Rogers camp suited its site.

LAKE OF THE WOODS MUSEUM, KENORA / 966.22.77

"The cottage was well organized for them," Gail Konantz writes in her biography of Edith.

There was always a boatman to care for the outdoor equipment as well as chauffeur people around the lake. A staff of three were in the house making and changing beds and cooking the meals. Edith would give them instructions in the morning, order the groceries from town and oversee any repairs around the house, creating an organization on the scale of a small hotel. When the guests arrived, and there were always guests, there were activities planned. Croquet on the lawn, bridge for rainy days, and long, leisurely trips down the lake for picnics and fishing when the weather was sunny.

Right: The Persse-Gooderham-Redmond-Heenan camp on Coney Island, circa 1915, with its pagoda roof and huge bay window.

Below: The breathtaking plan of the Rogers camp, with its enormous octagonal sunroom. The building was uninsulated, but the master bedroom and kitchen had wood-burning stoves, making them habitable into the cooler months.

DOCUMENTATION OF LAKE OF THE WOODS CAMPS / UNIVERSITY OF MANITOBA

178

THE OCTAGON, a popular style known as Queen Anne Revival, became a distinguishing characteristic of Lake of the Woods camps; Oriental pagoda roofs were the fashion for boathouses and other outbuildings. Some campers built a tower or lookout with a spectacular view of the lake. Ralph Connor built a small, two-storey octagon a few yards from his main camp. The screened-in top floor served as the master bedroom at night, and his study during the day. "He wrote with a heavy pencil in children's Jumbo exercise books," his daughter Lois recalls. "He sat on the edge of the bed, and wrote on one of the wooden shutters that folded down." The ground floor was an office where his secretary typed up his manuscripts.

Ironically, most men who could afford to build these retreats worked all week in the city; from Monday to Friday, camps were harems of women and children. Families were large, and children usually brought a friend or two; children couldn't get lost on an island, or attacked by wild animals (though bears can swim) and once chores were done even the strictest mothers allowed their children to make their own fun. Girls wore dresses or blouses and skirts but they could be tomboys, and children joyfully gave up their beds to guests for a chance to sleep in a tent.

"Mother loved her tent with the balsam boughs on the floor, later to be replaced by a wood floor," Alice Galt Weiss recalls in a memoir, *A Little Girl Remembers*.

The second tent was mine with a double cot in which Connie Milroy and I and the cat spent the summer. How could I be so lucky! We cut evergreen boughs for smudging the tent if there were mosquitoes. Connie and I would go to bed with our books and our chocolate bars and then a voice came from the house, 'Put out your light.' Then we'd creep out to a well-planted ladder, on to the roof and look through the skylight. Of course the lamp was shining down on the table.

They played poker in those days. It was sort of fun to watch. We thought they looked very devilish and they never caught on they were being watched.

Mother was nervous of storms and always insisted that we come into the house during a thunderstorm. We protested loudly as we really preferred the tent and would have liked to have stayed in bed and watched. There was no window but a tent doesn't need a window. When there's lightning you could see right through the canvas.

Oh, who would sleep in the house,
'Tis a perfect fool to the tent.
There we never feel the sun,
Though on waking us he's bent.
We have hedgehogs in our bed,
And the geese caw overhead,
But the breakfast bell's
The only thing
Can rouse us worth a cent.

A THIRD TENT WAS OFF IN THE WOODS for men visiting and there was a second backhouse (or biffy) nearby. Children were allowed to stay up late, especially if there was a bonfire, with cocoa and marshmallows to roast on a stick. One young visitor wrote an ode in the Galt's guest book:

O roast potatoes spread with salt
And thick with cinders too
And butter blended with a stick
How beautiful are you.

Many childhood friendships blossomed into romance at the lake; Old Lake families often grew into interlocking clans. Courting couples went fishing or canoeing to Ash Rapids or Whitefish Bay; Alice Weiss went on a week-long canoe trip when she was about nineteen with an engaged couple acting as chaperones.

We were six girls and four boys. One of the boys was captain of each of the three canoes. Daddy took us by launch to Whitefish Bay and then we paddled in a circle of lakes. Food for the whole week had to be carried along with the tents and canoes over many portages. We had a whole side of bacon, a sack of flour, a sack of potatoes and 12 dozen eggs in a wooden crate. We used the flour to mix our own pancakes.

We had never been on a long canoe trip before and hardly knew what clothing to take. We wore heavy pleated wool skirts which weighed a ton when we got wet walking through the wet bush in the rain. I don't think any of us had as much as a bandaid. There was a large tent for the

girls. We had our position on the floor each night and kept it so that if you got over a log or a stone or an ant hill it was just bad luck. We didn't have an air pillow or a mattress, just two blankets, one to lie on and one to put over. The boys slept under the canoes.

The trip was longer than we planned and we ran a little short of food. We had intended to catch our supper every night but when we landed the fishing wasn't very good so we resorted to bacon and eggs. We took one day off to fish but it rained.

THE TRIP WAS A SUCCESS: three couples married. An invitation to The Lake was the acid test of any city romance; few survived. Even a "lake girl" like Alice found it hard to manage when she and her husband Karl Weiss built their own camp on Galt Island. "We went down to the lake in July 1923 when Karl Jr. was three months old," she says.

There was no boathouse, and no launch, just a dock and a boardwalk over the sand leading to many steep steps up the hill. Karl settled us in over the long weekend then returned to Winnipeg, leaving me with the four young children, a cook and a nursemaid, Ellen Reedman, 'Nin' as we called her.

My Day: Nin stuck her head in the door to my bedroom saying, 'The water pressure's low.' I shook in my shoes because that meant I had to go down to the pump house to tackle the nasty engine that ran the pump. It took a lot of pressure to get the water up to the tank and always at some time during this procedure the pump got a little annoyed and tried to kick me out of the pump house. However, I did get the tank full of water.

'I'm out of wood,' said the cook. Karl had said we wouldn't have to worry about wood for the stove. 'There's enough lying around, all you'll need till I come down Friday.' Well, all the wood I needed took me to lunchtime Tuesday! He didn't realize that leftover shingles burn up like paper and with a baby needing a bottle in the middle of the night, the woodstove had to be lit to get hot water no matter how hot the night. That stove was the hungriest thing! There was nothing to do but get out the crosscut saw and start in on the woodpile. All that week I had to get up extra early to cut enough wood to heat the bottle, wash the children and cook the meals.

Next it was time to tackle the ice. The ice was cut in the winter and brought up the hill by a team of horses. Large chunks were packed in sawdust in the ice house. It had double Dutch doors. At the beginning of the summer, when the ice house was full, you'd enter by the top door, climb up on top of the pile of sawdust, work a crowbar between the squares of ice and then push on the other end of the crowbar. One might think it was a nice job to work in an ice house but it was one of the hottest places you could possibly imagine. The pieces of ice were carried with tongs to the back step; there was an outdoor tap I used to wash all the sawdust off. The chunks were split and then lifted into the large wooden icebox. However, it wasn't a very efficient icebox and in time took on a distinct smell of damp wood. Thunderstorms turned the milk sour.

THE WEISS MENAGE consumed six quarts of milk a day, double on weekends. Some families tried keeping a cow, but cows, like bears, could swim; the Gordons' cow was called Rainbow, as in "I am always chasing Rainbow ..." Alice bought a motor launch, *Bell Four*, to run the eight kilometres into Kenora for milk and groceries, but the Weiss camp had no boathouse:

The first storm came out of the west during the night. I was alone in camp with Nin and the children and a guest – a girl who got a sore throat if she got her feet wet. I went down to see what I could do about my new boat which was kept tied to the dock. The boat had broken loose and was bumping against a large rock. There were big waves. I figured that if I could just get it over the rock on the lee side I'd be able to beach it. I could just get it to go over the top, then the wave would recede, taking it back again. Every time, it came back to hit me. I was black and blue from my chin to my heels. I tried and tried to hold that boat as it went off the rock but it was always too quick for me. Finally, I got an old straw-filled mattress and tied it to the boulder so the boat would hit the padding. I tumbled into bed, having been up all night. I had done all I could.

My vegetable garden was a complete failure. The raspberries were terrible. The roses crossed with wild roses and grew among the raspberries – very thorny but beautiful with deep pink petals. When it was time for cutting the canes, it was as much as your life was worth with all those thorns.

Everything at the lake seemed to have a bit of work attached to it. We made our own ice cream, cranking it by hand. I did a certain amount of cooking. Worst of all were Thursdays, the cook's day off. I'd take the help into town and leave them at the dock. I think they had a pretty dull time and it seemed there was always a thunderstorm when I went to pick them up. Collecting the tools was always a Friday job so that they were in the place where they were expected to be. The new boat, the canoe and the rowboat were sponged dry before Karl's arrival for the weekend.

CONTINUED ON PAGE 185

IMAGES THIS PAGE: DENNIS FAST

The interior of the Konantz's log cabin conveys an elegant rusticity much in keeping with the history of Lake of the Woods. It was built by the Allan family in the 1920s

POLITICIANS

THE LAKE OF THE WOODS AREA tends to attract people who seek anonymity and obscurity, at least for a few weeks in the summer, but John Turner, a Liberal cabinet minister from 1967 to 1976, prime minister of Canada during the summer of 1984, and leader of the Opposition until 1990, still turns heads as he trundles his shopping cart down the aisles in the Kenora Safeway; Turner's brother-in-law, David Kilgour, MP for Edmonton Southeast and Secretary of State (Asia-Pacific), has served in the House of Commons as a Conservative, then a Liberal, since 1979. In 1972, Prime Minister Pierre Trudeau, his wife Margaret and infant son Justin, were guests of Turner's cabinet colleague and neighbour on Coney Island, James Richardson. Another neighbour was Senator William Benidickson and his wife Agnes, James Richardson's sister. Elected as MP for Kenora-Rainy River in 1945, Benidickson, a Kenora lawyer, was undefeated until he was appointed to the Senate in 1965. Although he was Minister of Mines in Lester Pearson's Liberal government, Benidickson was elected as an unusual hybrid, a Liberal-Labour candidate.

The Liberal-Labour coalition in northwestern Ontario grew out of the Independent Labour Party, an organization of anti-Marxist, anti-Socialist working men founded in the political upheaval that followed the end of the First World War. In the Kenora area, the ILP was supported by railroaders fed up with long, irregular hours, frozen wages and dangerous conditions. In 1919, they elected Peter Heenan, local chairman of the Brotherhood of Engineers, to the Ontario provincial parliament; Heenan, a fiesty red-haired Irishman, smoothed the way for the construction of the Kenora pulp and paper mill in 1923, and "Heenan's Highway", the road through Sioux Narrows and Nestor Falls linking the lake's north and south shores.

In 1925, Liberal prime minister Mackenzie King, teetering on the brink of defeat, invited Heenan to run as a Liberal in the new federal riding of Kenora-Rainy River. After long deliberation, the ILP agreed, on condition that the Liberals implement their promise of old age pensions. Two separate conventions were held in Kenora, one ILP, one Liberal: both nominated Peter Heenan. In the election, the parties combined their resources and Heenan defeated the Conservative candidate, lawyer H.A. Machin, by 135 votes. King delivered the old age pension, and Kenora-Rainy River has been a federal Liberal stronghold ever since. Labour influence dwindled away with the railroaders, and now organized labour in the area supports the New Democratic Party.

One of the founders of the NDP's parent, the Co-operative Commonwealth Federation, was Ralph Connor's son, King Gordon. Gordon, together with University of Toronto professor Frank Underhill, drafted the CCF's Socialist platform, the "Regina Manifesto" for the founding convention in 1933. On their way west, they stopped at Lake of the Woods; some of the manifesto's most eloquent passages may have been inspired by the view down the lake from The Lookout.

When it came to radical action, however, it was a Liberal, Edith Rogers, who in 1920 became the first and only woman elected to the Manitoba legislature in the first election in which women could vote. She had courage; the vote had been won in 1916 in the face of scurrilous opposition from the defeated Conservative premier, Sir Rodmund Roblin. Finding the idea of women's suffrage "abhorrent, unthinkable," Conservatives like Roblin conjured up "a Dante-esque vision of disintegrating families and neglected children moaning through the mists of vacant houses in search of their vanished mums," writes Edith's biographer Gail Konantz: "Politics was considered a dirty game, one with which those 'nice ladies' shouldn't concern themselves."

EDITH, a mother of four and one of the wealthiest women in Winnipeg, was elected because of her years of dedicated, unpaid "dirty work" on behalf of Winnipeg's most destitute families. As president of the Patriotic Fund's Auxiliary during the First World War, Edith sent money to needy wives of men serving overseas, visited their homes and listened to their troubles; when the Patriotic Fund ended with the war, she advocated for aid to unemployed veterans. As an MLA, Edith campaigned for old age pensions and mothers' allowances; in 1922 she championed the province's first Child Welfare Act. At a time when racial and religious bigotry were rife, and Winnipeg was riven by class warfare, Edith was at home with immigrants, soldiers and trade unionists, unwed mothers, ragged orphans and missionaries of all denominations.

"Perhaps because of her own severed family situation during the years she was growing up, she was particularly sensitive to the needs, unexpressed longings and frustrations of others," says Konantz. Edith had been born in Norway House, Manitoba, in 1876, the daughter of HBC fur trader Donald MacTavish and his wife Lydia; two years later, the MacTavishes moved to an even more isolated post, Rupert House, on James Bay. Her mother died of tuberculosis when Edith was only ten; she was raised by her father's sister Emily in Colborne, Ontario, and sent to boarding school in Montreal.

Yet Edith MacTavish belonged to Canada's fur trade aristocracy. Her maternal great-grandfather, Alexander Christie, was Governor of Assiniboia; her maternal grandmother, Mary Sinclair, was a descendent of HBC chief trader William Sinclair and his Cree wife, Nahoway (also called Margaret). Her MacTavish grandmother, Maria, was an illegitimate daughter of the HBC's famous "Little Emperor", Sir George Simpson. For generations, canoes carrying Sinclairs, Christies, MacTavishes and Sir George himself had passed the point in the channel on Lake of the Woods where the Rogers built their camp in 1910.

Edith retired from politics undefeated in 1932. After her death in 1947, the camp was inherited by her eldest daughter, Margaret Konantz. Margaret, her mother's most passionate campaign worker, became Liberal MP for Winnipeg South from 1963 to 1965; she had been made an Officer of the Order of the British Empire in 1946 for her philanthropic work.

In the early years of the twentieth century, the lake's most powerful and flamboyant politician was a Conservative, Robert Rogers,

PROVINCIAL ARCHIVES OF MANITOBA

This lovely log cabin, built by the Allan family, now belongs to Gordon and Gail Konantz. Gordon is Edith Rogers' grandson; he and Gail travel from Vancouver to carry on the family tradition of summering at Lake of the Woods.

DENNIS FAST

POLITICIANS

a cabinet minister in the Manitoba and, later, federal governments. A genial pork barrel politician, the "Honourable Bob" used his magnificent Lake of the Woods summer home as an English aristocrat's country estate; some weekends he had so many guests he didn't get around to meeting them all. The Rogers' guest book includes the signatures of young Winston Churchill and Edward, Prince of Wales, but his most memorable coup was a brief visit on July 25, 1916, by Canada's governor general, His Royal Highness, Prince Arthur, Duke of Connaught, accompanied by the Duchess and their daughter, Princess Patricia.

THE VISIT GOT OFF TO A FINE START, with cheering crowds at the Kenora station and a motorcade, led by the town's brass band, to the Main Street dock. Rogers' speedboat, the *Robert R.* took the royals to the yacht club – the duke graciously suggested the club apply for the title "Royal" – then to lunch at Rogers' camp; on their return to Kenora, the launches carrying the Connaughts were joined by a flotilla of boats of all shapes and sizes, gaily decorated with flags and bunting, in a noisy, churning parade through Devil's Gap to Kenora Bay. But the motorboat traffic made it impossible for the Kenora Rowing Club to hold the final races of its regatta, and as the *Robert R.* moored at the Main Street dock, a steam tug, the *John S. Minor*, began to tow a log boom into place to cordon off the race course.

"Some of the launches were caught unawares," writes lake historian Lori Nelson. "Although they hailed the captain and crew of the *John S. Minor*, their shouts were unheeded. Hon. Robert Rogers' launch was crushed between the boom and the *Keenora*, wrenching the stern and causing the boat to take on water. The passengers were hastily transferred to another boat without danger." The Duchess was evacuated from her launch when it too was crushed and sprang a leak.

Their Royal Highnesses were unharmed, but the accident was an unlucky omen: ten days later Canada was at war with Germany. After the war, Rogers lost his political influence when the Liberals won the 1921 federal election, and he lost his fortune in the 1929 stock market crash. The family was forced to sell their camp. His granddaughter, Eve, recalls how the new owner refused to allow her mother on the island to retrieve her personal belongings, and her own hurt at seeing another girl driving around the lake in Eve's boat. The camp changed hands over the years until it was abandoned and vandalized. It burned to the ground in 1975.

Boats of all kinds lined up to use Kenora's Main Street Dock in 1917, just as they do today.

Meeting the train on Friday night was the social event of the week. Armadas of boats converged on the Kenora and Keewatin docks, boatmen and campers exchanging greetings and gossip while they waited. In Kenora, boys ran up to the station, ready to carry Dad's bags; the Keewatin station was so close to the dock baggage was tossed down a chute. Camps were tidied, the children scrubbed and combed.

For many campers, life at the lake was as hectic as it was in Winnipeg, but others sought silence and solitude. Lake of the Woods attracted Winnipeg clergymen — one island was called "Preachers' Island" — who craved a simpler life. The Anglican church bought the O'Gradys' island, B'nai Brith ran a camp for Jewish children and the YMCA operated Camp Stephens for city boys and girls. At the lake, religion tended to be a common rejoicing in God's country.

NO WINNIPEG CAMPERS lived closer to nature than Reverend Gardner and Ada Freeman and their children. As minister of King Memorial Presbyterian Church in a working-class area of Winnipeg, Freeman preached and practiced the Social Gospel — the transformation of society into a living embodiment of the teachings and spirit of Jesus. In 1923, the Cecilia Jeffrey Indian Residential School at Shoal Lake became part of his mission field, and while Freeman approved of converting the Ojibwe to Christianity, he adopted their way of life during his one-month summer vacation.

"An Indian made us a 16' birchbark freight canoe guaranteed to hold a ton," recalls the Freemans' son John. "We took all our stuff for the month so we didn't have to go back to Kenora. It was a huge mound of stuff — macaroni, rice, beans, potatoes, canned goods, back bacon." The canoe was equipped with oars, paddles and a sail; the five children sat on top of the load or took turns paddling. The youngest — John was only six months old on his first canoe trip — were bundled up in Ojibwe *tikinagans* (cradle boards). They took the family dog along.

Paddling three or four hours a day, the Freemans set up their tents in the remote bays of the Aulneau Peninsula or the islands on Whitefish Bay. They fished and picked blueberries, becoming sooty from cooking over camp fires and brown from the sun. "My mother was a formidable camper," says the oldest son, George. "In the morning she'd paddle out with two fishing lines clenched in her teeth. When she got a bite, she'd haul the fish in and kill it. She'd have eight fish in no time." The Freemans seldom saw anyone.

One of their favourite camp sites was an island about eighteen kilometres southeast of Kenora. "One day the James Richardson family drove up in their boat and told us they had bought the island," says John. "We moved to another one, then a third." The Freemans could have bought the island, but property ownership went against their grain, and the law required them to build some sort of permanent structure. It was Muriel Richardson who resolved Gard Freeman's dilemma: "You buy the island, I'll donate a summer porch and you can sleep in the tent and look like an Indian for the rest of your life!" Gard and Ada Freeman bought the island, used the Richardsons' old sunroom as a woodshed and slept in the tent.

Any camp demanded a commitment of infinite time, energy and money; if the ravages of winter were not repaired in the summer, frame buildings were soon reclaimed by the bush. Closing up for the winter meant storing bedding and linens in mouse-proof trunks, or in a storeroom lined with wire mesh; one family piled mattresses

IMAGES COURTESY OF JOHN FREEMAN

Above, John Freeman and his twin sister Marjorie seemed delighted with their first canoe trip in July 1925. Four years later, two canoes (background photo) were needed to convey the twins, their parents and three siblings from island to island.

on the dining room table and set its feet in tin cans to keep the mice from climbing up. Chimneys had to be plugged, windows and screens shuttered. The "mansions" built before 1914 were deserted during World War I; men had enlisted, women devoted their time to the Red Cross and other charities. Augustus Nanton converted his Keewatin Beach camp into a convalescent home for the wounded. Many lake families suffered financially from the collapse of the grain trade and real estate market; the Depression bankrupted more. Children moved away, lost interest, or could not afford the upkeep; elderly parents agonized over who should inherit, and fratricidal quarrels broke out when their children could not agree. Sometimes the camp went to the child who could afford to buy the others out, or it was sold to strangers, an act lake loyalists consider a mortal sin. Yet every summer descendants of the original campers fly and drive thousands of kilometres to The Lake. Ralph Connor's grandson, Ottawa writer Charles Gordon, is one of them. In his book, *At the Cottage*, he tells why:

> After an uneventful voyage the boat, still leaking and still conking out at slow speeds, arrives at its destination and crashes into the dock. In the semi-darkness, a child slips on the same loose board as last year and scrapes his knee. A parent promises a Band-Aid, once they are inside.
>
> The shutter covering the front door hangs at a funny angle. The door itself is covered with scratches and opens too easily. In the kitchen, unidentifiable bits of something - food perhaps – cover the floor. Small animal droppings – that is, droppings from a small animal – are on the floor in the living room, along with the contents of what were once seat cushions. No Band-Aids in the medicine cabinet. The child's scraped knee bleeds on the chair that was the subject of last year's argument about whether or not it was a bit too fancy for the cottage. A member of a hardy breed of spring fly buzzes in through gaping holes in a screen. Half a tree is on the roof. The other half looks as if it soon might be.

THE COTTAGE, carefully cleaned and swept in September, has to be cleaned and swept again. The pump refuses to fit together, the toilet is making that funny sound again, and the children are refusing to go outside because they saw something large in the woods. Tomorrow the parents will find messes that cannot remotely be identified, but smell bad and have to be cleaned up anyway. The parents will get grease all over themselves trying to fix the pump. They will have to carry the heavy shutters and put them under the house, bumping their heads on things. They will get angry at each other. They know this.

Their backs will get sorer and they will have to jump into water that is colder than it has ever been in the history of the lake, partly to get clean, because the pump doesn't work, and partly because the children say it is a 'tradition', and if they don't do it they are old. The Stanley Cup finals are on television and there is no television. There is radio. Experience tells them that the game is on the radio, but only in French, and indistinctly at that.

The parents look at each other. 'It sure is nice to be here,' one says, and means it. The other, to his surprise, agrees.

Left: Edith Rogers and George Allan found the lake a much needed respite from busy lives.

PAUL KANE

WHEN **ARTIST** PAUL KANE RETURNED EAST across Lake of the Woods in the fall of 1848, having spent two years in the Northwest, he brought with him, in addition to some 500 sketches, bundles of Aboriginal artifacts he had collected: hide shirts and leggings, pipes, war clubs, beadwork and quillwork, a saddle, even a scalp. In his Toronto studio, Kane painted 100 colourful, dramatic oil canvases based on his sketches; in 1853, a wealthy patron of the arts, George W. Allan, bought all of his oils, 300 sketches and the "Indian curiosities" for $20,000. Allan, equally passionate about art, horticulture, music, history and politics – he was mayor of Toronto and Speaker of the Canadian Senate – displayed his collection in the family's mansion, Moss Park, until his death in 1901. The art works were sold – they were later given to the Royal Ontario Museum – but Allan's son, George Jr. inherited most, or all, of the artifacts. George, a corporate lawyer and insurance company president, had moved to Winnipeg, and when he and his wife Muriel, nicknamed "Mooge", built their Lake of the Woods island camp in 1904, they displayed Kane's collection. When the building was demolished in the 1940s, their daughter Jocelyn donated the collection to the Manitoba Museum in Winnipeg.

Paul Kane's *Lacaway, the Loud Speaker*, was painted in 1846. An oil on paper, it is among the collection of Queen's University's Agnes Etherington Art Centre.

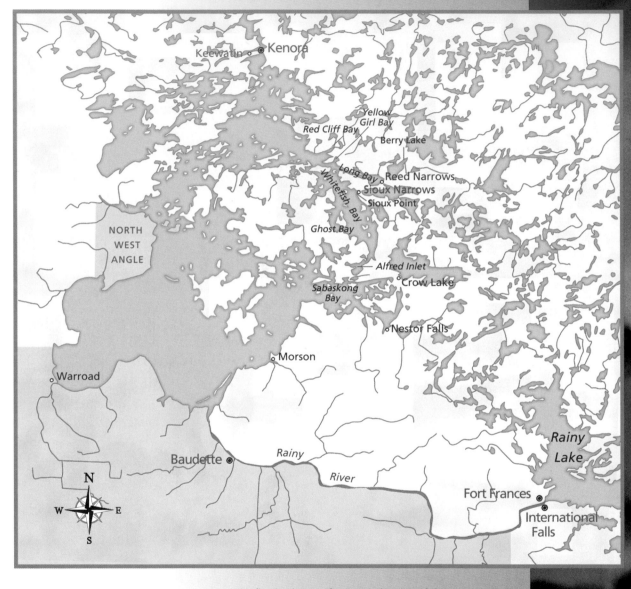

The flaming leaves of autumn, the glint of the summer sun
on the water, the dark mystery of the forests; this was the
magic of Lake of the Woods. Add the "mod cons"
and it seemed a combination that couldn't miss.

THE SARATOGA OF THE WEST

THE SARATOGA OF THE WEST

Kenora's Tourist Hotel, renamed the Kenricia, was designed to be one half of a hotel and resort combination that would draw fashionable clients from all corners of North America. It didn't quite work out that way ...

EARLY IN THE TWENTIETH CENTURY, Kenora began promoting itself as "the Saratoga of the west", a reference to a fashionable resort at Saratoga Springs in upper New York state. But Kenora had no mineral hot springs, and Banff, farther west on the CPR line, had both hot springs and the Rocky Mountains. When the CPR declined to build a luxury hotel equivalent to the Banff Springs Hotel, Kenora businessman Harding Rideout persuaded a group of Chicago investors to build a first-class hotel in town, and a private resort on Rideout's island in the lake.

Construction of Kenora's Tourist Hotel, designed by renowned architect Frank Newell, began in 1907. It was elegant and modern, but Newell's design for the island's Buena Vista Club resembled a medieval fortress surrounded by Swiss chalets and an Atlantic City boardwalk. Buena Vista was intended to accommodate 500 guests and a staff of 100, including four cooks, twenty-six waiters and fifteen chambermaids; it would be steam-heated, with Turkish baths and an indoor swimming pool. For rainy days, Newell included bowling alleys and a billiard room, a stage and ballroom for evening entertainments. To raise the $300,000 needed to build the club, 500 memberships were advertised at $100 each, 25,000 associate memberships for $10. Members would have to pay up to $25 a week to stay at the club, plus their railway fare from Chicago.

The club was never built. Investors, however, may have been swindled: rumour in Kenora had it that a member of the syndicate disappeared with all the money. The most likely culprit was Harding Rideout. President of the Tourist Hotel Company and mayor in 1908, Rideout abruptly left town. His half-built hotel, taken over by the town and renamed Kenricia, opened in 1910.

If the Buena Vista Club was ephemeral, Minaki Lodge has been a phoenix with multiple reincarnations. Built by the Grand Trunk Pacific Railway where its line crossed the Winnipeg River about forty-five kilometres north of Kenora, the Minaki Inn opened weeks before war broke out in August 1914. It closed immediately and the GTP went bankrupt. The inn, taken over by the CNR, was renovated in 1925, but it burned down the day before its scheduled opening on June 12th. In 1927, the CNR replaced it with a beautiful log and stone lodge surrounded by log cabins, tennis courts and a nine-hole golf course. Aiming to blend "the primitive with the elegance of civilization," Minaki

Tourist Hotel, Kenora, Ont.

Minaki was not the only retreat on the Winnipeg River. Holst Point Lodge, seen above in 1910, and from the air (inset) fifteen years later, was another wilderness lodge aimed at luring those who did not own cottages to the vast Canadian Shield.

At least some felt that Kenora's motor boat landing was postcard perfect ... and you couldn't beat the price!

KENORA BOAT COMPANY LTD.

GASOLINE PUMP

$2.00
Return
ONE-DAY

BARGAIN TRIP
TO
KENORA
Wed. July 12

Lv. Winnipeg   8.30 a.m.
Lv. Ingolf   10.35 a.m.
Lv. Laclu   11.05 a.m.
Lv. Keewatin   11.20 a.m.
Ar. Kenora   11.30 a.m.

RETURNING
Lv. Kenora   7.30 p.m.
Lv. Keewatin   7.40 p.m.
Lv. Laclu   7.50 p.m.
Lv. Ingolf   8.20 p.m.
Ar. Winnipeg   10.30 p.m.

Day Coach Accommodation
No Baggage Checked
Children, 5 years and under 12,
half fare.

Delightful short boat trips on
Lake of the Woods. Visit Devil's
Gap Chalet Bungalow Camp

For information phone
City Ticket Office   903 211-2-3
Depot Ticket Office   903 216-7

CANADIAN
PACIFIC
World's Greatest Travel System

Lodge achieved neither; it was too swank for fishermen and elegant civilization ended with the stock market crash in 1929. It struggled on, a stately pleasure dome in the middle of nowhere.

By the mid-1960s, a crude, tortuous road linked Minaki to the TransCanada Highway, but the only people brave enough to drive the Minaki Road were fishermen, the Waabisimoong First Nation, village residents and campers. Passenger train service dwindled until it stopped. In 1974, the Ontario govern-ment bought the lodge, intending to operate it as a year-round convention centre. At a cost of about $50 million, it built an airport, rebuilt the road, replaced the lodge's rustic cabins with rows of concrete condo-style suites and added to the dining room, which seated 200, a kitchen capable of feeding 2,000. The Radisson and Four Seasons hotel chains made stabs at running the lodge, but it was too small and remote for major conventions, and guests on a wilderness get-away didn't want to share it with a crowd. The lodge's most loyal patrons were the area's campers: they could golf, have a drink in the bar and enjoy a gourmet meal. But management disapproved: men were instructed to wear a jacket at dinner, and the Sunday brunch, which attracted hordes of sloppy locals, was restricted to the lodge's few guests. Minaki Lodge never did open in the winter and changed hands several times before it closed in the mid-1990s. It opened again, briefly, in the spring of 2003.

When the CPR opened its Devil's Gap Bungalow Camp southeast of Kenora in 1923, it hastened to reassure customers that "it has nothing at all to do with tents. On the contrary, it is like living in one's private house, without the bother of meals or servants – living on one floor, in bungalows, without elevators, bell-hops or the usual enamel of a summer hotel, and yet with all the conveniences." Twenty-two private chalets perched on the rocks around a main lodge that served as a dining room, lounge and entertainment centre; the view overlooking the channel was magnificent. For $5 per person a day, Devil's Gap Camp provided electricity, laundry and maid service; it offered tennis, volleyball and badminton, canoes, boats, and, after 1929, access to the Kenora golf club. Children were welcome.

Guests, ferried by motor launch from the Kenora station, were met on the dock by white-gloved bellhops, but once in their cabins they could do as they pleased in the "Land of Loaf." Families booked their cabins years in advance, year after year, but by 1960 they were travelling by car, not train, so the CPR sold the camp. A road was put in from Kenora in 1965, but the camp closed in 1974 and the cabins were individually sold.

The lake's rugged southeastern bays attracted an entirely different tourist: Americans in pursuit of trophy fish. In 1910, Rainy River druggist E.C. Calvert, a keen fisherman, invited two doctors from Philadelphia on a fishing trip; it was so successful Calvert found himself running a little hobby business. Using canoes, or his sailboat, equipped with the newfangled, single-stroke outboard motor, Calvert took fishermen camping in tents on Cedar Island in Sabaskong Bay. He built a permanent Cedar Island camp in 1920, and by 1926 he had a second camp in Whitefish Bay. He bought the *Clipper* to transport some 700 guests a year from the train station in Rainy River.

TO THE NORTH, on the shore of Long Bay, a French-Canadian homesteader, Joe Soissons, expanded his log cabin into a humble inn for lake travellers. Soissons was an expert guide, and in 1913, a party of Kenora hunters adopted "Old Joe"'s cabin, called "Long Baloney" because of its low ceiling and string of makeshift additions, as their annual autumn headquarters. They returned for thirty years. Long Baloney, probably the lake's first hunting lodge, set a high standard of masculine roughing it for camps that followed.

The lake's settlers, with no electricity, hot running water or flush toilets, were puzzled that city people would pay money to share their deprivations, yet tourists landed on camps that were not yet built. In 1929, A.G. "Dad" Crawford, his wife Lily and their three sons built a home on Big Pine Lake at the end of the new dirt road running north from Highway 11 to Nestor Falls. The boys were building a cabin in the yard for themselves when the Pearsons, a couple from Bartlesville, Oklahoma, drove in looking for a vacation spot. Crawford said that if they came back the next day, the cabin would be finished. The Pearsons returned and stayed for two months, using nine-year-old Ed as a fishing guide.

A pair of visitors to Calvert's White Fish Camp unveil one of the secrets to the camp's success: professionals and businessmen could escape their real lives for a few days to play woodsman ... and bring back photographs guaranteed to astound their colleagues

NORMAN CHARLES QUICK / NATIONAL ARCHIVES OF CANADA / PA-802272

Spotting a trend, the Crawfords moved north with the road, setting up camps at Crow Lake, Reed Narrows and Sioux Narrows. The opening of the Sioux Narrows bridge on July 1, 1936 attracted a Chicago couple, Stanley and Mary Goodell. Mary writes:

Stanley wrote Crawford's Camp for the reservation of a cabin. No reply was received so we decided to bring a tent. We packed our car with the necessary equipment; this included all food since there were no stores in the vicinity at the time. The road was being built and we became mired many times. The men working on the road would hitch a team of horses to the front of the car and pull us through. We arrived at Crawford's Camp tired and ready to relax and were greeted by Mr. Crawford with: 'We haven't any cabins for vacationers. We are boarding and housing the men and horses working on the road.' Mrs. Crawford, who operated the dining room, told us that if we wanted to pitch our tent across the channel we could have two meals a day in their dining room served family style. We accepted her offer and the meals were delicious.

So we lived in a tent and slept in a pine bough bed. Except for moose trying to get out of the water, a few bear roaming about, heavy rain and strong winds, it was quite comfortable. As to fishing, each day we would catch our limit of walleye within thirty minutes by anchoring in the channel close to the bridge.

Camps provided local guides, usually Métis or Ojibwe, to take guests to the best fishing spots. Norman MacLeod's Camp at Sioux Point charged $5.50 a day for a guide and $2.50 for an outboard motor and gas; the boat was included in the $5 daily rate for a cabin and meals. For less than $15 a day, a fisherman could land lake trout, pike or muskellunge weighing up to eighteen kilos, and plenty of walleye for a shore lunch. Camp owners spent

LAKE OF THE WOODS MUSEUM, KENORA

long hours filleting the fish and icing them down; they got up before dawn to make breakfast and entertained their guests with stories and song well into the night. While guests were out on the lake, they cleaned cabins, did the laundry, fixed the outboards, baked pies and kept an eye on the weather: fishermen frequently ran out of gas, got lost or were caught in storms.

The season opened with the spring bear hunt in March and ended with the bear, deer and moose hunts before the lake froze. During the winters, the men trapped, worked in the bush and put up ice. Cleo Gaudry, owner of Split Rock Camp at Nestor Falls and an outpost at Dryberry Lake, advertised his business by touring the United States with a winter sports show. Dressed in lumberjack's boots, jodhpurs and a bright red shirt emblazoned: Gaudry's Camps, Kenora, Canada, Gaudry paid for his booth by showing off his skill at log rolling and canoe jousting. Gaudry, his wife Alice and six sons later took over a trading post at Regina Bay, buying fish, wild rice and blueberries from the Ojibwe; Alice smoked trout and whitefish, Cleo logged, freighted, sawed lumber and prospected.

THE DISCOVERY OF GOLD in eastern Ontario and northern Quebec rekindled gold fever at Lake of the Woods. In 1929, George Marwick brought his family from the gold mines of Kirkland Lake to the old, abandoned Horseshoe Gold Mine on Regina Bay. "They resided in a old fortress-like white house built into the side of a solid rock outcropping," recalls their daughter Betty Kerr.

The architect, Col. Wilkinson, a retired British Army officer, firmly believed that the ferocious natives who were his neighbours close by were skulking about in the bushes awaiting the opportune moment to divest him of his scalp-lock.

The walls were a half-metre thick granite and cement, part of the floor solid rock with an ancient furnace tucked away into its niche. A comfortable place, warm in winter, cool in summer. A gigantic iron stove and a heavy, hand-hewn log table and benches dominated the room. Shelves were stocked with hundreds of jars of preserved berries, fruits, jams, jellies, fish, fowl and game. Another pantry contained the bulk foods and canned goods that one was forced to stock over freeze-up and break-up. A lot of dried fruits in wooden boxes, 60-pound wooden cases of butter, 50-pound tin pails of lard and shortening, 100-pound sacks of sugar and flour. We remember

Jimmy Robinson, one of those fearsome natives, driving across the ice with his pony and sleigh to take entire families to enjoy Christmas celebrations in their round house on the reserve. Ferocious indeed!

It took stamina to spend the long, bitter winters in these isolated bays, yet for Betty, winter meant "visits to good friends where, after a big supper, children, tired at play, curled up to sleep by the old pot-bellied stove, while parents played cards and talked their loneliness away. The long walk home over thundering new ice, air thick with frost, myriads of twinkling stars reflected in the newly-fallen snow crystals; breathtakingly beautiful!"

Camp owners' children were taught at home by correspondence; the older ones boarded in Kenora or Fort Frances. At Christmas, they came home by taxi or truck on the ice road, jolting over the raised hummocks; when the road ended, they walked the rest of the way prodding the ice with a long pole to test its strength. In summer, they booked passage on mail and freight boats. Betty vividly remembers Tommy Harrison's "blueberry special."

It was a coal burning, fire-spitting barge, often overloaded, its gunwales barely surfacing above water, plowing and slogging its merry way, willy-nilly, into all sorts of weird places. Often the passengers were a day or so late as Tommy would frequently pull into shore, any old shore would do, tie up and proceed to have some pretty potent liquid refreshment – no rush. When under steam, Tommy would be found below deck, pounding the engine into submission with a ball-peen hammer. He would pop up periodically to see if we were still on course. Not that it really mattered; that old scow had a shattering acquaintance with every shoal and reef on its route –

CONTINUED ON PAGE 199

Fishing on remote lakes accessed by float plane is popular in many places on Lake of the Woods. Near Sioux Narrows, vacationers and sightseers mingle with fishermen at several lodges and the drone of single-engine planes often accompanies breakfast.

THE LEGEND OF SIOUX NARROWS

Legends differ about how Sioux Narrows was named; this, printed in
The Colonist *magazine in 1893, rings truest.*

"KEEWATIN IS THE SITE OF AN OLD CHIPPEWA [or Ojibwe] camp, where a powerful chief ruled over some 250 warriors with their squaws and papooses. Iasawash, as this chief was named, had gone through many a fierce fight with the Sioux [as the Dakota were then called], and had brought home from his forays scores of scalps of his enemies. He was advancing in years, and he had no sons left for three of them had met their death in war with the hated enemy, and two of their scalps were supposed to be ornamenting the tepees of the Sioux. He had one child, Cheekanaguaybeek, or the Lake Lily, a daughter, the fame of whose accomplishments had spread among all the Chippewa bands on the lake. She had seen but little of warfare from her childhood, and had only shared in the rejoicing and the spoils, when the warriors of her tribe came home from a successful foray into the Sioux country. Still she had the inborn admiration for the daring and the brave.

"Keeshcahminisay, or the Kingfisher, had attracted her attention more than any other, for his bound was the most agile, his arrow was the truest in aim, his hooks and his nets seemed to bring in more fish, and his canoe had time and again defied the wildest storms. His love for the Lake Lily was as pure as his heart was brave." Iasawash, however, rejected Kingfisher's suit until he had proven himself in battle:

"One day, Iasawash called together and met the braves of his tribe in council of war. He told them how his heart, though older and beating more slowly, was as brave as ever, and as fierce against their enemies, the Sioux. He longed to wipe out the blood of his lost sons in a deluge of Sioux blood; and he had determined to attack the Sioux once more in their own yellow land. Not to make a foray with a few, who would hurry back in the night with the spoil; but to go there with every brave of his tribe, and deal out a blow that their enemies would long remember, and tremble when they thought over it. Some of his braves loved peace, and did not care to go to war. They were secure in their present camp. But he asked them to once more for the last time follow him to the fight, he was their chief and their medicine man also, his wisdom had kept them strong and free from disease, and had done much to guarantee them their present rest and safety. Once more he asked them to trust to his wisdom on the war path, and to be ready next morning to start on a war expedition against the Sioux. In the closing of his speech he pointed to his only child, on the outside of the ring of warriors in council, and said: 'There is my light of eye, the center of my heart. She shall be given as the squaw of the brave who brings home the most scalps' It is needless to say that every brave of the tribe agreed to follow their old chief once more on the war path, and that night all was bustle and preparation.

"By grey dawn Iasawash and twelve score of his braves manned their birch bark canoes, each warrior in his war paint and armed for the fray. Their course was across a portion of the open lake to Buffalo Bay. Here they reached in safety, and cached their canoes before camping for the night, carefully obliterating every trail that would lead to the hiding place. Early next morning they were on the march westward, and at night selected a safe camp near a small lake.

"On the morning every brave was puzzled to note the troubled look on the face of their chief, and all were astonished to learn that he proposed an immediate return to their home. He had dreamed a terrible dream, and he felt certain all was not well with the unprotected families they had left in their home camp. Former dreams of Iasawash had

Prisoners were expected to cut and stack a cord of firewood a day. In the fall, when the heat and bugs were gone and the forests flamed with colour, many found it was pure delight to be in the woods.

POWs. Two camps, Alfred Inlet and Ghost Bay, were on the Aulneau Peninsula, the others at Yellow Girl Bay, Oak Point, Red Cliff Bay and Berry Lake. They had no barbed wire: bush, bears, wolves and blizzards were considered sufficient. An uninsulated bunkhouse made of rough siding covered with tarpaper, heated by a central stove, housed twenty men. Their living conditions were luxurious compared to the old logging camps; in addition to a stable, storehouses and outhouses, a POW camp had a dining hall and kitchen, an entertainment cabin, a wash house, a first aid room for the

visiting doctor, and separate cabins for the camp boss, the company foreman and a half-dozen guards. The guards were Canadian veterans too old for active service, the camp boss a German POW with senior military rank.

The POWs were paid fifty cents a day to cut and stack one cord of wood; once they finished, they had the day off. Johannes Lieberwirth, captured in North Africa in 1941, arrived at Red Cliff Bay Camp in April, 1944. He describes a typical day: "We got up I guess 6 or 6:30 a.m. Then we had our breakfast and we were going into the bush around

DENNIS FAST

200

7 a.m. And we all had our lunch boxes with us and a pot of tea. We had an axe, a swede saw and a measure stick, 8' long. In the middle was a little ribbon around so you knew that's only 4', because we had to make it 4' by 4' by 8'. But it was not a big deal. After you get some routine you can make it in five hours or so. But we decided not to make more than we had to. At that time, 50 cents was a lot of money in our lives. I think a package of cigarettes was 25 cents, Pepsi Cola 5 cents."

At Red Cliff Camp, twenty of the 100 POWs worked as stable hands, blacksmiths, cooks and kitchen help. "The food was excellent, really excellent," says Lieberwirth. "We didn't starve at all, even at that time, and we were told that at the end of the war there were some rations in Canada, butter I think and meat. We didn't feel that. You could eat as much as you wanted. But, forbidden was alcohol, liquor – officially. That was one side of the coin. Some of us, we had a gear made to distill liquor and we put it in between the walls of the cabin so nobody could see it. But since the Veteran Guards always got a little bit from what we had made, they never discovered it, or tried to. So that was not a big problem."

THE POWs were so young they were treated almost as sons by the Veteran Guards: at some camps, guards took their prisoners duck hunting. The POWs appreciated their kindness: when two armed guards escorting POWs to the dentist in Kenora spent too much time in the beer parlor, the POWs, carrying the guards' rifles, helped them back into the boat.

"There was no enemy-like life," says Lieberwirth. "Everyday we had a roll call, of course. They came in and said: 'How many people are there?' Nobody escaped. There was no reason for it. We had nowhere to go." Two POWs at Yellow Girl Camp escaped in November, – their frozen corpses were found the following spring.

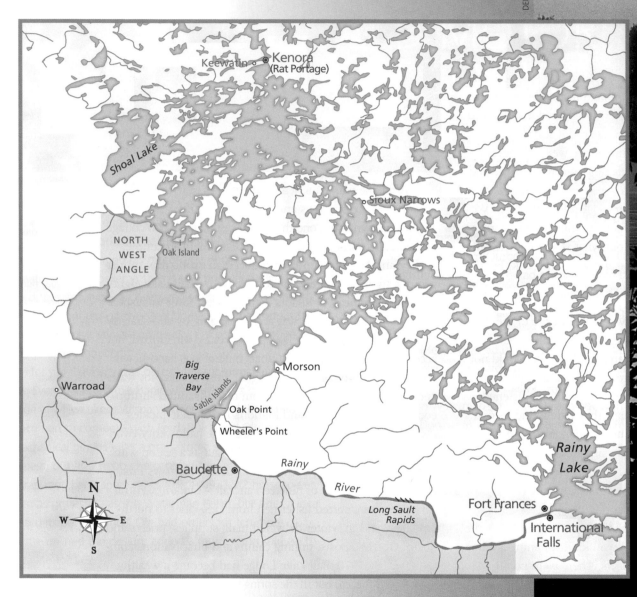

Keewatin
Kenora
(Rat Portage)

Shoal Lake

Sioux Narrows

NORTH
WEST
ANGLE

Oak Island

Big
Traverse
Bay

Morson

Sable Islands

Warroad

Oak Point

Wheeler's Point

Rainy

Baudette

River

Rainy
Lake

N
W E
S

Long Sault
Rapids

Fort Frances

International
Falls

In many places, Lake of the Woods
seems pristine, untouched, but beneath
the golden surface, fish populations are
in grave danger.

FROM CAVIAR TO CATASTROPHE

winter "we chopped holes in the ice and set the net with a line run under the ice with a jigger. If the ice was clear, you could see it. Sometimes we lost it, though, and that meant starting all over again." It was cold, harsh work and prices were low. McKeever hauled their catch over the ice to Warroad by horse-drawn sled; in summer the *Resolute* or *Scout* picked up their cleaned, iced fish and delivered them to the Booth Fisheries station on Oak Island.

Lifting nets by hand required enormous strength. Even when bigger boats and powerful gasoline engines made their jobs easier, the "lake men" had to be tough, resourceful and fearless. Risking their lives on the lake, often alone, made them independent but they were clannish too: over the years fishing families grew into dynasties with names like Arnesen, Brewster, Boucha, Selvog, Moyer, Kreger, Vickaryous and Johnston. "These sturdy lake people loved the lake and always thought of it as feminine (she's calm, she's rough etc.)," Alvin Johnston writes in his memoir, *A Time to Fish and A Time to Dry Nets*. "They knew she could do wild and wicked things but, if she did, they knew she could not help it. She would take family members or friends away from them, but they never blamed the lake. They knew every day is a new day, that to be a survivor in this wild and untamed land you must be lucky, that without luck you might not return from a day's fishing. If that happened to you, the unknown tale would remain her secret, buried under the sandbars and beneath the waves forever."

Boats capsized, fishermen fell overboard. Alvin Johnston's father, Albert, a barroom bare-knuckle boxer before he took up fishing, survived a freak accident on board his seven-metre *Vernabelle:*

On the way to lift my gill nets at Buffalo Point,
I was bucking a north wind gusting to 30 mph.
I was alone on board when a huge wave rolled over the front deck, breaking the anchor loose

and causing it to ship back and forth across the deck. Moving the throttle to slow, I lashed the steering wheel so the boat would hold a straight course while I climbed out on the deck and lashed the anchor. A big wave rolled over the bow, washing me into the lake. Unable to swim, I was under water until another wave rolled me to the surface just in time to see the *Vernabelle's* stern sliding past. I saw the stern tie rope dragging in the water. Catching the tie rope, I was towed along behind. Exhausted, I inched forward far enough to pull myself back on board.

THE FALL FISHERY lasted until the lake froze over in November. October was feared for its storms: north winds whipped freezing spray into black, blinding clouds that swirled on top of the whitecaps. A boat could sink under the weight of ice, or break apart from the pounding of the waves. In winter, ice fishermen contended with snowdrifts, pressure ridges, slush, open water and wind chill temperatures of -60°. Fearful of losing their catch and their nets, they often risked their lives.

One day in the winter of 1930, Albert Johnston, his

Though there are days when it is pure pleasure, right, ice fishing can be frigid work, but transportation is greatly improved. Instead of horses, many fishermen use snowmobiles to deliver them to and from their fishing shacks, above, out on the lake. Snowmobiles also provide hours of winter entertainment; the lake has hundreds of miles of mapped and marked trails.

IMAGES THIS PAGE: DENNIS FAST

209

Keewatin ○ ● Kenora

Sioux Narrows

NORTH
WEST
ANGLE

Oak Island

Morson

Warroad ○

N
W   E
S

Baudette ○

Rainy

River

Fort Frances ○

International
Falls

*Rainy
Lake*

Like moths drawn to a lamp, sailboats and their
motor-driven cousins cluster along the shore near
the Royal Lake of the Woods Yacht Club.

A PASSION FOR SAILING

A PASSION FOR SAILING

ROYAL LAKE OF THE WOODS YACHT CLUB

It wasn't only men who enjoyed sailing; nattily attired Alice Galt Weiss was one of many girls who developed a passion for the sport.

COURTESY OF JANE MATHER

AMONG THE FIRST SUMMER CAMPERS on Lake of the Woods was a group of Winnipeg businessmen who shared a passion for sailing. They raced on Sundays, using an island as their base. Their favourite route was up Keewatin Channel to George Galt's camp, Nebinatawin, for a buffet lunch before they sailed home in time to catch the Campers' Special back to the city. The Lake of the Woods Yacht Club was formally organized in 1903, and its clubhouse included bedrooms for city sailors who came for the weekend; thirty boats competed in six classes ranging from 14-foot dinghies to 25-foot sloops. Six years later, the club purchased its own island.

The yacht club became the lake's weekend social centre; racing day was changed to Saturday and the *Argyle* brought crowds to watch. Sailing rules and dress code were strictly enforced, but there were motor boat races as well and competitions in swimming, paddling and rowing. Women gathered for tea in the clubhouse or on the verandah, and some sailed: in 1909 Elsie Gordon won the Hugo Ross cup for ladies' dinghies, a Miss Peters in *Jinjur* took the Patton cup in 1911 and the Macara cup in 1912, and that year Jean Mather won the Peters cup.

All eyes, however, were on the race for the lake's first international challenge cup, a three-day competition between two 32-foot scows, L.W. Caldwell's *Daphne*, representing the Lake of the Woods Yacht Club, and Lou Ordway's *Quaker Girl* from the White Bear Yacht Club of St. Paul, Minnesota. Members of the two clubs had become friendly competing in rowing regattas in Winnipeg and St. Paul, and it was agreed that the sailing competition would alternate annually between the two lakes. White Bear won the 1912 challenge, and all that followed until an angry dispute ended the competition in 1925.

The Lake of the Woods Yacht Club, buoyed by the King's permission to add "Royal" to its name, had been confident it finally had a winner, *Phantom*, a lightweight scow designed by her veteran skipper, N.J. Dinnen, and built in Keewatin by H.W. Cossey. *Phantom* was the fastest boat on Lake of the Woods, but at White Bear she was competing in a best-of-five regatta against Dick Ordway's undefeated American champion, *Kawa*. Two races were marred by disqualifications on both sides; a third was called for lack of wind. On the fourth day, *Kawa* nipped *Phantom* at the finish line. Dinnen asked for a measurement of *Kawa's* sails; as he had guessed, they were oversized. Dinnen lodged a protest, but Ordway objected that Egyptian cotton sails normally stretched with use, and his sails had measured perfectly at the beginning of the season. Dinnen had followed the British practice of cutting his sails smaller to allow for stretching, and he refused to accept Ordway's explanation. Race officials dithered. Dinnen lost his temper and accused Ordway of cheating; Ordway, who had followed standard American rules, was insulted. The fifth race was never held. The Canadians huffed off home, and awkward attempts to revive the challenge ended with the Depression.

COURTESY OF FRANCEAN CAMPBELL

Above: George Huestis Campbell and friends on a day outing at Lake of the Woods. Campbell's boat, *Hillyho*, was built in Winnipeg and shipped to the lake.

Inset: Sailing took a number of forms, as this twin batwing sailing canoe belonging to Bertha Stone demonstrates.

LAKE OF THE WOODS MUSEUM, KENORA / 2001.15.6

215

Sailing, Kenora, Ont.

This early twentieth century view of Kenora Bay, crowded with boats of every description, is a clear indication of the enormous popularity of sailing and boating generally prior to the Great War.
Inset: Lake of the Woods Yacht Club, 1915

Nine years of economic collapse followed by six years of war nearly ended the RLWYC. Closed for years, it was kept afloat by a few dedicated members under long-serving commodores Norman Paterson and Gordon E. Konantz. When it got back on its feet in 1946, the rules were modernized – all sails were now measured prior to a major regatta – boats were smaller and easier to handle,

the crowd younger, dress less formal and dances the biggest attraction. By the late 1950s, wooden boats were being replaced by the fibreglass Lightning, then by the small one-person Laser; both were hugely popular, but the technology of sailboat design and construction was advancing so rapidly that few summer campers had the enthusiasm or the money to maintain prize-winning racing boats.

EMPHASIZING SAILING FOR FUN, the club hired an instructor to teach children. Two of the best young Lightning sailors, Jim Richardson Jr. and Sandford Riley, dreamed of competing in the Olympics – Sandy's uncle, Derek Riley, had been an Olympic rower – and in 1971 they brought Olympic-class, one-person Finn boats to Lake of the Woods. The only other sailor on the lake with a Finn was Gordon Konantz Jr., and all summer the three of them raced up and down the Yacht Club channel. "The Finn is bigger than a Laser," says Riley, "a powerful boat that is difficult to sail in strong winds. We had high winds every day that summer. I loved those winds."

They learned by trial and error, and after months of training in Europe, they competed to make Canada's 1972 Olympic team. Riley finished fourth, Richardson seventh; Riley, only twenty-one, was chosen to be the winner's training partner. Riley continued to sail out of Toronto's Royal Canadian Yacht Club as he studied law and in 1975, his boat proudly flying the colours of the Royal Lake of the Woods Yacht Club, he became the first Canadian to win the U.S. Finn championship. In 1976, Riley represented Canada in the Olympics in Kingston, Ontario. He finished eighth.

Sailboats were getting bigger, big enough to stow camping gear and supplies for several days, and now that the lake was charted, the channels and reefs marked with buoys, sailing into strange coves and bays was safer. Auxiliary engines countered the vagaries of the wind, and radios

For many years in mid-century, family sailing outings and the sight of great sails on the lake were little more than a memory. It would take a combination of technology and individual talent to resuscitate sailing at Lake of the Woods.

Right: Sandy Riley's enthusiasm and success helped to revive the popularity of sailing on the lake.

reduced the risk of getting lost, but American boaters were so fearful of the Big Traverse they rarely ventured beyond the river mouth harbours.

IN 1965, Clyde and Shirley Ryberg of Minneapolis and their two children, Donald, sixteen, and Marguerite, twelve, daringly circumnavigated the lake in an E class racing scow. Towing tents, sleeping bags and their grub in a canoe, they sailed from Baudette on a 450-kilometre route via Oak Island, Kenora, Sioux Narrows, Morson and home; they camped in pristine coves, caught fish for breakfast and dinner and made friends with the Canadians. They had their share of anxiety and misfortune – their mast broke leaving Baudette, storms blew down their tents and kept them windbound – but, as Shirley wrote later, "We had action! Our real love was sailing, and this we had in such full measure we can't wait to sail this lake again."

The Ryberg's Discovery of "the most wonderful cruising water on the North American continent" inspired sailing enthusiasts in Minnesota and Ontario to form the Lake of the Woods International Sailing Association. LOWISA organized an annual regatta to follow the Rybergs' route, and every second year the starting point would be Kenora. Participants could choose to race, or cruise at their own speed; they were free to sleep in the boat, camp out, or book a room at a tourist lodge. All boats were required to carry essential safety equipment and the fleet would be

patrolled by rescue boats. Float planes were on standby. Every boat was supplied with charts, and a baggage boat transported their gear.

On August 15, 1966, fifty-five boats, five Canadian, set off from Baudette. They were all shapes and sizes, from a 38-foot scow to a 12-foot homemade catamaran, and their crews totalled 176, including children. The start was inauspicious: the officials' boat got lost in fog. All made it safely to Oak Island, but the wind died and only four arrived under sail. The race was voided. Day 2 dawned dead calm, and boats without engines had to be towed before the wind freshened; many got lost, others took a shortcut. Kenora gave the flotilla a warm welcome during a one-day layover, but the next leg, to Sioux Narrows, was terrifying. Bob Oas of Duluth, racing his C class boat, describes his experience:

When we started off this morning there was lightning flashing across the sky all around us and the winds were about 25 mph, but no one wanted to turn back and be left to navigate for themselves so on we all went. Each time we came to open water our hearts sank as the waves were getting bigger all the time. One by one, the boats were tipping over. One gust of wind capsized six boats, all sailing together, at one time. When we were only 2 1/2 miles from the finish line, by this time sailing in steady 50 mph winds and about 4-foot waves, we were suddenly hit by a harder gust and over we went. Luckily, there were three runabouts to our rescue almost immediately.

FLOATING GEAR WAS RESCUED, but Oas and his partner lost their radio, camera, binoculars, shoes and boat pump; a rescue boat damaged their sail and boom. Six boats limped in with broken masts, five boats went missing until they were found safely on shore the next morning. One solo sailor, whose small boat tipped nine times, said: "I have never been so scared so often and so long in my life."

After a day of rest and repairs, thirty-nine boats left Sioux Narrows for Morson and Baudette; winds were so light the crews fished. The regatta ended with a banquet, trophies, no loss of life and no serious injuries. Bob Oas highly recommended the LOWISA regatta to his sailing club, describing his adventure as "the best week we had ever spent anywhere." LOWISA thrived, and grew to as many as 130 boats. In 1975, Hank and Virgina Henderson of Warroad organized ESCAPE, the Exciting Scenic Canadian American Powerboat Excursion, to encourage inexperienced boaters to explore the lake together during a sociable four-day guided cruise. For boaters who prefer solitude,

Henderson, a veteran of the U.S. Navy and Border Patrol, a pilot and sailing instructor, has published a handbook, *The Vacation and Cruising Guide to Lake of the Woods*, wryly subtitled "Women and Children First, Follow Me! I'm your Captain."

COURTESY OF THE TOOLE FAMILY

Sailing is increasingly popular, particularly among the younger summer residents of Lake of the Woods., including Aynsley Toole, above left, sailing a Laser Radial with Krista Harris. Toole served as Manitoba's provincial coach for several years in the late 1990s, taking teams to regional and national competitions.

Like a red sky in the morning, there is
menace beneath the beauty of
Lake of the Woods.

MAKING PEACE WITH THE MANITOUS

MAKING PEACE
WITH THE
MANITOUS

Right: The 1954 wreck of the Camper's Special illustrated yet again how unsafe rail travel could be in the era of steam engines. Seven years earlier, in 1947, the CNR's Campers' Special wrecked at Dugald, Manitoba, and passengers were burned alive.

CONFLICT, NATURAL DISASTER AND HUMAN tragedy continue to shape the history of Lake of the Woods. At about 8:30 p.m. on Friday, July 16, 1954, the CPR's Campers' Special, carrying 200 passengers, ran off the rails sixty-two kilometres west of Kenora. *The Winnipeg Tribune* reported: "The locomotive jumped the track on a curve, bounced along the ties of the parallel westbound track for 200 yards, then plunged down an embankment. The baggage car followed." The first three cars rolled on their sides into a swamp; passengers, cut and bruised, smashed windows and climbed out. An elderly woman, Isabel Maconnell, was crushed to death in a washroom doorway; the front end brakeman, James Szabo, was fatally scalded by steam from the engine's ruptured boiler. The five rear cars left the track but remained upright. Hours later, a freight train took the passengers to Keewatin and Kenora in boxcars; forty-five were treated in hospital.

Among the people waiting anxiously at the Keewatin dock were Gordon Gage's two young sons, Stewart and Ross, and his boatman, John McLeod. When Gordon arrived, uninjured, he took the wheel of his sleek, speedy motorboat, *Red Devil*,

FINAL THE WINNIPEG TRIB

WINNIPEG, SATURDAY, JULY 17, 1954

64th Year   No. 169

2 Die, 45 Hurt As 'Special' D
HOLIDAY TRAIN WI

and headed out into Portage Bay. The night was dark and Gage, who usually docked in Kenora, was unfamiliar with the channels in the narrow bay. Within minutes, the *Red Devil* smashed into an unmarked log boom. The boat sank in thirty seconds; the Gages swam safely to the boom, but McLeod went down with the boat.

The following year, Ogilvie Mills bought the Lake of the Woods Milling Company and shut down the oldest of Keewatin's two flour mills. In 1957, Keewatin's tiny business district was devastated by a succession of mysterious fires. No lives were lost, but the fires damaged the Bay City hotel, Allan's tea room, a tailor shop and a shoe repair; Moore's Fuel, the North American Lumber Company and the town's own fire hall, including a fire truck, were destroyed. The swift, fierce blazes, which broke out between 2 a.m. and 3 a.m., suggested arson but no arrests were made. Ten years later, on July 3, 1967, Canada's Centennial weekend, the remaining flour mill, the backbone of the community for sixty years, went up in a gigantic fireball at 4 a.m. The thirty employees on shift escaped, but strong north winds blew chunks of burning debris on to nearby roofs. On July 5th, the tie mill, the last of the Mathers' legacies, burned to the ground.

Fire was a familiar foe, but mercury poisoning was new and insidious. In 1956, Japanese doctors had begun to investigate a deadly disease of the central nervous system, much like cerebral palsy, that afflicted the fishing families of Japan's Minamata Bay. Children were born deformed and brain damaged, and both adults and children developed symptoms that included staggering, slurred speech, blindness and delirium. After testing the fish and the sediment on the ocean floor, the scientists concluded in 1962 that "Minamata Disease" was caused by eating seafood highly contaminated with the mercury Minamata's giant petrochemical company, Chisso, had been discharging into the bay since 1932.

The Lake of the Woods Milling Company, once an economic catalyst for the whole region, ends its days in an inferno.

MERCURY WAS ALSO USED by petrochemical and pulp and paper industries in Canada, and they discharged their noxious effluent into lakes and streams. Yet it was 1968 before Ontario, prodded by a visiting mercury specialist from Norway, Norvald Fimreite, began to test fish downstream from the Dryden Chemical and Dryden Pulp and Paper companies on the Wabigoon-English River system east of Lake of the Woods. Test results showed mercury levels substantially above the provincial standard of .5 parts per million. In the spring of 1970, a week before the fishing camps opened for the season, the Ontario government issued a "pollution alert" for the Wabigoon-English River system, advising fishermen to "fish for fun" and return their catches to the water. But publicity about the horrors of Minamata disease had created a climate of fear, and "fish for fun" implied that no fish was safe to eat. The pollution alert covered the whole watershed; the Rainy River, Lake of the Woods and the Winnipeg River were all downstream from pulp and paper mills.

Having sounded the alarm, and triggered an avalanche of cancelled reservations, the government tried to cover up the danger by scoffing at "pollution hysteria". Leo Bernier, the area's MPP, joked that he had eaten fish from the Wabigoon-English River chain for years and nothing had happened to him. "By his words and actions he encouraged the delusions of the worried camp operators," George Hutchison and Dick Wallace write in *Grassy Narrows*. "With large amounts of capital at risk, most were prepared to do whatever was required to get over the rough period, which, they had been assured by the politicians, would be short." Camp owners along the river route were mum on the subject; no literature on mercury pollution was prepared and when visitors inquired about the problem at Kenora's tourist offices, the staff generally responded by ridiculing the whole issue.

Barney and Marion Lamm, concerned about the health of their guides as well as their guests, refused to join in this conspiracy of silence. Closing their Ball Lake Lodge, they devoted their energies to gathering and publicizing information about mercury pollution. The Lamms' crusade made them profoundly unpopular in Kenora, but it turned an international spotlight on the English River home of their Ojibwe guides, Grassy Narrows First Nation. The people of Grassy had been eating a steady diet of fish as long as the Dryden mill had been dumping mercury into the rivers, and some of them showed symptoms – tunnel vision, staggering, and violent or irrational behavior – that resembled Minamata Disease. Alcoholism had been blamed, as it had been earlier in Minamata, but in 1973 Dr. Peter Newberry became convinced that fifteen of the seventeen Grassy Narrows volunteers he tested were in the early stages of Minamata Disease. The government denied that mercury poisoning had been proven, then told the residents of Grassy Narrows, and White Dog First Nation downstream, not to eat the fish.

What else could they eat? They had fished forever, and it was no fault of theirs that the fish were contaminated. When Ball Lake Lodge closed, Grassy's guides lost jobs that had been in their families for twenty-five years, and wages and tips that had tided them over the off-season. They could work as guides for lodges that remained open, but they would have to fry up a shore lunch of fish for unwitting Americans: the government did not close the watershed to sport fishing. It did provide Grassy with a freezer and shipped in frozen fish from Manitoba; when the freezer broke down, the fish rotted.

The pollution was stopped, although the mercury will remain for years in the lake bottoms and riverbeds, but the plight of the Kenora area Ojibwe had roused public concern. Canadians were beginning to feel guilty and ashamed of their governments' complicity in the squalor, hopelessness and violence characteristic of so many First Nations

PETER ST. JOHN

IT WAS HARD TO BELIEVE, MANY FELT, THAT THE WATER OF THE LAKE AND ITS TRIBUTARIES WAS UNSAFE.

Disastrous fires were nothing new for Kenora; the Hilliard House fire in January of 1902 (bottom) destroyed one of the community's most elegant hotels, while the Short's Tie Mill fire of 1914 ruined livelihoods as well as one of the region's largest mills.

LAKE OF THE WOODS MUSEUM, KENORA / 964.16.25

LAKE OF THE WOODS MUSEUM, KENORA / 975.31.8

communities, and nowhere were misery and poverty more visible than in Kenora. The 3,000 Ojibwe who lived on the Canadian circumference of Lake of the Woods came to Kenora because it was the nearest place to shop, see a doctor, go to a movie or, if they lived on a reserve that banned liquor, drink. Kenora was still a hard-drinking town. Ted Burton, Crown attorney at the time, attributes it to the area's boom-or-bust economy and seasonal work: "When people have time on their hands, they drink, and when they drink, they fight. It's that simple. People who do that sort of thing also steal, though often not very successfully. The majority of lawbreakers in these parts are stupid or unfortunate."

FISHERMAN DRANK LIKE FISH, so did summer campers; a stretch of Coney Island lakefront was dubbed "Cocktail Alley," and, before the telephone, one island hostess bellowed "Drinks at 5:30!" to her neighbours across the channel through a megaphone. Kenora's teens drank illegally at parties; "There was a culture of drinking," says a well-educated, middle-class woman who grew up in Kenora in the 1970s. "The attitude was: 'Okay, as long as the police don't come knocking on the door.'"

The Ojibwe liked to drink outdoors, gathering in convivial, sometimes fractious knots in the parks, alleys and shopping malls, on boulevards and along the waterfront. Hadn't the First People, after all, been camping here for thousands of years? If they were a long way from home, and had walked all the way on the railway tracks, it was pleasant to curl up for a snooze in the shade of a tree. Passers-by tended to look away when couples copulated, or a man peed against a wall. When a shopper stepped around a grimy, comatose figure in a doorway, it was less a sign of indifference than of accommodation to an unknown and inexplicable way of life.

The police went through the motions: in 1973, nearly 7,000 arrests were made for public intoxication. Many were the same people; they had no money to pay fines, and jail was a clean place to dry out or do time in the winter. The Ojibwe were part of the streetscape, yet their appearance was alarming: young mens' faces were disfigured with livid scars from knife wounds, many were missing legs and arms. Women, young and old, looked thin and bloated, their clothes and hair unkempt, bodies stooped and twisted from illness or malnutrition. Limping, shuffling, the street people looked like refugees from some terrible secret war.

In 1973, the 100th anniversary of Treaty #3, Grand Council Treaty #3 published the war's most recent casualty figures in a report, While People Sleep. One hundred and eighty-nine Kenora-area Ojibwe had died violently since January 1970: twenty-four committed suicide, twenty-five died from exposure, thirty in fires, forty-two drowned, sixteen died in car crashes and thirty eight died by stabbing, gunshot and hanging. Sixty-six of the victims were under twenty, and seventy per cent of the deaths were linked to intoxication. The mortality rate was the equivalent of 10,000

death; inspired by the militant American Indian Movement, Keesick, with Louis Cameron of White Dog, organized the Ojibway Warriors Society. Mayor Davidson reluctantly gave the Warriors permission to hold a four-day conference on Indian rights at Anicinabe Park, a campground and trailer park on Kenora's outskirts, July 19th to 22nd, 1974. The Warriors invited AIM's Dennis Banks, the Dakota hero of a violent 1973 stand-off with U.S. authorities at Wounded Knee, South Dakota, to be the keynote speaker.

Campers and Kenora residents feared a bloodbath, but Banks was temperate, the 300 conference participants quiet and orderly. Liquor and firearms were forbidden. The choice of site, however, was provocative: the Ojibwe believed that Anicinabe Park, as its name suggests, belonged to them, and that it had been sold to the town years before without their permission. At midnight on Monday, July 22nd, a group of 150 young militants, led by Louis Cameron, announced they would occupy the park until the town council listened to their grievances.

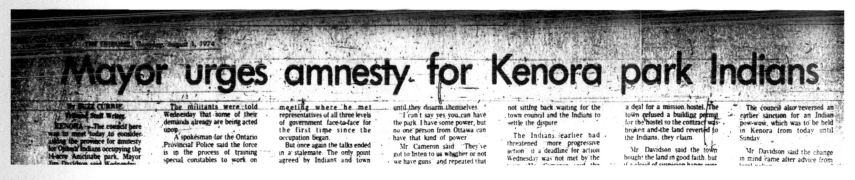

violent deaths a year in Toronto. In May 1974, a posse of Ontario cabinet ministers toured Kenora's waterfront, expressed dismay at what Mayor Jim Davidson called the "moral pollution" of alcohol abuse, and proposed a study of the whole "social problem".

Tommy Keesick, the newly-elected, twenty-five-year-old chief at Grassy Narrows, didn't intend to be studied to

Mayor Davidson had invited the Warriors to meet with the council at 7 p.m. that evening, but in the afternoon Cameron had been arrested in Kenora and charged with carrying a "dangerous weapon", a sheathed, five-inch hunting knife. Cameron was freed, but the outraged Warriors boycotted the council meeting and barricaded the entrance to the park; rifles, shotguns, spears, knives and molotov

For Kenora's Ojibwe population, death had become a familiar companion, and the cemetery a place that almost every family knew too well.

cocktails appeared from nowhere. The "kamikazis" in the park were ready to die for their cause, Cameron told the press, and AIM organizer Harvey Major threatened, "If just one of our Indian people is hit by a bullet, Kenora will go up in smoke."

Their demands were innocuous – transportation to and from the reserves, interpreters for government agencies, employment opportunities and fairer treatment by the police – but the Warriors, with their long black hair, headbands, naked torsos and guns, were menacing and unpredictable. One put a gun to the head of a Toronto reporter, others fired shots randomly into the air. The incessant beating of drums could be heard far out on the lake; campers relaxed a little when they learned that the drumming, broadcast by loudspeakers, was on tape.

The park's occupation was supported by the area's liberal-minded campers and locals – radical was chic in 1974 – but the Ojibwe chiefs and elders almost unanimously deplored it. Elders whose children and teenagers were in the park tried to act as mediators. The Ontario Provincial Police brought in ninety extra officers to patrol the road in front of the park's entrance, but the Warriors remained free to come and go, bring in food and use the park's barbeques, electricity, running water and telephone.

Were the Warriors revolutionaries, or, in the words of Mayor Davidson, "those dumb kids"? Who knew? The stalemate dragged on into August; futile attempts at negotiation caused mutual acrimony and mistrust. Harvey Major taunted the OPP officers as "pigs" and "General Custer", but the OPP behaved with such restraint hostile townspeople wanted to call in the army. By August 15th, Crown attorney Ted Burton, who knew everyone on both sides of the fence, sensed that the Warriors might welcome a face-saving truce if they could surrender their weapons to their elders. Dennis Banks, who had returned to the United States before the occupation, agreed to act as conciliator. On August 18th, the

Warriors put down their rusty, worn-out guns pending an amnesty and a ten-day negotiating period; Anicinabe Park, vandalized and strewn with garbage, was vacated by September 3rd.

"It was a near thing," says John Reid, Member of Parliament for Kenora-Rainy River from 1965 to 1984 and a camper on the lake at the time. Like Burton and Davidson, Reid worked feverishly behind the scenes to calm fears, soothe tempers and avert violence.

Mayor Davidson, a model of common sense throughout the crisis, was defeated by two votes in the next election, and Tommy Keesick, who had played no public role in the occupation, was deposed as chief at Grassy Narrows. The Warriors' grievances disappeared into the bureaucracy's omnivorous maw. However, the key issue of the occupation – did Anicinabe Park rightfully belong to the Ojibwe? – was pursued by Treaty #3's researchers.

I N 1929, the Department of Indian Affairs had bought the 5.6-hectare lakeshore property from Hattie Louise Cameron for $2,500. It was designated as a campground for Native Canadians who were working or shopping in town, visiting their children in the residential schools, or going back and forth to hospital. A crude lodge, "Indian House", was staffed by a caretaker and his wife. In the 1940s, the Presbyterian Mission proposed building a hostel, but the town of Kenora, calling the site "insanitary" and "detrimental to the town," wanted to buy the land and relocate the campground. The squabble between the church, the town and Indian Affairs continued until June 30, 1959, when Indian Affairs sold the campground to Kenora for $1875. The Presbyterians were offered land elsewhere – they opened a Fellowship Centre on Water Street in 1961 – but the Ojibwe were not compensated. Although early Indian Affairs records list "Kenora Camping Ground #38D" as Rat Portage reserve land, possibly purchased with the band's

LAKE OF THE WOODS MUSEUM, KENORA / 971.52.6

The Ojibwe had a long claim on Kenora's waterfront; for example it was here in 1881, almost a century before the occupation of Anicinable Park, that a pow-wow was held in honour of Canada's governor general, the Marquis of Lorne. His wife, Princess Louise, was a daughter of Queen Victoria.

own revenue from timber leases, government lawyers classified it as Crown property.

Leasing and selling reserve land had been Canadian government policy. In a 1926 speech about "the Indian problem", Kenora district Indian Agent Frank Edwards described his duties: "To protect the Indians from fraud, trespass and other illegal acts of white men, to improve their living conditions, to encourage them in farming and stock-raising, to educate their children, assist the sick and destitute, to secure surrenders of land, to make payments on Treaty, to handle correspondence and prepare reports. The Indian is fathered by the Department from his birth until his death, being a ward of the Crown. As such, he cannot be sued for debt. No one can legally purchase hay,

CONTINUED ON PAGE 232

Adapted from Journal of a Country Lawyer by E. C. (Ted) Burton

THE MAD BOMBER

A FEW MINUTES BEFORE 3 P.M..ON MAY 10, 1973, a short, middle-aged man wearing bush clothes and a checked fedora walked into the CIBC branch on Kenora's Main Street and took a chair in manager Al Reid's office. His backpack and a satchel slung around his neck suggested a hitchhiker, but when Reid asked what he wanted, the stranger pulled a revolver from his pocket. "Phone the police," he said. "Tell them I am here and I want the money from the bank." As Reid put through the call, the stranger produced a device resembling a large clothespin connected to wires leading into his satchel. He had a bomb in his bag, he said, and if the ends of the deadman switch connected, the bomb would go off. He pulled a black balaclava over his head, ordered Reid to clear the bank and inserted the switch between his teeth.

Three police officers were already in the lobby. They shooed out the staff and customers, then left the robber alone with Reid while they cordoned off the street. Word was spreading quickly. CJRL radio announcers Chris Paulson and John Berry, who had a bird's-eye view of the bank, broadcast a running commentary. A huge crowd collected. Inside, the robber took a rifle out of a kitbag he had stowed near the door and used it to pry open the tellers' drawers. Stuffing bills into his bag, he told Reid: "I want the cash out of the main vault or I'll blow the place up!" Reid had to phone his accountant

THE WINNIPEG TRIBUNE / MAY 11, 1973

for the combination. The human bomb waited calmly, the deadman switch clenched between his teeth or held apart by his gloved fingers when he was talking to Reid. His serious, quiet manner convinced Reid the bomb was real.

When the vault was opened, the bomber filled all his bags with cash, then demanded that the police send over an unarmed man with a pickup truck. Reid phoned in the request as Constable Don Milliard was coming on duty. Milliard changed into plainclothes, grabbed a municipal half-ton truck and drove to the bank. He walked in shortly after 4 p.m.; the bomber had been in the building more than an hour. The windows and roofs of surrounding stores and offices were crammed with spectators; police officers armed with rifles had stationed themselves at stragetic points. Among them, only fifty metres from the truck, was Sergeant Bob Letain, a crack shot with a .308.

"A few minutes later," writes Ted Burton, "Milliard and the robber came out into the open, Milliard carrying the duffel bag, the robber a step behind, awkwardly carrying a bag, a backpack and the dynamite satchel. One hand was up by his shoulder, the automatic dangling cumbersomely from his fingers. The deadman protruded from his mouth like an open duck's bill. Milliard could see perhaps a dozen of his colleagues with

Thousand see deadly drama unfold

The entire front of the Canadian Imperial Bank of Commerce has just exploded. A helicopter is flying over now. Windows have been blown out literally all over the place."

Letain's bullet blew the bomber to smithereens. Milliard was knocked to the ground, his trousers shredded and the flesh on one hip and leg burnt raw. The street, choked with acrid smoke, was strewn with money, shrapnel, broken glass and body parts; police obtained the bomber's fingerprints from a hand blown through the window of Johnson's Pharmacy. The prints proved only that he had no criminal record.

Who was he? The Mad Bomber, as Burton dubbed him, had registered at the Kenricia Hotel using a fictitious name, Paul Higgins, and a non-existent Toronto address. Described as having brownish hair and a reddish beard, he had hung

their guns trained in the direction of the robber." The pair suddenly wheeled and went back in the bank; the robber had forgotten his rifle. When they came out again, Milliard, walking a few paces ahead, caught Letain's eye; Letain, seeing Milliard partly shielded by the truck, fired.

The sound of the shot, followed by an explosion, was broadcast over CJRL. "Bloody hell, the bomb's gone off!" Chris Paulson shouted into his microphone. "The bomb has gone off, the bomb has gone off," cried John Berry, then together: "The bomb has gone off! Ladies and gentlemen, get off the street. A policeman has been shot ... a man ... men are running ... two cars are completely heavily damaged.

around town for several days. Maps, tools and camping gear found in his bags suggested a drifter, but he left a portable television set and neatly-folded clothes in his hotel room. He carried Canadian and American money. In spite of a long, meticulous investigation, his plans, motives and identity remain a mystery. A recent investigation has produced no new information.

Wealth from the great lake's many resources, once at the heart of the western Ojibwe empire, was now largely out of reach.

grain, cattle etc. from a Treaty Indian without the sanction of the Department. This arrangement is made to prevent the Indian from being defrauded by the white. No land or timber can be taken from the Indian without first being surrendered by them, and the monies received from the sales are placed in a trust fund for the benefit of the band."

THE OJIBWE HAD BECOME PRISONERS in their own land, and on Rainy River they had been cajoled and coerced into surrendering more than eighty per cent of their property. In 1873, they had reserved more than 45,000 acres (18,000 hectares) at their traditional fishing and camping grounds, Manitou and Long Sault Rapids and Hungry Hall, including a 20,000-acre or eight thousand - hectare "Wild Land" rich in wildlife. Indian agents reported that the Ojibwe lived in comfortable log homes with shingled roofs, enjoyed good hunting and fishing, and the men found employment in the lumber camps, sawmills and on the riverboats. They showed no interest in farming or raising cattle.

Wild land was waste land to politicians convinced of the moral and economic virtues of agriculture. In 1914, the Department of Indian Affairs, pressured by Ontario, "persuaded" the Rainy River Ojibwe to surrender for sale six of their seven reserves; over the next five years, nearly 200 people were relocated to the Manitou reserve and their land was sold to homesteaders. Gone were their gardens, woodlots, hunting and trapping grounds and the ancient mounds at Hungry Hall and Long Sault, the sacred site of their spring festivities. As well, their sturgeon fishery had been destroyed by commercial exploitation and the river polluted by effluent from the pulp and paper mills. The Indian Act made it impossible for an individual Ojibwe to buy a commercial fishing licence, and he was forbidden to sell fish without one. Ancestral fur trapping grounds had to be licensed and shared with interlopers. Punitive laws reduced

DENNIS FAST

commerce with "the white man" to a form of underground barter, and when the Ojibwe had money, they had to spend it in a white man's town: Main Street was not allowed on their own reserves.

Segregation sprang from nineteenth century British theories that dark-skinned Aboriginal peoples represented stages in human evolution doomed to extinction: on a Native reserve, as on a game preserve, an exotic species might live out its final days in peace. Indian agents fed the hungry, church missions clothed the poor and doctors treated the sick: vaccinations and medical examinations were part of annual Treaty Day celebrations. By 1920, despite all predictions, Canada's Aboriginal birth rate began inching ahead of mortality. Duncan Campbell Scott, deputy superintendent of Indian Affairs, declared a new strategy: "I want to get rid of the Indian problem. Our object is to continue until there is not a single Indian in Canada that has not been absorbed into the body politic."

Native women lost their treaty status when they married white men. Native men were paid $50 and their share of the band's savings if they forfeited membership and left the reserve; their wives and children as well became "enfranchised". Children aged seven to fifteen were required to attend a Christian day or residential school; in Ontario they were taught in English and forbidden to speak their own language.

LAKE OF THE WOODS OJIBWE were ambivalent about schools; Whitefish Bay had a day school, but North West Angle refused a school. Some parents sent their children to the Roman Catholic residential school in Kenora, others to Cecilia Jeffrey, the Presbyterian school at Shoal Lake. The Ojibwe welcomed education, but not Christianity. "In 1849, the Grand Council of Chiefs of Lake of the Woods had proscribed missionary activity altogether, forbidding a planned mission station and school on the Rainy River,"

Victoria Freeman writes in her evaluation of Cecilia Jeffrey in *Distant Relations*. "They issued a warning that warriors would dismantle any structures. Even when Allen Salt, an Ojibwa missionary, arrived at Rainy Lake in 1854, he was told he was not welcome to live among the Anishinabe. Although the Anishinabe were not interested in Christianity,

LAKE OF THE WOODS MUSEUM, KENORA / 986.64.74

they were open to accepting specific knowledge and technology from the Euro-Canadians – with no strings attached. They were interested in sending their children to school to learn to read, if they could have schooling without Christianity. When secular schooling was denied them, they rejected schools altogether."

The Department of Indian Affairs abhorred all Aboriginal spiritual practices. "The members of this band are all pagan," agents regularly reported from Lake of the Woods. At White Dog, the site of an Anglican mission, the Ojibwe still drummed and danced during their seasonal feasts, and the young men tied up their hair with ribbons

At residential schools, attempts were made to completely acculturate Ojibwe children; for at least the first six decades of the twentieth century, that acculturation was accompanied by religious instruction aimed at eliminating Aboriginal spirituality.

The intent of the schools was to separate the children from their families and the influence of traditional Ojibwe life. Sent to school as young as six — barely out of the *tikinagan* — yet not accepted in white society, many Ojibwe found themselves in a "no-man's" land, social outcasts in both cultures.

and painted their faces. Children who did attend school had to read, write and speak English, a language they rarely heard at home, and they were cruelly punished if they spoke their own, even out of class. Teachers spoke no Ojibwe. In an 1895 curriculum devised by Indian Affairs, students were not taught to count to 100 until grade three, science wasn't taught at all, and teachers were advised to avoid "the unnecessary use of textbooks." If students made it to grade six, which few did, they studied: "Patriotism. Evils of Indian isolation. Enfranchisement. Labour the law of life." The intent of the school was not to educate but to "civilize": emphasis was placed on cleanliness, obedience, neatness and "proper behavior".

AT THE RESIDENTIAL SCHOOLS boys spent half the day working in the gardens and barns to supply the school's food. Girls sewed, ironed, cooked and did housework. Visits from parents were discouraged, and homesick children regularly ran away. Parents' complaints about abusive and incompetent teachers fell on deaf ears. In 1929, in spite of protests from the Shoal Lake band, the Cecilia Jeffrey school relocated to Round Lake east of Kenora, a distance of seventy kilometres. The band lost access to their children, the services of the school's nurse and a major market for their fish, game, berries and firewood.

With rare exceptions, the meagre education provided by the residential schools did not compensate for their harm. Children were told that they were lazy, dirty, sinful and ignorant. Emma Paishk's description of her life at Cecilia Jeffrey is quoted in *Distant Relations*: "I was abducted from my safe, familiar environment and plunged into a stark, cruel existence that was as foreign to me as the language. I began to regress into a very quiet little girl, terrified of the new world around me,

using gestures and facial expressions to communicate with others. I lived in a silent world of hurt, rejection and most of all loneliness. I often experienced the lashes of those studded hard brown leather straps when I was caught speaking my own language or making an attempt to run away. I lived in such fear of those people that ran the school that my throat was always constricted with unshed tears." Freeman describes Paishk's terror as "the everyday wearing down of the spirit"; others call it cultural genocide.

The consequences of segregating Ojibwe children while educating them for assimilation were reported by Kenora's Indian agent Frank Edwards as early as 1938: "The great difficulty is finding a place for children who have finished school, in order that they may be gainfully employed. They have forgotten to live like Indians, they are not content to be sent back to a reserve to live in a tepee under most primitive conditions, and yet what effort have we made to assimilate them into our civilization, after bringing them up in it? If commercial fishing and trapping were left in the hands of the Indians, their children could be taught a regular business and occupation, but it isn't so there is really nothing for them to go back to. They are becoming greatly discouraged and demoralized at being unable to earn a living. Our Indians should be given training that would enable them to make a living out of natural resources, which should be kept exclusively for them."

Edwards' advice would be remembered by the Ojibwe, but the spiral of anger, alienation and impoverishment continued. By 1965, the peak of the civil rights movement in the United States, the similarities between the Ojibwe of Kenora and black Americans had become embarrassingly obvious. Barely a dozen Ojibwe were employed in the town, none in the mill; some businesses refused to serve them or made them unwelcome. One laundromat was for white people only. There were no public washrooms. The Friendship Centre turned away people who were drinking. The jail population was almost exclusively Aboriginal. Children with parents in jail fed themselves by rummaging through garbage cans; 350 were in the custody of the Children's Aid Society. Thirty families, fifty adults and thirty-eight children, lived under docks or in derelict shacks. Townspeople ignored and despised the "drunks", or helplessly wrung their hands, and Indian Affairs wanted nothing to do with Pete Seymour, an Ojibwe war veteran and Rat Portage band councillor who revitalized Grand Council Treaty #3 in the summer of 1965. Said Seymour:

> We needed financial assistance to organize ourselves as a government. We wanted to all speak with one voice. We wrote to the government official, the top man in Ottawa, asking for help. We got no reply. Nothing. I waited two or three months. Then I started talking to the boys 'We're gonna have to do something else, something drastic.'

THE SOMETHING DRASTIC happened on the evening of November 22, 1965: 400 Ojibwe, led by their chiefs, marched solemnly through Kenora's cold, snowy streets to petition the town council for assistance in solving their problems of poverty, isolation and alcoholism. Walking four-abreast in their dark winter jackets, women in floral cotton skirts carrying their babies in cradle boards, they formed, as *The Winnipeg Tribune* reported, "the most impressive display of Indian unity this region has ever seen." Except for the police, reporters and cameramen, the streets were virtually deserted.

A young Ojibwe spokesman, Fred Kelly, had warned of Indian "uprisings," but once they were seated they watched impassively as Kelly reassured the councillors that they came in peace, "a peace based upon dignity, equality and justice for the Indian people." As neighbours, Kelly said, the Indians wanted to work with the people of Kenora to find mutual solutions to problems "so many, so varied, so intense we hardly know where to begin." They were asking for Kenora's "time and commitment", not handouts: "We deeply resent the welfare cheque solution. We want to earn our income, not beg for it."

Seeking time and commitment

400 march for equality

Kenora Indians air grievances

By DUART FARQUHARSON
Tribune Staff Writer

KENORA, Ont. — More than 400 Indian men, women and children marched in dignity before a white man's town council here Monday in the most impressive display of Indian unity this region has ever seen.

The council reacted with a sigh of relief and a proposal that Indian chiefs meet Thursday with council and a federal-provincial Indian co-ordinating sub-committee.

In a brief asking only for Kenora's time and commitment, the Indians described problems of poverty, unemployment, discrimination and alcohol before calling upon the town for four specific undertakings.

Awaiting the meeting's outcome

Kenora district Indians march for equality

Mayor Edward Norton breathed a sigh of relief when the delegation presented its four demands: an Indian-white "mayor's committee" to develop long-term cooperation, radio telephones on reserves, a longer trapping season, and treatment, not jail, for alcoholism. The council agreed with alacrity. The Ojibwe walked quietly back to Knox United Church for sandwiches and coffee, then boarded buses for the trip home.

The Kenora march marked the beginning of Canada's

Aboriginal civil rights movement. "Indians don't march!" cried one astonished onlooker. Fred Kelly was fired from his job with the Kenora Children's Aid Society. The "mayor's committee" dissolved in acrimony. Radio telephones were installed in locked band offices. Ontario boosted welfare to national standards.

"Bah! We're worse off than ever!" said a disillusioned Pete Seymour. "Welfare has doubled or tripled in this area. Lots of money around. Lots more alcohol. More people are on relief than ever before. Anybody can get it. It's easier for the government to give, to buy them off. We never asked for welfare!" Tough, taciturn, a reputed medicine man, Seymour had mobilized the march. Nine years later, a new generation of Ojibwe Warriors occupied Anicinabe Park.

BY 1974, Kenora townspeople were fed up with being depicted as racist rednecks. "Why should you get more than I just because your skin is brown?" Judy Parkes wrote to the local newspaper in response to the Warriors' demands. "If your argument is that you were bought out by the white man, whose fault is that? This isn't your country any more than it is mine. You speak of racism, bigotry and discrimination. It's about time you realized that white people share these problems too. You Ojibway are just as much to blame for discrimination as anyone. You're too busy crying over it to get out and do something constructive about it. When was the last time you spoke to a white person except to use the news media to get publicity? You blame the Indian Affairs for their Indian policies. Well then, let's abolish Indian Affairs. That's our tax dollars, not yours. Let's see you work for a living to build and buy your own homes and pay for your own education. If you want equality, seriously, then cut your ties with the government and their juicy grants and free houses. Pick up your load and walk with us for a mile. The grass isn't any greener over here, you know."

Parkes expressed the frustration and resentment many

locals felt. Who had bailed out the workers when the flour mills closed and burned, or the families of workers at the pulp and paper mill, now owned by Boise Cascade, who had suffered hardship when a strike had shut down the mill in 1973? Organized labour was a power to be reckoned with in Milltown. The International Brotherhood of Locomotive Engineers had arrived with the first trains. They were followed by the Brotherhoods of Firemen, Operating Engineers and Trainmen, and in 1885, local contractors joined the Brotherhood of Carpenters and Joiners. Hourly employees at the pulp and paper mill had been unionized since 1925, but, depending on their trade, they belonged to one of six unions. When a wildcat strike broke out in the summer of 1978, mill workers fought the company, the police and, most bitterly, each other.

The strike began at the Fort Frances mill when 140 members of Local 2693, Lumber and Sawmill Workers Union, walked out to protest the hiring of an independent contractor to harvest timber with his own equipment. Privatization threatened their jobs, and bush workers could not afford to replace their chain saws with heavy machinery. When the union's contract expired on October 11th, Kenora's Local 2693 struck in support. The union picketed the mills' shipping gates, then, on November 10th, blocked all entrances. Members of the five other unions did not cross. The mills shut down.

No one was happy. Picketers huddled in plywood shelters in freezing temperatures and heavy snow; everyone was going broke. On November 21st, Lyle Hudson, president of Local 1330, United Paperworkers International, wrote to Boise Cascade: "Now is the time for the Company negotiators to get off their ass, take their hands out of their pockets and settle the issues quickly. YOU CAN DO IT: SETTLE WITH L.S.W.U. AND LETS GET TO WORK." But Hudson blamed the strikers for causing "resentment and hard feelings among union members," and urged the LSWU to withdraw their pickets so his members could return to work. On November 28th, the United Paperworkers ratified a new contract; by 8 a.m. the next morning, the first shift, lunch pails in hand, had mobilized in front of the Kenora mill.

Angry strikers, wearing protective snowmobile helmets, swarmed in front of the entrance; Kenora police, augmented by the OPP, stood guard. At 8 a.m. the mill workers surged towards the door. "Fists began to fly," reported the *Kenora Miner and News*. "At one point, strikers, mill workers and members of the police were in a pile in front of the double doors." When the police picked themselves up out of the snowbanks, they urged the mill workers to retreat. "We know all the people," said Sgt. Carl Hager. "I've got relatives on both sides. That's the problem in a small town."

Logging trucks and workers in buses with boarded-up windows, protected by squads of OPP, broke through the picket lines. Five of the six unions joined the strike, but by the end of the year the mills in Kenora and Fort Frances were up and running. By April 1979, all the unions except Local 2693, Lumber and Sawmill Workers, had caved in. Local 2693's militants refused to concede, but loggers drifted away in search of work. For fifty-five years, a

job at the mill had been a cherished heirloom passed down from father to son to grandson; this strike set families against each other, impoverished everyone and resolved nothing.

Labour strife, Aboriginal misery, polluted water and economic depression forced the lake's residents, including the summer campers, to take a hard look at themselves. The reckoning began in 1971 when Ontario, responding

Economically, as well as socially and geographically, Kenora's pulp and paper mills were at the centre of the community.

Strike On, But Some Work

to the mercury crisis, upgraded its water quality standards and new cottage subdivisions planned for Lake of the Woods failed to meet the sewage regulations. In fact, the lake had no sewage regulations; even Kenora dumped its raw sewage into the Winnipeg River. Campers had been in the habit of tossing cans, bottles, stoves, furniture and anything else that sank into the lake; municipal garbage was dumped in open landfills and burned. Most of Lake of the Woods was Unorganized Territory – no local government, no bureaucracy, no laws – and Ontario belatedly realized that it had no idea who was out there and what they were doing. In 1972, Richard Hanlan, a planner with the ministry of natural resources, spearheaded an intensive, five-year Land Use Inventory of the lake's Ontario watershed (excluding the upper Rainy River).

HANLAN'S TEAM CAME UP WITH some alarming information. The area's economy was dependent on recreation, but facilities were overcrowded and sport fish in Lake of the Woods were disappearing: anglers and commercial fishermen were catching more than a million pounds of walleye a year, far more than the fish population could sustain. Hanlan drew up a land use plan with one primary goal: "The area's high quality environment is essential and it must not be allowed to deteriorate."

Once Kenora realized the extent of its environmental problems, it began to make efforts to remedy them on many fronts. The result can be seen today in the town's gleaming waterfront, below, and heard in the occasional grumbling of cottagers over environmental regulations that some feel are "ridiculously strict".

Ontario closed Shoal Lake to commercial fishing, cut quotas and began to buy out licences; fish, shoreline habitat and water quality were monitored. Logs disappeared from the lake; the last boom was towed in 1985 and the tug, John McMillan, put on display. The shabby old waterfront was landscaped, and a public promenade and parking lot were built where wharfs, warehouses and the Rowing Club's boathouse had once stood. A by-pass on the TransCanada highway was blasted out of the granite cliffs to the north of town to relieve traffic congestion and air pollution. Kenora began treating its sewage.

The Ojibwe still camp today in the parks and parking lots. "They are like the chorus of a Greek play," observes Karen Chapeskie, a consultant to local First Nations on traditional land use projects. "We see them every day. They are witnessing, reminding us that we haven't dealt with this yet." But the Ojibwe are healthier and well dressed, and more of them are inside the stores, shopping, their new trucks parked out front. The hundreds of millions of dollars governments have invested in First Nations economic development have enabled the Ojibwe to manage their own social services, create jobs and hire scholars to research their history. Wauzhushk Onigum First Nation (Rat Portage) runs a charity casino. Band members who live and work off-reserve are no longer disenfranchised; traditional political structures, ceremonies and beliefs are being revived.

Every May, on the Friday before the fishing season opens, the Rainy River First Nations host a fish fry at Long Sault rapids. The feast is free, a come one and all, all-you-can-eat gourmet buffet, served outdoors, picnic style, with the rapids whispering beyond the trees. It lasts for hours, huge bowls of fried walleye, smoked sturgeon, wild rice and bannock refilled as they are emptied by hundreds of ravenous guests. Many are neighbouring farmers and towns-people; their faces are white, and the Aboriginal menu has changed over 2,200 years, but the people of the river are celebrating spring.

The river's people have become its guardians, and Lake of the Woods is struggling to survive its legacy of exploitation, carelessness and urbanization. In 1999, the lake was included in Ontario's "Living Legacy Land Use Strategy": thousands of Crown-owned islands became conservation areas and wildlife habitats were protected as nature reserves. Debates still rage over water levels, algae and cottage sub-divisions, the health of the fishery, clearcutting the forest and Aboriginal rights. In summer, Kenora is festooned with flowers, its waterfront buzzes with boat and plane excursions, plays, concerts and fishing derbies, but when Kenora, Keewatin and Jaffray Melick amalgamated into the City of Kenora in 2000, with a combined population of less than 17,000, the mayor kept his day job at the mill and the new city's offices occupied Kenora's quaint old Post Office.

Murals painted on the blank walls of business blocks recreate the past, and the past is present in city's former show-piece, the CPR station, now a decrepit warehouse. Kenora's cemetery is a tourist attraction; during weekly summer walkabouts custodian Barbara Manson tells lively tales about the graves' occupants. The imprint of old Rat Portage remains in the city's muskrat maze of streets and alleys, and the Legion Hall is the ghost of the railroaders' boarding house. The point of land on Tunnel Island where La Marteblanche may have parlayed with La Vérendrye is much as it was in 1732; Keewatin's public works yard offers a passage across ancient *wazhushk onigum*, rat portage. The site of Mather's first sawmill is a park. Kenora is like the well-worn clothes summer campers rediscover every year: full of holes where mills and roundhouses and railyards used to be, but familiar, comfortable and loved.

In the soaring interior of the roundhouse, even Euro-Canadians can hear the echoes of the many cultures that once lived and died here, at the Place of the Long Rapids.

IMAGES THIS PAGE: DENNIS FAST

Left: Kay-Nah-Chi-Wah-Nung Historical Centre at Manitou Mounds on the Rainy River, is just one of many indications of the revitalization of the region's Aboriginal past.

239

Keewatin ○ ◉ Kenora

Sioux Narrows

NORTH
WEST
ANGLE

*Buffalo
Bay*

Buffalo Point

○ Warroad

○ Morson

Rainy

Baudette ◉

River

*Rainy
Lake*

Fort Frances ◉

International
Falls

N
W   E
S

Autumn brings stunning colour to the forests around
Lake of the Wooks, and fills the skies with migrating
waterfowl. But in Warroad, Minnesota, the reds and
golds of autumn mean that hockey season is here again.

HOCKEYTOWN U.S.A.

HOCKEY TOWN U.S.A.

IN 1972, SIXTY-FIVE YEARS after the Kenora Thistles won the Stanley Cup, Henry Boucha of Warroad became the first Lake of the Woods hockey player to be drafted into the National Hockey League, and one of its few players of Aboriginal ancestry. A fast, stylish skater with a hard shot and a charismatic presence on the ice, Boucha had been a high school hockey sensation before joining the Winnipeg Jets' Junior A team in 1969, then the U.S. National Team that won an Olympic silver medal in 1972.

Boucha came from a hockey-mad town (pop. 1,400) that produced more great hockey players per capita than any other community in North America. The 1958 U.S. National Team included four members of the Warroad Lakers, Gordon, Roger and Bill Christian and Dan McKinnon, and its coach, Cal Marvin, was the Warroad businessman who had organized the Lakers in 1947. In 1960, Roger and Bill Christian played on the gold medal U.S. Olympic team. The Christian brothers opened a hockey stick factory in Warroad, an industry that was soon second only to Marvin Windows, an international sash-and-door manufacturer that grew out of the small lumber yard and grain elevator started by George Marvin in 1904. By the time the Warroad Lakers folded in 1997, the team had won almost every Canadian amateur championship, including three successive Allan Cups, and Bill Christian's son David, a U.S. gold medal Olympian in 1980, had followed Henry Boucha into the NHL.

Boucha's NHL career was cut tragically short in 1975. Like many NHL players in the 1970s, Boucha did not wear a helmet. He used a headband to keep his long black hair out of his eyes and his classic "Indian" appearance earned him the fans' affectionate nickname "Chief". Boucha took the jokes and tom-tom music in stride – he was proud of his Ojibwe heritage – but his popularity aroused the jealousy of other players and he became a target for his opponents' goons, big, tough players whose purpose in the game is to grab, slash, hook, elbow and punch. On January 4, 1975, when Boucha was playing for the Minnesota North Stars against the Boston Bruins, he was harassed by a Bruins' enforcer, Dave Forbes. In her biography, *Henry Boucha: Star of the North*, Mary Halverson Schofield describes the play as Boucha carried the puck out of his own end: Dave Forbes took a vicious run at Henry, elbows high. Henry saw him from the corner of his eye. He dead-stopped to slip Forbes – Forbes sailed past Henry and smashed into the glass. Fists flew as Henry and Forbes fought. Henry got the best of the fight, but

The sprawling Christian Brothers hockey stick factory – a remarkable small-town success story.

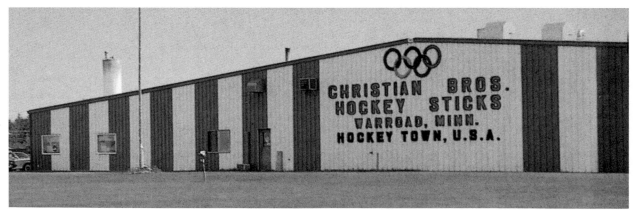

COURTESY OF THE WARROAD HERITAGE CENTER / WARROAD, MINNESOTA.

LAKE OF THE WOODS MUSEUM, KENORA / 974.39.1

when they went down in a pile, Bruins' goon Terry O'Reilly jumped on Henry's back. Henry and Forbes both went to the penalty box for two minutes for roughing and a five-minute fighting penalty. O'Reilly was kicked out of the game.

Forbes and Boucha shouted insults at each other through the glass. According to the *Minneapolis Star,* "Forbes held up a clenched fist and shouted across to Boucha, 'I'll get you and I won't use this, I'll shove my stick down your throat." As they both jumped out of the box at the end of

The 1907 Kenora Thistles – the only small-town hockey team ever to win the Stanley Cup.

Boucha under the knife

ST. PAUL, Minn. (AP) — Henry Boucha, injured in a stick-swinging fight with Dave Forbes of Boston Bruins last January, underwent further surgery on his injured right eye Tuesday.

Boucha played for Minnesota North Stars of the National Hockey League when the fight took place but since has announced that he has signed with Minnesota Fighting Saints of the World Hockey Association.

A Saints spokesman said

Mayo Clinic physicians performed the surgery at Methodist Hospital in Rochester, Minn. A hospital spokesman said it would take one to two weeks before the swelling around Boucha's eye goes down.

The hospital spokesman said the surgeon had "accomplished everything he has set out to do until the swelling goes down."

Boucha is expected to be released from the hospital Thursday.

Forbes was subsequently charged with aggravated assault but a Hennepin County District Court jury deadlocked on whether he should be convicted on a charge of simple assault.

County Attorney Gary Flakne announced earlier this month that Forbes would not be brought to trial a second time, and the charge was dropped.

Boucha saw little action after the injury and twice underwent surgery.

Henry Boucha, popular, talented and Aboriginal, was an obvious target for the hitmen of other NHL teams in an era when on-ice violence was not only condoned but encouraged. The injuries he suffered and the resulting assault charges were among the first steps in changing perceptions about violence in the NHL.

the penalty, Boucha glanced towards his bench. "In that split second," writes Scholfield:

> Henry heard a fan shout 'Look out!' He turned just in time to see the blunt end of Forbes' stick inches in front of his eye. Dave Forbes was a very strong man. He attacked from behind. The force was brutal. All the pain in the universe cracked through Henry's body. He felt the bone shatter. He felt the eye pushed in as he fell to the ice, blood from his eye spurting onto the ice. The stunned crowd screamed in fury. Henry did not fight back; he was unconscious to semi-conscious. He hands intuitively covered his face.
>
> Then, in an unparalleled episode in American sports history, Forbes jumped on Henry's back and continued punching him, beating him, beating him, punching him and banging Henry's lifeless-looking head on the ice. All the time the blood was spilling and flying, leaving the ice looking like the finger-painting of a mad man.

The officials did not intervene, but Boucha's teammates pulled Forbes off and formed a protective cordon until police and an ambulance arrived. Boucha recovered in hospital, but his eyesight was permanently damaged. His pro hockey career was over; he was just twenty-three. The Minnesota county charged Forbes with assault; his trial ended in hung jury, but Boucha won a civil suit for damages against the NHL, the Bruins and the team's coach, Don Cherry. In the 1980s, Boucha returned to Warroad to start a second career

selling real estate, teaching and coaching hockey and becoming a scholar and teacher of Ojibwe traditional knowledge, ceremonies, history and genealogy. In 2000, after years of effort, Henry reclaimed his Treaty #3 status as a member of the North West Angle First Nation: he is a citizen of three nations – Ojibwe, the United States and Canada.

Boucha's parents, George and Alice, were French Canadian Métis – Boucha is a phonetic spelling of Boucher – with a distinguished Ojibwe ancestry; George's grandfather, Johnathan Morrisseau, had been Captain Butler's guide when the Wolseley expedition crossed the lake in 1870, and Alice was the granddaughter and great-granddaughter of two chiefs who had signed Treaty #3: Powassan of North West Angle and Ay-ash-wash of Buffalo Point and Warroad. Treaty #3 negotiators seem to have overlooked the fact that Ay-ash-wash's camp at the mouth of the Warroad River was in Minnesota, and his band was part of the state's Red Lake reservation. This anomaly would involve Henry Boucha in a bitter, complicated and as yet unresolved political dispute at Manitoba's Buffalo Point First Nation.

FOR AY-ASH-WASH'S BAND, Buffalo Point was a temporary summer camp for fishing and festivals; their main settlement, Kah-Bay-Kah-Nong, "End of Trail", guarded the "war road" that led into the heart of Minnesota and Dakota territory. This camp was of strategic defensive importance for all Lake of the Woods Ojibwe: Ay-ash-wash claimed to have been scalped and left for dead during a great battle with the Dakota in the mid-nineteenth century. After Treaty #3 was signed, Ay-ash-wash, with his several wives, children and extended family, still camped at Warroad, and they remained there when the Red Lake band ceded this part of their reservation to the U.S. government in 1889. They welcomed the American settlers, and the government granted Ay-ash-wash's son, Nay-may-poke, 113 acres (forty-five hectares) of land on the south shore of the river – the site of his village – and a similar parcel to a younger son, Ka-Kay-gee-Schick, on Muskeg Bay. The eldest son, Ah-ne-me-Keene, "Little Thunder", became a chief at Red Lake, Minnesota.

Since, at that time, no band members lived year-round on Buffalo Point's 3,005-hectare reserve – their schools, hospitals, jobs and stores were all in Warroad – the role of chief was largely symbolic. Little Thunder's descendants were elected by consensus according to custom. From 1941 to 1969, Warren "Shorty" Thunder served as chief. He had no children, and when he wanted to retire, the only available candidate was his nephew, Jim Thunder. But Jim was white. When Sarah Conover, a white American, had married Shorty's brother Tom, she had brought her three children, including Jim, from a previous marriage to a white man. Tom Thunder adopted the children, and he and Sarah had two more, Frank and Dorothy. Shorty and the elders preferred Frank for chief, but he was serving with the U.S. Marines in Vietnam. They accepted Jim Thunder until Frank came home, and Jim had an attractive plan for Buffalo Point: a tourist development with cottages and a marina, golf course and hotel. Revenue, held in trust for the First Nation, would be used for their common benefit, and tourism would create jobs for them in construction, maintenance and service industries. In 1970, Thunder created the Buffalo Point Development Corporation with himself as president and the band's two councillors as directors; in 1969 he had quietly used the "band custom" provision in the Indian Act to declare himself hereditary chief.

With Canadian and provincial governments falling all over each other to invest billions of dollars in First Nations' economies, Jim Thunder had no difficulty leasing reserve land to 250 non-native cottage owners or in getting personal loans to build a 300-berth marina, the largest on Lake of the Woods. Over the years, he added a restaurant, a laundromat and guest cabins. Buffalo Point was held up to the world as a rare example of First Nations' prosperity, but to Ojibwe elders like Charles "Sam" Gibbons, the investment seemed to benefit only outsiders and the Thunder family. "James 'Thunder' (Conover) has systematically excluded any participation in the affairs of the community of all of us Buffalo Point people who are Ojibwe," Gibbons wrote in an open letter in 1996. "We have never been able to review his leadership. He controls all of the financial affairs of Buffalo Point."

How many millions had been invested in Buffalo Point, and where had the revenue gone? The corporation's president and two directors held their shares in trust for the benefit of the band, but the scattered band members, few of whom had ever lived at Buffalo Point, received no financial reports or dividends. There was no spiffy new housing development for them at Buffalo Point First Nation, and most of the seventy-five full-time residents were not band members. Money had gone to roads, septic fields and hydro to service the cottages, but the reserve had no school or health care facility. The Indian Act gave chief Jim Thunder virtually dictatorial powers to appoint and pay officials – his son John served simultaneously as a band councillor, corporate director and band manager – regulate band meetings, licence businesses, hire employees, allocate reserve land, decide who could live there and remove and punish trespassers.

TO OJIBWE ELDERS LIKE GIBBONS, Jim Thunder's adoptive, unaccountable family fiefdom was not hereditary custom, but the community was at an impasse. Canada's Indian Affairs department, a band member's only recourse, shrugged off protests and calls for an inquiry. After all, the band numbered fewer than ninety people, most of them lived in the United States, and Buffalo Point was a showpiece.

Jim Thunder stepped down as chief in favour of his son John in 1997. When John bragged to the media about his plans to build a $20 million hotel and casino, the elders wondered who would profit, and were outraged that he

245

intended to bulldoze a burial ground, Ay-ash-wash's resting place, for a golf course. On December 4, 1999, three Buffalo Point Ojibwe women and their children occupied the band's new $1.2 million administration building and demanded a meeting with the chief; Thunder refused, and during the next two weeks the number of protesters increased. Thunder dismissed them as malcontents trying to sabotage his bid for a casino; they demanded accountability and free elections, starting with "the white chief's" resignation. Thunder cut off the hydro and telephone to the band office, and got a court injunction to have the demonstrators forcibly removed by the RCMP. "We do not recognize him as our chief," said protestor Ernest Cobiness. "No chief would do that."

BY FEBRUARY 2000, the dissidents, claiming to represent seventy per cent of the First Nation's eighty-six members, had formed the Buffalo Point Membership Committee; its spokesmen were Henry Boucha and elder Robert KaKayGeesick, a grandson of Ay-ash-wash's second son, a medicine man revered in Warroad who, by all accounts, had died at the age of 124 in 1968. To placate the angry elders, John Thunder had appointed KaKayGeesick as a band councillor and corporate director in 1997 – Jim Thunder was the other – but while KaKayGeesick was asked to sign various documents, he was not invited to meetings, if any were held, or given financial statements. Suspicious and frustrated, KaKayGeesick filed a law suit in Manitoba's Court of Queen's Bench in January 2001, asking the court to seize all the corporation's financial records and minute books, order an investigation of its practices and replace the Thunders as directors. Questioned by KaKayGeesick's lawyer, Norman Boudreau, John Thunder admitted that no directors' meeting had been held since 1991, and most of the businesses on the reserve, including the marina, restaurant, laundromat and a miniature golf course, were privately owned by himself and other family members. He claimed that these ventures had been financed by personal loans from banks, businessmen and government agencies, and that he regarded the First Nation and the corporation as "one and the same". Because the suit had not included the First Nation, Boudreau was not allowed to question Thunder about the millions of dollars of Canadian taxpayers' money, some claim as much as $800,000 a year, that for more than thirty years has been invested in the tiny Ojibwe population of Buffalo Point First Nation.

Legal costs have prevented KaKayGeesick from proceeding with the suit. Indian Affairs states that the band's books are audited and that the controversy, a matter of "internal resolution", is "not our business". The Indian Act does give the minister of Indian Affairs the power to investigate any band's governance and financial affairs, but intervention requires a federal court order the Buffalo Point Membership Committee can't afford to apply for. Proposed amendments to the Indian Act, known as the First Nations Governance Act, offer only faint hope for resolution; the new legislation still recognizes "custom rules" for selecting a band council that do not require elections.

The simmering dispute has created bitter antagonism between band members who feel their democratic and treaty rights have been "hijacked", and those who find economic development beneficial; fifty-four of the 125 people who live full-time on the reserve are band members. Chief Thunder's administration has become more open, but Thunder praises his good fortune "to have the ability to look at things from a business perspective without political interference."

ENDNOTES

INTRODUCTION

p.10 John Tanner led a troubled, conflicted life. Culturally, he became Ojibwe, Shaw-shaw-wa-ne-ba-se, the Falcon, a successful hunter devoted to his family. By 1816, however, his red hair, blue eyes and ruddy face had attracted the attention of the Earl of Selkirk at Red River. Selkirk alerted the Americans, and Tanner was persuaded to reunite with his birth relatives in Kentucky. The attempt failed; he spoke no English and could not bear to sleep in a house. He readily returned to Garden Island on Lake of the Woods. But now he antagonized the Ojibwe by insisting on taking his two daughters to an American boarding school in Sault Ste. Marie. On the way, he was ambushed, shot and left for dead. His wife and daughters fled back to Lake of the Woods. Tanner was rescued by fur traders, recovered and found work as an interpreter for the U.S. government in Sault Ste. Marie. Proud, quarrelsome, at home nowhere, Tanner disappeared after he was accused of murdering the Indian agent's brother. No trace of him was ever found.

p.13 Many travellers noticed the mounds and camping grounds along the Rainy River. The mounds were sometimes described by local people as "underground houses" or refuges for women and children in times of warfare. They were neglected and plundered by souvenir hunters until the 1950s, when they were in danger of being bulldozed. Rainy River First Nation protested, and archaeologists realized that the site, Kay-Nah-Chi-Wah-Nung in Ojibwe, is the largest collection of burial mounds, and the largest surviving prehistoric structure, in Canada. It was declared a national historic site in 1970.

p.18 Colonel Wolseley was windbound and wandering on the lake for six days.

CHAPTER ONE – THE CREATION STORY

p.24 George Mercer Dawson was only twenty-three when he began his painstaking study of the geology and natural resources of the area north of the 49th parallel between Lake of the Woods and the Rocky Mountains, but he was already recognized as one of Canada's pre-eminent geologists. Dawson spent the next 20 years investigating coal deposits and dinosaur fossils in Alberta, the formation of the Rocky Mountains, the Haida of the Queen Charlotte Islands and gold deposits in Yukon. Dawson City is named for him. Dawson wasn't always right – draining Lake of the Woods was reckless advice – but he was curious, systematic and brave; spinal tuberculosis in childhood had left him hunched and dwarfed, but he endured without complaint the severe hardships of field work. Promoted to head of the Geological Survey of Canada and showered with international honours, Dawson died of bronchitis in 1901.

CHAPTER THREE – THE FIRST PEOPLES

p.46 There is intense controversy over when the first people arrived in the Americas, and where they came from. Recent archaeological discoveries date human occupation to more than 25,000 years ago; these people were not necessarily Asian, and theories other than migration across the Bering land bridge have been posed. Here, as in several other places in Canada, it's believed that North American populations travelled north as the ice melted at the end of the last glaciation. Jack Steinbring, however, could not find funding to continue his excavations at Rush Bay, and Bill Ross vehemently rejects any speculation that people were in the Lake of the Woods/Lake Superior corridor as early as Steinbring claims. Ross believes that the Blackduck pottery people migrated from the Lake Ontario area; Leigh Syms, curator of archaeology at the Manitoba Museum, postulates the abduction of women, but finds cultural evolution a simpler and more convincing possibility. Of course, many North American Aboriginal people believe that they have always been here.

CHAPTER FOUR – THE SEARCH FOR THE WESTERN SEA

p.66 The literature on La Vérendrye presents a romanticized, Eurocentric portrait of an intrepid explorer striking off to discover an unknown country. In fact, he was helpless without his Aboriginal guides. The La Vérendryes seem to have wandered largely where their hosts felt like hunting, trading or making war, and their guides' cooperation depended on the generosity of La Vérendrye's gifts.

p.67 The site of Fort St. Charles, remembered by an Ojibwe chief, Powassan, was unearthed in 1908 by a group of scholars from Manitoba's St. Boniface College. During their excavations, they discovered the headless skeletons of Aulneau and Jean-Baptiste La Vérendrye and, in a separate common grave, the 19 skulls of the canoemen. Aulneau's bones were taken to St. Boniface College where they were stored in the museum with great reverence; they were destroyed when the college burned to the ground in 1921. In 1949-50, the Fourth Degree Knights of Columbus of Minnesota reconstructed Fort St. Charles' pallisade, two bastions and chapel; flat stones mark the two graves.

p.73 A packet of Aulneau's letters to his mother and his colleagues, as well as their letters to her and to each other, was retrieved from the Aulneau home in France in 1889. The letters reveal Aulneau to have been a troubled martyr. The eldest son of landed gentry, he had been in Canada barely a year when, at age 30, he was sent west to replace ailing Father Mesaiger. In a letter to a fellow priest, Aulneau wrote: "My superior sends me without consulting me, in spite of my natural repugnance ... I humbly confess that it was not without a pang that I brought myself to obey." Physically healthy and robust, Aulneau suffered from spiritual malaise and a profound distaste for the people he was to bring to God. "I have already seen a few of almost all the tribes, and there is no more repulsive sight," he wrote to his mother soon after arriving in Montréal. The trip to Fort St. Charles did not lift his spirits. He wrote: "We journeyed nearly all the way through fire and a thick, stifling smoke, which prevented us even once from catching a glimpse of the sun." Finding nothing "deserving of attention" in "this wretched country", Aulneau dismissed the fort as "a few rough log cabins constructed with logs and clay and covered with bark," and he complained that during the winter of 1735 "we had no other nourishment than tainted pike, boiled or dried over the fire." He called his mission "the severest trial I could meet with in life. I confess that I can only look upon my destination with fear and trembling for my eternity." Aulneau was horrified at the prospect of wandering for years "in the midst of wild beasts," and "as for the Indians who dwell here, I do not believe, unless it be by miracle, that they can ever be persuaded to embrace the faith." Aulneau's life at Lake of the Woods was a martyrdom from which death was a merciful release.

p.73 La Vérendrye identified the massacre site only as "a little island" about seven leagues towards the Rainy River from Fort St. Charles. No evidence of the massacre has been found at any of the possible sites. By 1890, local legend had identified it as a relatively large, inhospitable island the Ojibwe called Manitou; the Jesuits erected a cross on its summit and renamed it Massacre Island. Older lake charts, however, identify an Ile du Massacre farther south in the United States. This small, low island, with a sheltered beach, is on the quickest, most popular route, and its distance almost matches La Vérendrye's estimate. In his *Narrative*, David Thompson, explorer, trader and astronomer, relates a story that suggest that by 1797 the 1736 massacre had become myth: "It seems that when the French from Canada first entered these furr countries, every summer a Priest came to instruct the Traders and their men in their religious duties: He had collected about twenty Men with a few of the Natives upon a small island, of rock; and while instructing them, a large war party of Sieux Indians came on them and began the work of death; not one escaped; whilst this was going on, the Priest kept walking backwards and forwards on a level rock of about fifty yards in length, with his eyes fixed on his book, without seeming to notice them; at length as he turned about, one of them sent an arrow through him and he fell dead. At this deed, the rocky isle trembled and shook; the Sieux Indians became afraid, and they retired without stripping the dead, or taking their scalps. These Isles, of which there are three, are to this day called "The Isles of the Dead (Les Isles aux Morts)."

p.79 Aboriginal slavery in Quebec pre-dated La Vérendrye's involvement, and was practised more enthusiastically, by both French and British, after his death. By 1787, public opinion, influenced by Christian evangelists, began to turn against slavery and it petered out in Canada in the early years of the 19th century. Since the vast majority of New France's "Panis" came from the southwest via the Mississippi and Ohio Rivers, French merchants were tapping into a continental Aboriginal trading network long before, and after, La Vérendrye struck out for the Western Sea.

CHAPTER FIVE – THE EMPIRE OF THE OJIBWE

p.84 Europeans may have introduced the practice of smoking tobacco in a stone or clay pipe. Archaeologists have not found pre-contact pipes used for smoking, and the Aboriginal pipe was often called by its French name, *calumet*. In his *Narrative of the Canadian Red River Exploring Expedition,* Henry Youle Hind describes how "an old Indian" showed him how to inhale tobacco smoke through a reed; the most sacred part of the ceremonial peace pipe was its long, beautifully decorated wooden stem.

p. 85 William Warren's history, rich with detail and incident, has the ring of truth, and he doesn't flinch from investigating touchy issues such as cannibalism. However, he is relying on others' memories and is highly biased in favour of his own people: his mother's Ojibwe/French family, the Cadottes, had been for generations the most powerful traders in the upper Mississippi watershed. In *Kinsmen of Another Kind,* (University of Nebraska Press) Dakota historian Gary Clayton Anderson argues that the woodland Dakota were moving west of their own accord: mysterious diseases were decimating the woodland game, while buffalo were plentiful on the prairie, and the plains people had acquired horses, guns and European goods by the mid-18th century.

p.90 Frances Densmore spent more than 20 summers among the Ojibwe of Minnesota during the early years of the 20th century, and the summer of 1919 at Manitou Rapids First Nation on the Rainy River. Densmore published numerous articles on their culture, medicines and music.

p.94 The true *megis* shell was *cypraea moneta.*

p.100 Simon Dawson (no relation to G.M. Dawson), advocated making a treaty with the Ojibwe in his 1868 report. Dawson was commissioned to do so, but the Ojibwe so hated him for his trespass on their land they refused to negotiate with him. Yet 20 years after Treaty #3 was signed in 1873, Simon Dawson was the only Canadian politician to advocate, in vain, for exclusive Ojibwe fishing rights on the Rainy River and Lake of the Woods.

p.102 Alexander Morris's book, *The Treaties of Canada with the Indians,* includes verbatim the important speeches at the great council, but Morris only hints at the unrecorded negotiations conducted day and night by his agents, who included the influential Métis, James McKay. The Ojibwe, renowned for their ability to memorize every word spoken in a parlay that lasted for hours, even days, then reproduce the entire dialogue years later, considered verbal commitments as binding as a written document. "Our hearts and brains are like paper," one chief warned Morris, "we never forget."

CHAPTER SIX – THE NORTH WEST ANGLE

p.106 Toronto scholar Bill Moreau, an expert on David Thompson, describes "Mr. Astronomer" as "hypersensitive, difficult, a loner who did not suffer fools." Thompson died at 87 in 1857, blind, impoverished and unrecognized. Thompson's reputation was tarnished when Canadians accused him of selling out to the Americans by drawing the boundary between Lake Superior and Lake of the Woods too far north, even though Thompson had no influence on this political decision. Settling with his wife and 13 children in Glengarry County in eastern Ontario, Thompson failed as a farmer, then as a merchant. Old, unemployed, he became so poor he had to pawn his instruments. Recognized now as Canada's pioneer geographer, Thompson was all but forgotten until 1916 when the Champlain Society published his immense, unfinished account of his travels.

p. 115 The hectare of land ceded by the United States to Canada was not the only surrender of land in U.S. history. In 1963, President Lyndon Johnson ceded the El Chamizal district of El Paso, Texas, 437 acres of land, to Mexico.

CHAPTER SEVEN – MILLTOWN

p.130 The reason Canadians gave to justify raising and stabilizing the lake level was to improve navigation, an argument supported by the U.S. government since it deepened the harbour at their border point, Warroad. Many Minnesota homesteaders seem to have been duped by real estate speculators who sold marshes as "temporarily flooded" farm land, but the farmers blamed Canada.

p.131 Of the fire that destroyed his mill in 1905, John Mather simply noted in his diary: "Sawmill at Keewatin burned on evening of 23rd." Canadian novelist Frederick Philip Grove seems to have used Keewatin as the setting for *The Master of the Mill,* but the characters and the story reflect the life and personality of E.W. Backus.

p.131 McLeod Park in Kenora is named for Dan McLeod. McLeod served the Mather mill and later the pulp and paper company as general manager and vice-president for 50 years.

p.140 The Rat Portage file in the Hudson's Bay Company gives entertaining glimpses into the parsimonious company's endless squabbles with the free traders, especially Laurenson [also Lawrenson]. The HBC post was moved from the island in the Winnipeg River to Rat Portage Bay in 1861, but the company did not develop its potentially lucrative land grant and slowly lost its retail struggle with the Main Street merchants. A handsome stone building replaced the log post in 1886, but the interior was cramped and dark. In 1888, and HBC official wrote: "The trader's house at Rat Portage is reported as small, unhealthy and infested with vermin." A Safeway store occupies the site of Laurenson's old post.

p.140 For decades, the railway line was the shortest pedestrian route linking Kenora to Keewatin and other outlying camps and communities; many people walking the tracks have been killed and maimed by trains.

CHAPTER NINE – THE SUMMER PEOPLE

p.170 Camping outdoors, with fresh air, sunshine and clean water, became popular after it was discovered that diseases were spread by bacteria, and thrived in dirt. The most effective treatment for tuberculosis was bed rest in an isolated wilderness sanatorium where patients slept in open-air verandas. The sanatorium concept was reflected in many early summer camps, where screened "sleeping verandas" were protected from wind and rain only by shutters or canvas blinds. Sleeping in cots was *de rigeur.* This fresh air fashion coincided with the last years of the Arts and Crafts movement, which cultivated an aesthetic approach to everyday living. At Lake of the Woods, city campers could indulge their creative passions for carpentry, gardening, rock collecting, boat building, painting and writing poetry without seeming eccentric to their neighbours, who were doing the same. Professional artists such as W.J. Phillips and the Group of Seven transformed the wilderness itself into an aesthetic experience.

p.185 In "The Invention of the Board Canoe," (Canadian Canoe Museum, Peterborough, ON) Ken Brown suggests that the first cedar board canoe may have been invented by explorer David Thompson on his journey to the Pacific Ocean in 1811. In his journal, Thompson describes sewing together split cedar boards for want of birchbark, and in 1837 he was building cedar canoes in Muskoka, Ontario. It took 50 years of experimentation by other builders before cedar and canvas-covered canoes went into mass production.

CHAPTER THIRTEEN – MAKING PEACE WITH THE MANITOUS

p.224 Marion Lamm's collection of research on mercury pollution is in the Harvard University Library.

p.238 Ontario fisheries scientist Dick Ryder developed a formula – the quantity of dissolved solids [nutrients] per volume of water – that accurately estimates the population of fish species. The higher the nutrient level, the more fish. In 1998, Ontario and Minnesota produced the "Boundary Waters Fisheries Atlas" that pinpoints the location and numbers of species in the area's two major lakes and rivers. Scientists also count the deer, moose, bear, elk and birds; the last of the woodland caribou have retreated north. Logging practices such as clearcutting, poaching, fishing and hunting regulations, algae and cottage developments continue to cause concern and controversy.

BIBLIOGRAPHY

Quotations not otherwise cited come from author interviews. *The Dictionary of Canadian Biography,* University of Toronto Press, is an authoritative and often entertaining source of information about historical figures who died prior to 1920.

INTRODUCTION:

Ashdown, J.H., "A Contemporary Explorer's Chart of Lake of the Woods," Royal Lake of the Woods Yacht Club, 1973.

Bigsby, John J., *The Shoe and Canoe,* New York, 1850.

Butler, William F., *The Great Lone Land,* London, 1872.

Chapin, Earl, *The Angle of Incidents,* Warroad Area Historical Society, 1970.

Delafield, Joseph, *The Unfortified Boundary,* New York,1943.

David Thompson's Narrative, ed. J.B. Tyrrell, Champlain Society, 1916.

Dewdney, Selwyn, "Stone-Age Art in the Canadian Shield," *Canadian Art,* XVI (3) 1959; *Indian Rock Paintings Of the Great Lakes,* (with Kenneth Kidd), University of Toronto Press, 1967; *The Sacred Scrolls of the Southern Ojibway,* University of Toronto Press, 1975.

Grant, George M., *Ocean to Ocean,* Toronto, 1873.

Henry, Alexander, *Travels and Adventures in Canada and the Indian Territories between the years 1760 and 1776,* New York, 1809.(pages 242-244)

Keating, William H., *Narrative of an Expedition to the Source of the St. Peter's River, Lake Winnepeek,Lake of the Woods etc,* 1824

Lund, Duane R., *Lake of the Woods Yesterday and Today: Our Historic Boundary Waters;* Adventure Publications, 1975, 1980.

Mackenzie, Alexander, *Voyages from Montreal on the River St. Laurence throughout the Continent of North America to the Frozen and Pacific Oceans...,* London, 1801.

Nute, Grace Lee, *Rainy River Country* and *The Voyageur's Highway,* Minnesota Historical Society, 1950, 1951.

Paul Kane's Frontier, ed. J. Russell Harper, University of Toronto Press, 1971.

Phillips, Walter J., "Wet Paint," unpublished mss.

Rajnovich, Grace, *Reading Rock Art,* Natural Heritage, 1994.

Wolseley, General Viscount, "Narrative of the Red River Expedition," *Blackwoods* Magazine, Dec. 1870-Feb.1871.

CHAPTER ONE – THE CREATION STORY

Bryce, George, "The Lake of the Woods: Its History, Geology, Mining and Manufacturing," Historical and Scientific Society of Manitoba, 1881.

Dawson, George Mercer, *Report on the Geology and Resources Of the Region in the Vicinity of the Forty-ninth Parallel, from Lake of the Woods to the Rocky Mountains,* Montreal, 1875.

Natural History of Manitoba: Legacy of the Ice Age, ed. James T. Teller, 1970.

Phillips, Brian A.M., "Shoreline Processes in South-East Lake of the Woods," unpublished report, 1994.

Williams, H.R. et al, "Tectonic Evolution of Ontario: Summary and Synthesis," Chapter 25, *Geology of Ontario,* Vol. 4, part 2, Ontario Geological Survey.

SIDEBAR
Johnston, Basil, *Ojibway Heritage,* McClelland & Stewart, 1976.

CHAPTER TWO – FOREST MEETS MEADOW

Bakowsky, W.D. & Oldham, M.J., "Summary Report on Significant Prairie and Savannah Vegetation, Vascular Plants and Natural Areas in Northwestern Ontario," Natural Heritage Information Centre, Ontario Ministry of Natural Resources, Peterborough, ON, 1998.

Banfield, A.W.F., *The Mammals of Canada,* University of Toronto Press, 1974.

Cook, Francis R., *Introduction to Canadian Amphibians and Reptiles,* National Museum of Natural Sciences, 1984.

Dunn, Gary, *Insects of the Great Lakes Region,* University Of Michigan Press, 1996.

Elder, Dave, "A Birder's Guide to the Rainy River Area" and "A Checklist of Birds of the Rainy River District," typescripts.

Ferguson, Robert S., "Summer Birds of the Northwest Angle Provincial Forest and Adjacent Southeastern Manitoba, Canada," Syllogeus 31, National Museum of Natural Sciences, Ottawa, ON, 1981.

Griffin, Kerstin, "Paleoecological aspects of the Red Lake Peatland, northern Minnesota," in *Patterned Peatlands Of Northern Minnesota,* University of Minnesota Press, 1992.

Lawrence, R.D., *The Natural History of Canada,* Key Porter, 1988

McAndrews, John H., "Holocene environment of a fossil bison from Kenora, Ontario," *Ontario Archaeology,* No.37, 1982.

Moon, Barbara, *The Canadian Shield: Illustrated Natural History of Canada,* 1970.

Newmaster, Stephen G; Harris, Allan G. & Kershaw, Linda J., *Wetland Plants of Ontario,* Lone Pine, Edmonton, AB, 1997.

Ontario Ministry of Natural Resources, Northwest Science Technology field guides: *Forest Ecosystem Classification for Northwestern Ontario (FG-03) 1997; Terrestrial and Wetland Ecosites of Northwestern Ontario (FG-02) 1996; Wetland Ecosystem Classification For Northwestern Ontario (FG-01) 1996.*

Scott, W.B.& Crossman, E.J., *Freshwater Fishes of Canada,* Royal Ontario Museum, Bulletin 184, 1973.

Sims, R.A.; Kershaw, H.M.& Wickwire, G.M., "The Autecology Of Major Tree Species in the North Central Region of Ontario," Canada-Ontario Forest Resource Development Agreement Report 3302, 1990.

CHAPTER THREE – THE FIRST PEOPLES

Arthurs, David, "Conservation Archaeology Report: Archaeological Investigations at the Long Sault Site (Manitou Mounds)," Report 7, Northwestern Region, Ministry of Culture, 1986.

Dewar, Elaine, *Bones: Discovering the First Americans,* Random House, 2001.

Erichsen-Brown, Charlotte, *Medicinal and Other Uses of North American Plants,* Dover, New York, 1979.

Forest Capital 1999 Tunnel Island Legacy Project, Draft Report, Towns of Kenora, Keewatin and Jaffray Melick.

Kenyon, Walter A., *Mounds of Sacred Earth: Burial Mounds of Ontario,* Royal Ontario Museum, 1986.

Mason, R.J., *Great Lakes Archaeology,* Academic Press, 1981.

Pettipas, Leo, *Aboriginal Migrations: A History of Movements in Southern Manitoba,* Manitoba Museum, 1996.

Phillips, Brian A.M., "A Paleogeographic Reconstruction of Shoreline Archaeological Sites around Thunder Bay, Ontario," *Geoarchaeology,* Vol.3, No.2, 1988.

Phillips, Brian A.M. & Ross, William, "The Glacial Period and Early Peoples," in *Thunder Bay: From Rivalry to Unity,* Thunder Bay Historical Museum Society, 1995.

Rajnovich, Grace, "Ballysadare (Dkkp-10): A Laurel Blackduck Site at the Source of the Winnipeg River," *Ontario Archaeology,* No. 33, 1980.

Reid, C.S, "Early Man in Northwestern Ontario: New Plano Evidence," *Ontario Archaeology,* No.33, 1980; "The 'Sacredness' of Carved Stone Pipes in the Ojibwa-Cree Area of the Northern Mid-Continent: A Spacial and Temporal Dilemma," *The Wisconsin Archaeologist,* Vol 76 (3-4)

Reid, C.S. & Rajnovich, Grace, "Laurel Architecture: Five Case Studies," *The Minnesota Archaeologist,* Vol.44, No.2, 1985; "Laurel: A Re-evaluation of the Spatial, Social, and Temporal Paradigms," *Canadian Journal of Archaeology,* Vol.15, 1991.

Ross, William, "The Interlakes Composite: A Re-definition Of the Initial Settlement of the Agassiz-Minong Peninsula," *The Wisconsin Archaeologist,* Vol.76 No.3-4, 1997.

Steinbring, Jack, "Elemental Forms of Rock Art and the Peopling of the Americas," paper delivered at the annual symposium of the American Rock Art Research Association, Ridgecrest, CA, May 25, 1998.

Steinbring, Jack; Danziger, Eve & Callaghan, Richard, "Middle Archaic Petroglyphs in Northern North America," *Rock Art Research,* Vol.4, No.1, 1987.

Two Conservation Archaeology Sites: The Lady Rapids and Fisk Sites, ed. C.S. Reid, Archaeology Research Report, 18, Ontario Ministry of Culture, 1982.

Wright, J.V., *A History of the Native People of Canada,* Canadian Museum of Civilization, 1995.

CHAPTER FOUR – THE MYTH OF THE WESTERN SEA
The Aulneau Collection, 1734-1745, ed. Rev. Arthur E. Jones, S.J., Archives of St, Mary's College, Montreal, 1893.

Burpee, Lawrence J., "The Lake of the Woods Tragedy," Royal Canadian Society Transactions, 1903; *The Search for The Western Sea,* Macmillan, Toronto, 1935.

Huck, Barbara, *Exploring the Fur Trade Routes of North America,* 2nd ed. Heartland, Winnipeg MB, 2002.

In Search of the Western Sea, Selected Journals of La Vérendrye, ed. Denis Combet, Great Plains, Winnipeg MB. 2001

Journals and Letters of Pierre Gaultier de Varennes de La Vérendrye and His Sons, edited with an introduction and notes by Lawrence J. Burpee, Champlain Society, Toronto, 1927. Reprinted 1968. Quotes are taken from this French/English edition.

Laut, A.C. *Pathfinders of the West,* Macmillan, 1904.

Nelson, Lori, "Where is the Real Massacre Island?", *Lake of The Woods Area News,* Vol.30, No.3, May, 2000.

Paquin, Rev. J., "The Discovery of the Relics of the Reverend Jean Pierre Aulneau, S.J.", S.J.[publisher] 1911.

Parkman, Francis, *LaSalle and the Discovery of the Great West,* Signet, 1963. First published, 1869.

Shanahan, Father Emmett A., "Minnesota's Forgotten Martyr," Diocese of Crookston, MN, 1949.

Trudel, Marcel, *L'esclavage au Canada francais,* [Slavery in French Canada], Les Presses Universitaires Laval, Quebec, 1960.

Warkentin, Germaine, *Canadian Exploration Literature: An Anthology,* Oxford University Press, Toronto, 1993.

CHAPTER FIVE – THE EMPIRE OF THE OJIBWE
Bishop, Charles A., *The Northern Ojibwa and the Fur Trade,* Holt, Rinehart and Winston, Toronto, 1974.

Brown, Jennifer S.H., *Strangers in Blood: Fur Trade Families in Indian Country,* University of British Columbia Press, 1980.

Densmore, Frances, *Chippewa Customs,* Minnesota Historical Society Press, 1979 (first published in 1929 by the Smithsonian Institute, Washington, DC).

Dunning, R.W., *Social and Economic Change among the Northern Ojibwa,* University of Toronto Press. 1972.

Huyshe, Captain G.L., *The Red River Expedition,* London, 1871.

McKay, John, *Post Journals,* Hudson's Bay Company Archives (Lac la Pluie post, B.195/a/1 and B.105/a/2.) Brief summaries have been published by Merv Ahrens, Devlin,ON.

McLoughlin, John, "The Indians from Fort William to Lake of the Woods," circa 1806, McGill University Rare Books and Special Collections, Montreal, Quebec.

Morris, Alexander, *The Treaties of Canada with the Indians,* Coles Canadiana Collection, 1971 (first published in1880).

Northern Ontario Fur Trade Archaeology: Recent Research, ed. C.S. Reid, Ontario Ministry of Culture, 1980.

Ray, Arthur J., *Indians in the Fur Trade: Their Roles as Trappers, Hunters and Middlemen in the Lands Southwest of Hudson Bay, 1660-1870,* University of Toronto Press, 1974.

Shenk, Theresa, "William W. Warren's *History of the Ojibway People:* Tradition, History and Context," in *Reading Beyond Words: Contexts for Native History,* ed.

Jennifer S.H. Brown and Elizabeth Vibert, Broadview Press, 1996; *The Voice of the Crane Echoes Afar: the Sociopolitical Organization of the Lake Superior Ojibwa, 1640-1855,* Garland, New York, 1997.

Van Kirk, Sylvia, *Many Tender Ties: Women in Fur Trade Society, 1670-1870,* Watson & Dwyer, Winnipeg, 1980.

Vennum, Thomas, *Wild Rice and the Ojibway People,* Minnesota Historical Society Press, 1988.

SIDEBARS
Arthur, Elizabeth, *Simon J. Dawson, C.E.* Thunder Bay Historical Museum, 1987.

Brown, Jennifer S.H.& Brightman, Robert, *The Orders of the Dreamed: George Nelson on Cree and Northern Ojibwa Religion and Myth, 1823,* University of Manitoba Press. 1988.

Dawson, Simon J., *Report of the Exploration of the Country Between Lake Superior and the Red River Settlement,* Toronto, 1859; *Report on Line of Route between Lake Superior and the Red River Settlement,* 1868.

Graham, Frederick Ulric, *Notes of a Sporting Expedition in The Far West of Canada, 1847,* London, 1898.

Hoffman, W.J., *The Midewiwin or Grand Medicine Society of The Ojibwa,* Smithsonian Institute, Washington, DC, 1891.

MacLeod, Margaret Arnett, "The Dawson Route," *Winnipeg Free Press,* Aug.2, 1940. Lady Dufferin's journal is quoted.

Manore, Jack, "Mr. Dawson's Road," *The Beaver,* Feb-March, 1991.

Morse, Eric, *Fur Trade Routes of Canada,* University of Toronto Press, 1969.

Narrative of the Captivity and Adventures of John Tanner, as told to Edwin James, M.D., London, 1830.

Palliser, Captain John, *Journals, Detailed Reports and Observations Relative to Captain Palliser's Exploration in British North America,* London, 1859-1863.

Paterson, Edith, "Passengers air complaints re Dawson Route – 1874," and "Dawson Route comes to an Inglorious end – 1878," *Winnipeg Free Press,* Oct. 19 & 26, 1974.

CHAPTER SIX – THE NORTH WEST ANGLE
Carroll, Francis M, *A Good and Wise Measure: The Search for The Canadian-American Boundary, 1783-1842,* University Of Toronto Press, 2001.

Lass, William E., *Minnesota's Boundary with Canada: Its Evolution since 1783,* Minnesota Historical Society Press, 1980.

Long, Stephen H., *The Northern Expeditions of Stephen H. Long,* Minnesota Historical Society Press, 1978.

Parsons, John E., *West on the 49th Parallel,* William Morrow NY, 1963.

Reports upon the Survey of the Boundary between the Territory of the United States and the Possessions Of Great Britain from the Lake of the Woods to the Summit of the Rocky Mountains, Dept. of State, Washington, DC, 1878.

Thompson, David, *Journal,* Notebook 55, David Thompson Collection, Archives of Ontario; microfilm MS 25, Reel 5, series 1, vol. 24.

CHAPTER SEVEN – MILLTOWN
A Colloquial History of Lake of the Woods, compiled by Patrice Nelson and Lori Nelson, 1978.

Berton, Pierre, *The National Dream,* McClelland & Stewart, 1970.

Burchill, John, "The Rat Portage War of 1883," typescript, LOW Museum, Kenora. Burchill incorporates parts of an eye-witness account by Alexander Begg in Begg's History of the North-West, Vol.III, Toronto, 1894-95.

Dion, Louis, "Logging on Lake of the Woods, 1870-1940," in Dion's report, *Historic Sites in Sioux Narrows-Lake of The Woods Area,* 1998.

Epp, Ernest, "The Lake of the Woods Milling Company: An Early Western Industry," in *The Canadian West,* ed. Henry C. Klassen, University of Calgary, 1976.

Final Report of the International Joint Commission of the Lake of the Woods Reference, Ottawa, Washington, 1917.

Five Fur Traders of the Northwest, ed. Charles Gates, Minnesota Historical Society, 1965.

King, Stuart, *Lake of the Woods: History & Heritage.*

McLeod, Donald (Dan), "Memorandum re Keewatin Lumbering and Manufacturing Company Limited, 1879 to 1906," and "Memorandum re Keewatin Lumber Company Limited, Kenora Paper Mills Limited and Allied Companies and their Operations, 1906 to 1943 & 1945;" McLeod papers, Don Cameron family archive, Kenora.

Mather, Jane; private archive

Mather, John, unpublished journals, Lake of the Woods Historical Society, Kenora; microfilm copies, Archives Of Ontario, Toronto.

Nelson, Lori, "The Race: Gaudaur vs. Towns", *Lake of the Woods Area News,* April, 2001.

Rat Portage and the Lake of the Woods: Diamond Jubilee Guide, 1897.

"Reports for Years 1917-1922," Mail Order and Liquor Branches, HBC Archives, Winnipeg.

Rich, E.E. *The Fur Trade and the Northwest to 1857,* McClelland & Stewart, 1976.

Ryan, John, "The Kenora-Keewatin Urban Area: A Geographic Study," MA thesis, Department of Geography, University Of Manitoba, 1964.

"Tracks/Chemin de fer," a history of the CPR in Kenora, Opportunities for Youth project, 1972; copy, LOW Museum, Kenora.

Waisberg, Leo & Hotzkamm, Tim, "From Ojibway Homeland to Reservoir: Flooding the Lake of the Woods Anishinaabeg," *Loss of Sacred Lands.*

Zazlow, Morris, "The Ontario Boundary Question," in *Profiles of A Province,* Ontario Historical Society, 1967.

CHAPTER EIGHT – SQUATTERS & SETTLERS
Bradof, Kristine L., "Ditching of Red Lake Peatland During The Homestead Era," in *The Patterned Peatlands of Minnesota*, University of Minnesota Press, 1992.

Between the Ripples: Stories of Chapple, Chapple Heritage Committee, Barwick, ON. 1997.

Gallinger, Rachel, "Finland, Ontario," typescript, Chapple Museum, Barwick.

Lake of the Woods County, The Lake of the Woods County Historical Society, 1997.

McKeever, Joe, interview in the Roseau *Times-Region*, April 4, 1977.

Memories of LacLu, LacLu Campers' Association, 1993.

Olsen, Emma, "The Town of Rainy River," typescript, 1947.

Schroder, Elsie Christianson, *Memoirs of the Christianson Families,* 1999.

"The History of Jaffray Mellick," typescript, Jaffray Women's Institute, 1945.

The River of Time: A History of Emo, Emo Historical Committee, 1978.

Wahlberg, Hazel, "Dakota Red," in *Northwest Angle: The Top Of the Nation,* 1987.

Warroad 100 Years Ago, 1899 and 1900; Warroad *Pioneer,* Centennial Edition, 2001; Warroad Area Historical Society.

CHAPTER NINE – THE SUMMER PEOPLE
Coyne, Susan, *Kingfisher Days,* Random House, 2001.

Gordon, Charles, *At the Cottage,* McClelland & Stewart, 1989. Interviews, Lois Gordon and family, Tanny Wells

Gordon, Charles (Ralph Connor), *Postscript to Adventure, The Autobiography of Ralph Connor,* McClelland & Stewart, 1975.

Inman, Robert, "A Summer Place: The History of the Winnipeg Summer Residents at Kenora," typescript, LOW Museum, Kenora.

Konantz, Gail, *Edith Rogers,* in the series *Profiles of Manitobans.*

Nelson, Lori, "Royalty Pays a Visit," in *Lake of the Woods Area News,* May, 1997.

Nelson, Lori, Nelson, Patti, "The Summer People: A History Of Kenora's Tourist Industry," typescript, LOW Museum, 1979.

O'Grady, Anna, handwritten memoir, LOW Museum.
Richards, R.W., *Royal Lake of the Woods Yacht Club: History to 1978,* RLWYC, 1978.

Weiss, Alice, "A Little Girl Remembers," typescript, LOW Museum

CHAPTER TEN – THE SARATOGA OF THE WEST
Dion, Louis, "German Prisoner of War Camps," in *Interim Report, Historic Sites in the Sioux Narrows-Lake of The Woods Area,* 1998.

Lieberwirth, Johannes, interviews, Kenora *Miner and News,* July 28, 1977, June 13, 1990; Kenora *Enterprise,* August 24, 1997.

Pamphlets re: Buena Vista Club, Devil's Gap Lodge; LOW Museum, Kenora

SIDEBARS
Hunn, Peter, *The Old Outboard Book,* International Marine, Camden, Me. 1994.

Lamm, Rochelle, Lamm family archive.

Webb, W.J., Carrick, Robert, *The Pictorial History of Outboard Motors,* Renaissance Editions, NY, 1967.

CHAPER ELEVEN – FROM CAVIAR TO CATASTROPHE
Johnston, Alvin, *A Time to Fish and a Time to Dry Nets: Lake of the Woods,* Lakewood Publishing, Warroad, MN 1996.

Holzkamm, Tim, Waisberg, Leo & Lovisek, Joan, "Rainy River: Heartland of the Grand Council Ojibway," in *Loss of Sacred Lands,*

Scott, W.B., Crossman, E.J., *Freshwater Fishes of Canada,* Bulletin 184, Fisheries Research Board of Canada, 1973.

Van West, John, "Ojibwa Fisheries, Commercial Fisheries Development and Fisheries Administration, 1873-1915: An Examination of Conflicting Interest and the Collapse of the Sturgeon Fisheries in the Lake of the Woods," *Native Studies Review,* Vol.6, No.1, 1990.

CHAPTER TWELVE – A PASSION FOR SAILING

CHAPTER THIRTEEN – MAKING PEACE WITH THE MANITOUS
Anicinabe Park occupation clipping file, LOW Museum.

Balka, Christine, "A History of Organized Labour in Kenora," typescript, Kenora and District Labour Council.

Burton, E.C., *Journal of a Country Lawyer: Crime, Sin And Damn Good Fun,* Hancock House, 1995.

Chapeskie, Andrew, "Land, Landscape, Culturescape: Aboriginal Relationships to Land and the Co-Management of Natural Resources," report for the Royal Commission on Aboriginal Peoples, 1994/95.

Cottam, Barry, "Federal/Provincial Disputes, Natural Resources and the Treaty #3 Ojibway, 1867-1924," PhD thesis, University of Ottawa, 1994.

Edwards, Frank, Edwards' archive, LOW Museum.

Forest Communities in the Third Millenium: Linking Research, Business and Policy towards a Sustainable Non-Timber Forest Product Sector, Ed. Iain Davidson-Hunt, Luc Duchesne and John Zasada, North Central Research Station, St. Paul, MN, 2001.

Freeman, Victoria, *Distant Relations: How My Ancestors Colonized North America,* McClelland & Stewart, 2000.

Kenora *Miner and News,* strike reports, October-November, 1978.

"Lake of the Woods General Land Use Plan," Ontario Ministry of Natural Resources, 1977; "Kenora District Land Use Guidelines," MNR, 1983.

Nobel, William, "An Historical Synthesis of the Manitou Mounds Site on the Rainy River, Ontario," Parks Canada. 1984.

Robertson, Heather, unpublished research on the 1965 Kenora march.

"We Have Kept Our Part of the Treaty: the Anishinaabe Understanding of Treaty #3," pamphlet, Grand Council, Treaty #3.

Winnipeg Tribune archive, University of Manitoba Archives; Stories on the 1954 wreck of the Campers' Special and The *Red Devil;* 1965 Kenora march; 1974 occupation of Anicinabe Park.

CHAPTER FOURTEEN – HOCKEY TOWN U.S.A.
Documents, Manitoba Court of Queen's Bench.

Henderson, Hank, *No Flag for My Coffin,* Wayward Wind Publications, Warroad, 1989; *Vacation and Cruising Guide to Lake of the Woods,* 1997.

Schofield, Mary Halverson, *Henry Boucha: Star of the North,* Snowshoe Press, Edina, MN, 1999.

Strandell, Warren, *Winning Under Two Flags: Cal and the Lakers,* Warroad MN

Winnipeg Free Press, stories re: Buffalo Point.

HEATHER ROBERTSON

Born and raised in Winnipeg, Heather Robertson is a graduate of Kelvin High School, the University of Manitoba (BA Hons English) and Columbia University, NY (MA. Eng Lit). Her writing career began as a reporter and editor with the U of M student newspaper, *The Manitoban*. She then worked as a reporter, drama and television critic with *The Winnipeg Tribune* and as a public affairs producer with CBC Winnipeg before becoming a fulltime author and magazine journalist in 1971.

Heather has published more than a dozen books of fiction and non-fiction, and has contributed to most of Canada's leading magazines. Her first novel, *Willie: A Romance*, won the Books in Canada prize for best first novel and the Canadian Authors' Assocation Fiction Prize for 1983; *Driving Force: the McLaughlin Family and the Age of the Car* won the National Business Book Award in 1995.

Heather is an active member of Canadian writers' organizations. In 1998, the University of Manitoba recognized her contribution by awarding her an honorary doctor of laws degree.

Heather lives in King City, ON with her husband, Andrew Marshall.